# Lilac Moon

## ALSO BY SHARON BUTALA

### NON-FICTION
Harvest
The Perfection of the Morning
Coyote's Morning Cry
Wild Stone Heart
Old Man On His Back

### NOVELS
Country of the Heart
The Gates of the Sun
Luna
Upstream
The Fourth Archangel
The Garden of Eden

### SHORT FICTION
Queen of the Headaches
Fever
Real Life

### PLAYS
Sweet Time
Natural Disasters
A Killing Frost
The Element of Fire
Rodeo Life

SHARON BUTALA

# LILAC MOON

*Dreaming of the Real West*

HarperCollins*PublishersLtd*

A PHYLLIS BRUCE BOOK

A Phyllis Bruce Book, published by HarperCollins Publishers Ltd

First edition

HarperCollins books may be purchased for educational, business, or sales promotional use through our Special Markets Department.

HarperCollins Publishers Ltd
2 Bloor Street East, 20th Floor
Toronto, Ontario, Canada
M4W 1A8

*www.harpercollins.ca*

Grateful acknowledgement is made to the following for permission to quote from published works:
Excerpts on pp. 58–59: Olive Dickason, *The Myth of the Savage: And the Beginnings of French Colonialism in the Americas*. University of Alberta Press, Edmonton, © 1984, 1997, p. 301.
Excerpt on pp. 70–71: Blair Stonechild and Bill Waiser, *Loyal Till Death: Indians and the North-West Rebellion*. Fifth House Ltd., Calgary, 1997, p. 224.
Excerpt on p. 122: Gerald Friesen, *The Canadian Prairies: A History*. University of Toronto Press, 1987, p. 301.
Excerpts on pp. 173–174: Ben Smillie, *Beyond the Social Gospel: Church Protests on the Prairies*. Fifth House Ltd., Calgary, 1991, p. 13.
Excerpt on p. 190: Henry Kreisel, "The Prairie: A State of Mind" in *Transactions of the Royal Society of Canada*, Vol. 6, 4th series. The Royal Society of Canada, Ottawa, 1968, p. 176.

Library and Archives Canada Cataloguing in Publication

Butala, Sharon, 1940–
Lilac moon : dreaming of the real West / Sharon Butala.

"A Phyllis Bruce Book."
ISBN-13: 978-0-00-200778-8
ISBN-10: 0-00-200778-9

1. Prairie Provinces. 2. Prairie Provinces – History.
3. Prairie Provinces – Social life and customs. 4. Regionalism – Prairie Provinces.
I. Title.

FC3237.B88 2005     971.2     C2004-905824-X

DWF 9 8 7 6 5 4 3 2 1

Printed and bound in Canada
Set in Monotype Baskerville

*THIS BOOK IS DEDICATED*
*TO MY GRANDPARENTS*

Jane Taylor Elder
Francis Ebenezer Graham
Edith Jeanne Le Blanc
Oliva Rudolphe Le Blanc

# Contents

*Preface*    A Western Family    xi

CHAPTER ONE    A Day in the Life of the Real West    1
CHAPTER TWO    The Last Great Wilderness    21
CHAPTER THREE    Shadows and Stars    51
CHAPTER FOUR    *Le pays d'en haut*    83
CHAPTER FIVE    A Loaf of Bread, a Piece of Sausage    106
CHAPTER SIX    Tough Stock    147
CHAPTER SEVEN    The West Wants In—or Out    167
CHAPTER EIGHT    Visions of the Prairie West    183
CHAPTER NINE    The Changing West    205

*Epilogue*    The Dream of the West    216

*Acknowledgements*    225
*Appendix A: Mother Remembers*    227
*Appendix B: Key Dates in Western History*    235
*Notes*    239
*Selected Bibliography*    248
*Index*    253

# A Western Family

FRIDAY, December 13, 2002: I am sixty-two years and three months old, and I have spent all but five of those years in Saskatchewan, and only four of those, August 1965 to June 1969, outside Western Canada. When my husband and I made the decision to bring our five-year-old son back home to begin school where we had gone to school, despite the eagerness with which I'd left—*at last, the wider world*—it was with relief and an absence of regret of any kind.

A poet said something about having to leave and come home again to know the place for the first time. So it was for me. We'd been driving for five days when we finally pulled up in front of a small shopping centre on the edge of Saskatoon. My husband went inside to buy some small item and I sat in the car, my little boy on my knee, and watched the people walking by. I saw faces that I hadn't seen for five years: I saw that they were Saskatchewan faces, and I was amazed, not knowing until that moment of return to my homeland that there was such a thing as a Saskatchewan face.

I'd begun my adulthood as a painter and so, for the four years we lived in Halifax, I was a frequent visitor to the travelling shows at the Nova Scotia College of Art and Design. Sometime near the end of our four years there, we went to see an exhibition of the works of the Regina Five: Art McKay, Kenneth Lochhead, Douglas Morton, Ted Godwin, Ron Bloore.

At that time, the "gallery" was actually simply a large hall where shows were hung temporarily. Expecting nothing special, we walked in, my husband setting down our child, me beginning to slide off my coat, and before I'd had time to do more than merely make a sweeping survey around the hall full of pictures—abstract works, not traditionally representative—I was hit so hard—I could *feel* the wind—that I, literally, nearly fell down. There it was: my prairie home, pale, bathed in light, vast, windswept, and open, everything that Nova Scotia, with its dense forests, its worn-down mountains, its hilly, winding roads, was not.

All this happened a long time ago, and that marriage has been dissolved for more years than it existed; my little boy has been a man for a long time and has two children himself, one of them the same age now as he was when we brought him back home to start school. I am no longer a painter; for twenty-five years I have been a writer, and for longer I've lived in the southwestern part of the province, although I was born in the northeastern (more accurately, central eastern, but it was north enough for us), and have lived in small towns and our two main cities as well.

From my eighteenth-century ancestor, François Le Blanc (called "Saswe" by his Native companions and "Franceways"— for François—by the English), to one of Calgary's first families to my pioneer parents, grandparents, and great-grandparents, with their farms in southern Manitoba established in the early

1880s, to my child's children, born in Vancouver and Saskatoon, I come from a Western family.

Today my family is scattered across the West, from St. Boniface in Winnipeg, Manitoba, and farms to the south, through Saskatchewan, into Calgary and small-town Alberta, to Kamloops, Penticton, Vancouver, the Sunshine Coast, and Victoria on "the island." We are Westerners, at home in any of the four provinces west of Ontario: Manitoba, Saskatchewan, Alberta, and British Columbia. Like many prairie people, then, I can never quite erase the inborn sense I have of the only natural landscape being a wide-open one.

But, of course, even to admit this is to perpetuate that old myth that so annoys all of us—the one about the three Prairie provinces being flat. It's surprising how little of the land actually fulfills that stereotype. In fact, most of them contain mountains, forests, lakes and rivers, or grassland (now farmland) that is actually rolling hills. Saskatchewan has waterfalls and the highest point (in the Cypress Hills) between the Rockies and the Laurentians; Manitoba has Riding Mountain National Park and enormous Lake Winnipeg, and Alberta has the mountains and the foothills. All three of the provinces have parklands, "bluffs" of trees around prairie, a most pleasing aspect. (I put quotes around *bluffs* because this usage is uniquely prairie. Elsewhere, a *bluff* means a bank or a cliff.)

Yet the state of mind that persists even among most people born on the prairies is that they *are* "wide open," with lots of space, surely the result of the fact that the majority of settlers stayed in the south, with its vast skies and rolling landscape, leaving the forested, watery parts to the north for the hardy few. And (with the exception of Alberta in the last twenty-five years) the generally sparse population, even in the south, left much distance between settlements, with wide, unpopulated farm fields separating them.

What the West is, what it means to be a Westerner, what the Western experience is and, thus, the Western soul, are what this book is about. From the Selkirk settlers, who arrived in the early nineteenth century, to the greatest in-migration of the late nineteenth and early twentieth centuries, we non-Aboriginal people can boast only one or two centuries on this western part of the continent—not long compared to European families, or to the people who were here already when the first of us came from Europe.

Again and again our poets have challenged us. Who are we, they ask? Not Europeans, most of us today never having set foot on that continent. In the face of Aboriginal people who have been here "since the world began," or at least since the end of the last ice age, fourteen thousand or more years ago, we claim only uncertainly to be "natives" of the new continent. Thus, we have no unchallengeable answer to that question, and our failure to find one, or our lack of certainty in what we do assert about who we are, is our basic, if unspoken, anxiety. It is one that haunts all Western Canadian people.

Nonetheless, this is *home* to us; we have no other home; if we do not belong here, neither do we belong anywhere else we can think of. If our ancestors did not love this place but dreamt instead of freedom, autonomy, prosperity, and far better lives for their children than they had, we newer generations have learned to love the prairies. We do not want to be anywhere else. But what do we need to think, or do, or have that would allow us to settle in, at last, as natives of this place?

I have pursued this question historically, more or less, by beginning with a day in my own life as a rural Westerner, then going all the way back to contemplating this Western land when it was what we EuroCanadians call a "wilderness." I have given a chapter to each of the Aboriginal people, the settlers, the French, and the women of the West (who have generally received short shrift in historical writing, despite their absolute importance, especially in Western Canada). We have lived and understood ourselves by certain fairly well set ideas about this place and, thus, about our situation in it. Sometimes, closer examination of these given ideas shows them to be false or, at least, in some degree inaccurate. In other cases, they are the closest thing to truth we can find.

Some of the questions I ask are these: Are we still a frontier society? Have we come to terms yet with the historical displacement of the Aboriginal people by the arrival of the couple of million settlers? How successful was that land-based settlement, and has the country lived up to its promise? Is this still "next year country"? Do we still live in the "last, best West"? We see ourselves as a group of Canadians not quite like any other Canadians, yet we believe, and wonder why, the rest of the country doesn't seem to understand us.

I have not always followed the standard stories about the West. My choice of subtopics and my emphasis are undeniably idiosyncratic, that is, those of someone who is a Westerner herself, and a woman, who is half-French by blood, who probably, although unproven, from somewhere in the dim past has a drop or two of Aboriginal blood herself, and who, having spent most of her life observing the hotbed of Saskatchewan politics, leans politically to the left rather than the right. I write about what most interests me, and what I think is most important, and in doing this, readers familiar with my work will find that *Lilac Moon* is not a departure from my earlier writing, but instead continues my own highly personal exploration of the lives, and the world, of Western Canadians.

Readers will notice that I have chosen to write about only the three Prairie provinces. This is primarily because to add the vast and varied province of British Columbia to the book would have required the addition of ideas not so congruent with what I am most interested in—the prairies. Nonetheless, to live on the prairies is to know British Columbia fairly well, to have visited and vacationed there often and since childhood, to have dozens of relatives who live there, many via retirement in that more benign climate. When I was a young woman, Vancouver was just coming into its own and, instead of Toronto, that was where prairie young people headed first in their quest to see the world. Many stayed, although just as many, like me, came back. As a consequence of all these forces, prairie people remain emotionally involved with that province, and it isn't possible to write a book about them without often mentioning British Columbia.

Most chapters have notes at the end of the book, where interesting, even essential, statistics reside, along with other information. I have also added an appendix, "Mother Remembers," consisting of most of the text of the story of my maternal great-grandparents who left Ireland in the 1860s, eventually arriving in southern Manitoba as settlers. It is a unique family story, but it is also a stand-in for many other settler-families' stories.

Although Manitoba became a province in 1870, it was then only a fraction of the size it is today, which it reached after 1905. Nevertheless, in 1970 Manitoba celebrated one hundred years of provincehood. Alberta and Saskatchewan, created at the same time, will celebrate their centenaries in 2005. It seems a fitting time to meditate on who we prairie-dwellers are today.

Through all of this I have tried not only to describe and recount what makes a Westerner, but also to discover and name the dream we all hold in common but never speak of, the one that is articulated perhaps only by our artists, and then, as is the way of artists, obliquely. What is *the dream of the West?*

# CHAPTER ONE

# A Day in the Life
# of the Real West

*The Wisdom of Horses*

A FEW DAYS before Christmas, I got up early and by a quarter to nine was on my way to a neighbouring town to pick up the new laptop we'd just bought at the computer store there. As Peter, my husband, was otherwise occupied that morning, I went alone. Since we had not had one flake of snow, I didn't have to go the long way around in order to drive on plowed roads, but took the more direct route on gravel roads—fifteen miles of them—before the last dozen miles of asphalt.

We live down in the Frenchman River valley, on land that is part of a flood irrigation project for growing hay. About twelve thousand years ago this valley was a great glacial meltwater river; its walls are as high as 160 feet and its width as much as a mile. Although the walls slope and sometimes flatten at a level higher than the valley floor, they are too rocky and steep to be plowed, and archaeologists and local people—

especially me—find many Aboriginal artefacts and features there. Because the valley is winding and the narrow little river that is all that is left of a once massive volume of water gets in the way, it takes about three miles of driving, past irrigation plot after irrigation plot—land that has been levelled and dyked in order to be flooded—to wend my way up onto the flat land above the valley.

That December morning I gained the top of the long hill and headed straight east, first passing a new steel storage shed, probably forty by sixty feet in size. I can never see it without remembering how its brand-new predecessor looked the day after it had been lifted fifty feet into the air, exploded, and then flattened by something meteorologists called a "plow wind," rather than a tornado, as everybody had first assumed. (The wind had come up from the southwest—I'd watched it as long as I dared, a roiling wall of wind, dusty pink in colour.) The same wind had first lifted and flattened a larger steel storage building to the south of us. As it swept on through our place, it took out steel gates and fences and, much worse, half of our trees, but miraculously it missed the house on one side of our road, where I'd run to, and the steel shed on the other side, where Peter had taken shelter.

Three miles beyond the shed I turned north. I saw then that the valley hills on my left to the west were still shadowed with deeper blue clefts, but a full, pale yellow moon was hanging in the sky just above them. As I drove—I had yet to meet or pass another vehicle—I watched the moon's slow descent into the pink haze that sat along the line of the hills. Then the colour changed—of both the hills and the moon—to a soft grey-pink. No, it was lilac. All the rugged landscape to the west had turned the colour of the blooms of the June lilacs that the first settlers had planted and that now rise to the roofline of the old log house I can see from my window as I sit writing this. (Once, about a week before I was to leave for Greece, I saw a green and yellow parrot—an "escapee," apparently—riding the lilac branches as they bounced in a strong wind. I stared and stared, then looked away; when I looked back, the parrot was gone.) I thought of how often in my writing I'd described our brilliant prairie sunsets and moonsets and their rises, and how often I'd used the words *mauve* and *lilac* to describe their colours (for some reason I shy away from the word *lavender*, perhaps because it seems precious and Victorian to a rugged, common-sensical prairie woman like myself).

Now I felt I'd been careless when I'd done that. I'd taken a glance and said to myself, not without a tinge of exasperation, oh, mauve, pink, or yellow, orange, because I saw the sun set and rise, and the moon too, often both, every day of my life. The palette doesn't vary all that much, just the brightness and the combination of shades, and what I was seeing now— as if I'd never really seen such a thing in my life before—was lilac, true lilac. The whole landscape had turned a soft, hazy lilac, and I was stricken with amazement, or awe, and a rare, inner speechlessness. I even laughed a little to myself as I sped down that noisy gravel road toward my new computer (about which I felt mostly bemusement), watching the now lilac moon as it descended on its stately journey to light the other side of the world.

On my left, a mile or so away, I noted that, as usual, an orange torch flared off gas from an oil well. Beside the moon's light and in the vastness of the rolling landscape of bare summerfallow or fields of dun-coloured grass or crop stubble, the lilac hills and buttes rising behind the fields, the flare was tiny and pale. Yet that tiny flare is almost ten feet high as it surges out of the mouth of the twenty- to thirty-foot-high steel pipe that contains it. It has been flaring there, as far as I can recall, most of the nearly thirty years I've been driving down this road, and I'm rarely even curious about it anymore.

At the highway at last (I still hadn't met another vehicle and there is only one occupied house on that twelve-mile stretch of road), I turned east again. Now I began to watch the sun rise, its first red rays striking flint along the eastern edge of the earth, then sending out rays of pure, molten gold. Good grief, I thought—I often catch myself thinking in phrases that were current in my grandmother's day or that went out of fashion when I was teenager in the fifties—good grief, how many people in Canada can drive down a road first thing in the morning in the dead of winter and watch the moon set on the one hand as the sun begins its rise on the other?

Well, Northerners can, and I suppose country people in rural areas from Newfoundland to Vancouver Island (except for mountains and trees in the way, and the fog, rain, and cloudy skies of coastal regions). Nowadays, though, most Canadians live in cities, and the bigger those cities are, the more likely their views of the sky are obstructed by buildings. As well, most city-dwellers are too busy or too preoccupied with other, more pressing things—traffic, people, business at hand—to notice the skies. At this moment, like rural-dwellers everywhere, I genuinely pitied them.

By this time the sun had risen fully above the eastern horizon and the landscape on all sides had turned a smoky pink. I turned up the radio in time to hear the announcer remark on the hazy pink light flooding the city of Regina, about two hundred miles east of me, and how beautiful it was. He went on to warn everybody about the approaching blizzard in the central to southeastern part of the province, telling them to stay off the roads, that visibility was nil in places and the roads ice-covered and far too dangerous for travel. I knew, as he did, that his

warning would be unlikely to stop anybody, not even grandmothers and rarely even school buses.

With the advent of cell phones and of roads and vehicles that
are much better than fifty years ago, it's rare for anybody to
freeze to death in a blizzard, as used to happen a couple of
times every winter. Now, people may disappear for a day or
two, having taken a back road and vanished into a snow-filled
ditch, but everybody gets out and searches for them. The radio
lets us know about the searchers' progress, and eventually the
lost persons are found, alive and well, rarely even frostbitten.
That is less true in the North, where the frozen bodies of the
lost do turn up. (Or in Saskatoon, where several winters ago,
shamefully, amazingly, horrifyingly, the body, frozen solid and
only half-dressed, of an Aboriginal man was found by an MLA
out for her morning jog, bringing the total of such bodies to
four, three that winter and one in 1990.)

I drove on as the sun rose higher and the pink turned to yellow and then to the normal, hyperclear light of a prairie winter
day. It was the kind of light that makes every fencepost, every
rock, every cleft in the hills stand out, so that, staring at them,
one wrinkles one's brow, puzzling, as if to ask, *Is God trying to tell
me something about that rock, that fencepost?* By then I'd reached the
town and, remembering my task, like any urbanite I began to
focus on it instead of the landscape and the wonderful sky.

The red-brick building that housed the computer business
used to be a Sears store and before that—well, I've forgotten,
but it's been doing duty one way or another for probably
eighty years, each owner tarting it up for its new incarnation.
But our laptop and printer weren't ready yet, so I went on to
the Co-op to pick up a few more grocery items for our Christmas dinner, and a few more gifts. I would have dilly-dallied
around town some more, but the morning was passing and I
had a funeral to attend that afternoon back in Eastend.

As it happens, the "other business" Peter had to take care of that morning was catching and saddling four horses, loading them into his stocktrailer, and hauling them to town. The afternoon's funeral was going to be a traditional Western "horseback" funeral, the first one held in town in a very long time. Three town-dwellers (although they never seem to perceive themselves as such, but think of themselves still as the cowboys and landsmen they were once raised to be) who kept their horses at our place were going to ride in the procession.

It would be a large funeral—the deceased had lived his whole life in the area and was well liked by everyone. Because the town hall, the only venue large enough, was in use for the schoolchildren's annual Christmas concert that afternoon, the funeral was being held in the church used jointly by the Catholics and the Lutherans. After a hasty lunch, we changed to our funeral-going clothes, plus some extra-warm items, and drove into Eastend, anxious not to arrive so late that we would have to stand outside the church on this breezy, chilly, but still snowless December day.

The deceased had so many relatives that nearly half the church's pews had been reserved for them; the choir loft was full of friends, neighbours, and acquaintances. I had no choice but to stand in the packed, freezing vestibule, the doors of which were open ostensibly so that those standing outside could hear the service, but they couldn't and chatted softly to each other, drowning it out so that those of us in the vestibule couldn't hear either.

Then it was over, the casket placed by the young pallbearers into the hearse, the family members dispersing into various vehicles. Before the service had ended, the riders had crossed the street to the vacant lot between the former building and the café, where their horses were tied to stocktrailers. They'd tightened their horses' cinches, changed halters for bridles, ridden them into the centre of the too-wide main street, and arranged themselves into seven straight rows of four horses each.

As the mourners slowly emerged from the church, we milled quietly about, most of us trying to find a good vantage point from which to watch the procession as it made its way down the main street toward the bend in the road that led to a long hill and the sudden, narrow turnoff to the cemetery, which sits high above the western edge of town.

The riders were dressed simply in their best casual jackets and jeans or riding pants. All wore light-coloured Stetsons (few wear black because around here black hats are reserved for the Hutterite men) and their riding boots. I don't remember seeing any chaps, spurs, or other cowboy gear, which might include the coiled rope tied to the saddle, the saddle-bag containing maybe fencing pliers, maybe a vial of cow or calf medication and a syringe, although they could have been on some saddles.

Slowly, the long grey hearse pulled out from the curb. It made its way, a few cars of immediate family following closely, past the crowd of silent mourners, skirting the lines of horses, to the front of the procession. Once there, somebody at the back shouted "Move out!" The call went through the riders to the front, and the twenty-eight horses (at least one ridden by a woman) began slowly, in formation, to clip-clop softly down the street in the grey, late-afternoon light.

The odd thing was that all twenty-eight horses had moved into position and stood quietly for perhaps fifteen minutes, waiting, not one of them acting up—prancing out of position, trying to bite or kick the horse next to it—not one resisting. Standing as I was in the vestibule, if one had even neighed, I would have heard it. "It was as if they knew it was a funeral," somebody said, and we mourners smiled a little and nodded sagely, a bit awed, a bit touched, by the horses' unusual good manners and the thought of what they might know, for which we rarely give them credit.

Behind them came a lone rider leading a dun-coloured quarter horse—saddled but riderless. Usually, at such funerals, the deceased's riding boots are placed backwards in the stirrups, but today the stirrups were empty and I wondered if nobody had wanted to bother the widow for her husband's boots, or if they felt such a gesture excessive, or if they'd simply forgotten the custom. Watching the horses as they disappeared down the street, I couldn't decide if this was mawkish, excessive, a gesture designed more for the glory of those riding the horses than as a statement of respect for the deceased, or if it was touching and beautiful, an old-fashioned folk rite one would rarely see except, maybe, at a state funeral in England.

It occurred to me that the riderless horse (with or without the backward-facing boots) might be a military custom. Did it come west with, say, the North-West Mounted Police in the 1870s, I wondered? Or had it come north with the many American settlers to this region? And if it did, was it through the American cavalry? I made a note to ask somebody about the riderless horse, because it had begun to seem to me a strange thing for ordinary people to do for other ordinary people.

But I knew that this gesture was reserved for and meant as an expression of the highest respect for one who had been a horseman, a stockman, all his life a man of the land. Later I asked my husband to explain what it was all about and after a long, reflective silence, he said, a touch glumly, "It's the last ride, I guess."

After that, many cars and half-tons full of mourners went slowly by on their way up to the cemetery. A large reception would be held later in the town hall, where coffee and tea, small sandwiches, and squares would be served to perhaps two hundred people, all this work done by local women—the hall board or women members of a church or club.

Because Peter had to help reload the horses later in the day and drive them home, he would attend the reception (viewed by those not close to the deceased or his family—although they'd probably never admit it—as an opportunity to "visit" and to catch up on all the news). I couldn't stay, though, because I had a weekly meeting to attend in a village thirty miles south of our home, and I had to drive home and change my clothes before I could go. It would be twilight on my way there—I would watch the sun set as I drove south—and dark on my way back; I'd have to drive more slowly than I'd like to because of the inevitable deer and sometimes antelope that often suddenly appear in my car's headlights. After my leisurely starlit drive back, Peter and I would meet at home around eight in the evening.

I would describe all of this, airily, as an ordinary day in the life of the West, and—other than the horseback funeral—it was: the severe yet commonplace wind damage, the long drives to do normal daily errands, rarely meeting another vehicle, the full view of both sunrise and sunset and the enormous gossamer moon floating over the hills in a lilac haze, the deer, the antelope, the huge community gathering (including many people who barely knew the deceased or didn't know him at all) because one well-liked, respected man had died, the oil rigs and gas flare we'd lived with so long we hardly noticed them. Perhaps I should say it was an ordinary day in the *rural* West.

I wondered briefly if I could describe a day in a Western city, and supposed that I could but that there wouldn't be much point in doing so. Most Canadians live in cities, and our television, movies, and radio assume all their listeners and viewers are urban—so everybody knows what a day in the life of a city is like.

I wondered if a day in the life of a Western city would be different from one in Central Canada or the Maritimes, and if it was (and I felt sure it would be) what the differences might be. I felt no need to examine rural life further; surely my just-finished day was, as the day of a Westerner only, self-explanatory.

I started to think about the West. I thought about Western alienation and Western radicalism, both of the political right and of the left, and about our so-called redneckism, that is, our supposed lack of culture and our rigid attitudes toward foreigners—visible minorities—and, indeed, toward those Canadians of French heritage and especially toward the French language itself. I thought of our vaunted tendency to love guns better than "Easterners" do. I thought too of British Columbia on the other side of the mountains, practically a country unto itself in the view of all Canada east of the Manitoba–Ontario border. I thought of Alberta's magnificent and growing wealth, which attracts people from all over the country, and of what is perceived of as our—and especially Alberta's—bumptiousness: political, Christian, and *nouveau riche*.

However, if you were to ask a Westerner who he or she is, the reply would have to do with our essential classlessness, with the vast opportunities here, and especially with our great love of the land, of nature, and of our wilderness. It would probably also have to do with growth and progress and our shiny future. And, inevitably, it would have to do with pioneering, with a reverence for our heroic past, how the present generation can never live up to that heroism, that courage, that toughness, how we are a tough breed, much tougher and more rugged than other Canadians, except perhaps for the fisher families of the Maritimes.

Men out here are always finding ways of proclaiming to the rest of the world that they are real men, guns being one way, cowboy boots on executives another. Westerners also see themselves as more direct, less devious, and more honest than other Canadians, especially Central Canadians. Yet we believe that we are seen as essentially a peasant society, and that the rest of the country looks down its nose at us.

Somewhere in the roots and at the core of these assumptions about the West—our own and those of the rest of Canada—I was sure the truth lay. But I was equally sure that it was not easily identified, was probably elusive. I began to wonder if I could ferret out the truth, if I could *say* it. And that is how this personal journey of exploration began.


If the best way to be a true Westerner is to be born here, preferably in the earliest of settlement days and preferably under suitably difficult conditions, that is, closest to nature (although not in a teepee, which might not count), another way to be a true Westerner is to rodeo—not to take part in rodeo, but in Western parlance, as a verb, *to rodeo*.

Although I didn't come from rodeo country but from "the bush," I've been living on a Saskatchewan cattle ranch for nearly thirty years. Here I have had to learn to ride a horse and chase cows, to know what a "stifle" is, and "bulldogging," and when to use a "breakaway hondo," not that I ever have. Rodeo is an integral part of this life, whether one actually rodeos or merely watches, and so I have had to learn about it, too. Over the years I've gone from being fascinated (in a slightly revolted, mildly terrified way), to being bored stiff, to telling my *non-country* friends that secretly I think there's no excuse for it.

Then Peter won a trip for two to the twenty-ninth Canadian Finals Rodeo (CFR) in Edmonton, something he's always wanted to attend, although it was not on my top ten list. I decided to go with him, as much out of curiosity as for a not-to-be-missed shopping opportunity. I made up my mind I'd sit through all three shows we'd been given tickets to while keeping my eyes wide open and my mouth firmly shut.

Our first tickets were for the Friday evening "performance," where we wedged ourselves into our seats high up in the stands above the chutes. We were surrounded by women my own age, with no-nonsense haircuts, new skin-tight blue jeans, and Western-cut blouses and vests, by toddlers wearing tiny cowboy boots and minute jeans, and by Stetson-hatted, blue-jeaned, boot-wearing men with serious bellies and weathered faces. The younger men had romantically drooping moustaches and the younger women had long (but never "big") hair—you can't work as hard as most of these women do and keep "big" hair.

Moving with the crowd into Edmonton's Skyreach Centre, we'd seen two police officers interrogating a young cowboy. We'd no idea what had happened, thinking at first there had been a fight, and then more likely that his wallet or gear had been stolen. He was pretty embarrassed, but I was struck by something familiar: that scrubbed look, a kind of freshness that radiates from all these young men, which I find unique to young rodeo cowboys. His was a choirboy's face, except for his eyes. They were somewhere between permanently startled and visionary, as if all he could see was the blue of the sky and the dream they carry of a world only they can see: of what a *man* is—invincible and pure—and how a *man* lives—wild and free. (You don't see that look on the old men, who appear merely exhausted, leathery, and often as hard as nails.)

Of course, we mustn't forget young cowboys who are so in love with their lifestyle, so proud of all that they believe it stands for, I suspect most of it learned from American Western movies. They dress as if it were the American frontier around 1860 or so, with that *desperado* look: carefully cultivated bushy moustaches, picturesquely dented Stetsons, nicely draped neckscarves with the knot at the back and the point below the chin, and sometimes leather vests, plus the ubiquitous Levi's and worn high-heeled boots (although lower heels are the fashion these days). But even given this carefully cultivated outward image, I hasten to add that these men are nevertheless not the drugstore variety, but are real working cowboys who can rope and ride with the best of the old-time cowboys they so revere.

That gear, however, evolved for good reasons, most of which still apply. I once did a radio piece explaining the purpose of each standard item of cowboy clothing. For example, the wide-brimmed hat is not an affectation but a necessity because out on the plains in the summer heat, the only shade is under that hat; the tight jeans are so that legs won't get rubbed raw when on horseback all day; the neckscarf covers the mouth and nose when the moving cattle create clouds of dust; the chaps provide warmth and/or protection when riding in bush. I ended by explaining that the big silver belt buckle is to stop bullets.

CFR is the culmination of a year of nearly sixty rodeos held across Western Canada; it's a strictly Western phenomenon (despite the fact that cowboys themselves can come from Texas, Quebec, or Queensland). However, competitors do have to belong to the Canadian Professional Rodeo Association (CPRA). To do this, a cowboy has to first become a semi-pro (by earning $1,000 in two seasons in the five major events: saddle bronc, bareback bronc, bull riding, calf roping, and steer wrestling). Then, as a semi-pro he must earn $1,000 in one season in a major event. As well, to make the Canadian Finals, he has to have earned points in the top ten for the year. Points are actual dollars won—in Canada, as much as $100,000 per year, but usually, for the top cowboys, in the $25,000 to $35,000 range. It's not much compared to pro hockey, and the expenses are higher: nobody provides his gear, the costs of his constant travel, or his entry fees.

Prize money has been climbing, but at the 2002 CFR, first to fourth in the five major events and barrel racing paid "$5,586, $4,189, $2,793, and $1,396," according to *Canadian Rodeo* (CPRA's official newspaper). That's called the "day money," meaning that the day's winner in any event is not necessarily the same person as the year's event winner, or even, in the longer rodeos, as the rodeo's winner. But you have only to sit through a rodeo to know that these boys aren't in it for the money.

Although I've been going to rodeos ever since I married Peter, the CFR was something new. In the early years of our marriage, every July we'd drive up to a small local rodeo called Murraydale, in the Cypress Hills, on land adjacent to the Nekaneet Reserve. Like all such rodeos, events took forever to unfold, the hapless announcer constantly urging the next event's participants to get down to the arena: "Ladies, barrel racing," he'd bellow, "you're up next, get them horses ready, let's go now," and so on, but no one was ever lined up and ready to go the instant the last calf-roper had coiled his rope.

Nobody really minded, though. We'd park our trucks on a grassy hillside with a view down to the dirt arena, high enough to escape the roiling clouds of dust that accompanied every event. Everybody had a picnic: fried chicken, watermelon, a few beers in a cooler for the men. Everybody knew everybody else, so when the countless team ropers got too boring to watch anymore or there was another in the endless series of delays—the arena empty except for little boys galloping on foot trying to rope each other and the chute end lined with companionable ranchers and cowboys of all ages—the rest of the crowd wandered around happily and visited. In the early days, I'm told, Murraydale lasted two or three days. People would sleep out all night under the stars and there would even be a "moccasin dance," that is, on the grass, on Saturday night.

Once, at the Maple Creek rodeo, I'd been lying with my husband and his friends on the grass outside the arena's high page-wire fence, when about four feet from us, a bareback bronc bucked so hard he fell over backwards *on* his rider. I burst into tears, sure the cowboy was dead. "Ah, he's just winded," a cowboy said to me. "Please, don't cry ma'am." The horse rolled and pulled himself to his feet, and then, the cowboy I'd expected to see as flat as a pancake dragged himself upright and, as the crowd cheered and clapped, slapped the dust off himself and walked gamely away, albeit with a slight crimp in his torso. That's how the small rodeos go, dusty, wild, and up close and personal.

But when the CFR started in Edmonton you'd have thought we were at a rock concert. Country and western music blasted out over the sound system, huge puffs of white smoke billowed up and spread out into the rafters, giant fireballs flared upward from two fire-pots on the coliseum floor, revolving floodlights flashed patterns, and big screens above showed horses, cowboys, and pretty cowgirls streaming by in full colour. Over the jumped-up audio system, the mellifluous announcer spoke mawkishly about rodeo.

Next, the previous day's event winners were introduced as, one by one, they walked forward into the spotlight, a row of flames marking their progress. Gorgeous blonde Miss Rodeo Canada, in her glittering shirt, followed, circling the arena at a fast gallop. Then, slowly, the lights came up, the volume was lowered minimally, the first bronc rider was out in the arena, and the eight-second horn sounded before I'd even realized the rodeo had begun.

It went that way the whole evening and the next and during

the Sunday-afternoon finals too: events whipped by within a two-hour limit. Not a delay, not a foul-up, not a second's pause for showboating (yes, even rodeo cowboys have been known to showboat). One nineteen-year-old steer wrestler was so pleased about his time that—to the crowd's delight—he did a few not-very-smooth disco steps and then, still wearing his chaps and protective vest, finished up with a clunky cartwheel. The announcer said, "He's a little thick in the middle to be doing those moves," and the clown (miked and down in the arena) replied, "Yeah, the French judge'll kill him on the figures."

As a former city girl, I'm only too aware of urban attitudes to rodeo. The biggest concern (although not one spoken of much in polite company) is what makes the horses and the bulls buck. The obvious answer is that they aren't "broke" animals and that they respond to the cowboy's unfamiliar presence by try-ing their best to get rid of him. More important, they've been bred to buck, on special ranches like the Calgary Stampede Ranch. But the fact is, as anybody familiar with horses and bulls knows, sometimes they don't buck, and if rodeo is going to be viable, a small incentive has to be provided.

For this, the flank strap is used. This is a sheepskin-covered leather strap that circles the animal's body around his flanks—that inward curve between the back of the belly and the swell of the hip, in *front* of the animal's genitals—with a "breakaway" fastening (meaning one jerk from the pickup man and it falls off ). The flank is a particularly sensitive area (my husband says you never touch a horse on his flank; he'll kick you for sure), and the horse or bull responds by trying to kick off the strap. It isn't pain he's feeling but a kind of irritation. If it were pain (and in the past those straps were sometimes pulled too tight), the horse would fall down and wouldn't be able to get up until the strap was loosened—not a profitable way to run a rodeo.

The events last only eight seconds and the pickup men are

there at once, leaning over their horses to jerk open the flank strap and let it fall away. Twenty seconds in total, maybe. Knowing this, and knowing also that this is rodeo stock— animals that have been through this lots of times and know what's going to happen—I watched the saddle, bareback-bronc, and bull-riding events without qualms for the animals. (The CPRA claims that horses and bulls are hurt more often in ranch life than they ever are in rodeo.)

As far as I know, the CPRA doesn't keep statistics on damage to cowboys, but I'd seen enough on television to know the horrifying possibilities. I'd seen cowboys whose entire faces were smashed, cowboys confined permanently to wheelchairs, cowboys with punctured lungs, busted teeth, ribs, legs, and spleens, or mentally disabled for life. I'd shaken my head more than once, saying, "They're crazy; they have to be crazy!"

There had been 15,348 people at the rodeo on Friday night, but on Saturday night there were more, and they were louder and more enthusiastic. You could feel the cowboys and cowgirls responding to the excitement. I felt it myself, and as salesmen raced up and down the stands carrying stacked trays of beer and the people around me concentrated hard on goings-on in the arena when they weren't intent on marking their small personal scorecards, I moved, just a little, into feeling a part of things.

When one calf-roper made his catch with such a jerk that the calf lifted into the air, spun sideways, and landed on the arena floor with a heart-stopping thud, I didn't want to leave. I was pleased that at least half the sixteen thousand people gave a collective roar of displeasure. Clearly, I wasn't the only one who found this unacceptable. (There are new rules now, designed to prevent this from happening.)

The roper then leaps off his horse (trained to allow a rider to mount and dismount from either side), runs to the calf, holding it down with a knee, grabs a front and two back legs, and ties them together. "Two rounds and a half-hitch," the announcer, himself a rodeo cowboy, intones. During this the horse keeps the rope around the calf's neck taut, but once the calf is tied, the cowboy remounts and slackens the rope, and the calf must stay immobilized for six seconds before the contestant gets a time. Then a couple of men race out and free the animal. A good calf-roping time is eight to nine seconds.

Calf roping is a part of ranch life: if a calf is separated from its mother and starving, or hurt, or sick, and the rancher is four miles from the nearest corral (and calves are notoriously hard to chase), it must be roped in order to doctor it or get it where it's supposed to be. But it's never much fun for the calf, no matter that it saves its life. In the rodeo arena, it was the event I found hardest to take, even though some effort is made to save animals discomfort: team-roping steers wear leather pads around their horns so the rope doesn't burn their hides; flank straps are covered in thick sheepskin; animals are well fed, rested, and kept clean—sick or weak animals can't perform— and many past abuses are now disallowed (at least, in competitions at this level).

It used to be, too, that rodeo contestants were ranch-raised, had grown up routinely calf roping and riding broncs. Sundays, young ranchers would often get together at somebody's ranch; cheering each other on, they would ride steers and unbroken horses, and sometimes even bulls. All one summer during the first years of our marriage, my husband would load his horse into his stocktrailer and head down to a friend's ranch, where a bunch of cowboys would stage an impromptu rodeo. I still occasionally hear from the other men who were there about the time somebody else's horse "blew up" and my husband, then nearly fifty, "rode 'im," instead of getting splattered on the ground. He grinned at me sheepishly when he told me about it, not having rodeoed as a young man because as an only son he was vital to the ranch, and useless with a broken leg.

At the CFR one cowboy had a medical degree and another, according to the announcer, "grew up in Quebec and learned about rodeo from television!" But he went on to remark, "I don't care where you grew up . . .," meaning, I suspect, that so many non-ranch-raised competitors are a bit of an embarrassment to professional rodeo. After all, rodeo is a cultural ritual, the embodiment of a culture's idea of itself. If anybody, ranch-raised or not, can learn to do it, the culture feels itself devalued.

That night I slid into my seat during saddle-bronc riding. The last rider had stayed on, but when the horn sounded, the pickup men were far back in the arena and the wildly bucking horse, his mane and tail streaming in the wind he'd created himself, made straight for our end. Gripping the rigging now with both hands, his hat still on, the cowboy fell into harmony with the horse's lunges and kicks. From above, but on an angle, I could see the rider's torso stretching and yielding in time with the horse.

Then it was that everything stopped, the very turning of the earth, and there was no one else in that vast place, just him and the horse in that dance together, all alone in the midst of—of that vision I'd first seen in the young cowboy's eyes on my way in on Friday night.

It was a truly masculine vision if ever there was one. Even the program lists the "five major events *and* ladies barrel racing," and as soon as the truck containing the barrels moves out into the arena, half the audience gets up and leaves for the bathroom, a leg stretch, or a hot dog. I've never been to a rodeo where that didn't happen. Not to say that the women don't have their supporters, that their horses aren't studied, discussed, and cheered, that their riding techniques aren't minutely watched, and that their times aren't marked on personal scoresheets too. Partway through the event all those leavers drift back to their seats.

The last event is always bull riding. It's the most exciting, the most dangerous, and the one the crowd most wants to see. (While steer wrestlers are usually big and heavy, bull riders tend to be small men.) It's the event requiring the most courage, too, because once the rider is off, the bull will turn on him to gore, stomp, or kick him, or all three. The worst time is when the rider *can't* get off, gets "hung up" in the rigging and hangs spinning and heaving with every spin and heave of the two-thousand-pound bull intent on ridding himself of an annoyance. This is life and death, pure and simple; no bull rider ever knows when he lowers himself onto the bull's back, gingerly, with shaking knees, whether he'll get off with all his faculties or never perform again. But he does it anyway.

Then it was all over. I came away chastened, moved even, my disapproval mitigated, almost gone. I even felt a little proud, that an (arguably) dying culture maintains such ardour—in the face of all sorts of opposition and criticism—for its unique rite. The participants understand it, even if others don't.

And that was when I saw finally what rodeo was all about—the meaning of what I'd seen when the world had stopped as I watched the cowboy ride, in triumph and joy, his wild horse. It was a moment's distillation of all the West had once stood for: freedom, and a valiant sharing in the last great wildness. It was a *dream of the West*.

# CHAPTER TWO

# The Last Great Wilderness

*What makes a Westerner?*
*Our relationship to the land.*

L ATE one afternoon just before Christmas, Peter and I were driving home to our hay farm on the Frenchman River near Eastend. It's in a valley that runs east and west for many miles and, as I've explained, the valley walls are the boundaries of a once-great glacial spillway. The valley bottom—a mile wide where we are situated—is cultivated to hay, and as it is also a flood irrigation project, it's often very busy with people coming and going. Because there was little snow, we were entering the hay farm by the well-used dirt trail along the river. As we approached the place where the road rises over a large culvert, we saw an animal come at right angles to our path out of the high grass, cross the road in front of us, and disappear into the opposite ditch. It was moving so fast it was barely more than a blur.

"*Did you see that?*" I asked Peter. "*What . . . ?*" He'd braked and we sat there, stunned, neither of us sure what we'd seen until we'd checked with the other.

"It wasn't a coyote," we agreed. It had been moving in the

wrong way, and more—something that even at that speed we'd both seen—it had a long, thin tail, like a cat, with a black tip on the end. I said, "It was more the colour of a Hereford calf" (a dark, reddish shade, although otherwise it was the wrong shape, and no Hereford on earth could run that fast). And a bobcat's tail is—check the name—very short. That left only—we hesitated, almost afraid to say it—the mountain lion. In the end we decided that there could be no other explanation, but it wasn't until I looked up "mountain lion" and read that its colours range from gold to a dark red (often all on one animal) that I could fully accept that there had been a mountain lion on our land.

Cougars, or mountain lions, also known variously as pumas, painters, panthers, and catamounts, are and have always been part of this landscape, a fact I hadn't known until a year or two earlier, about the time that a woman was killed in a cougar attack at Banff and another was saved from one at the last moment. Closer to home, though, I remembered that a cougar had been spotted in Swift Current (a hundred miles northeast) near a walking path along Swift Current Creek. A naturalist friend told us that although they are normally here, we rarely see them because they travel out of sight through the deep, branching, and sometimes wooded coulees characteristic of this landscape. They are nocturnal animals, although they will hunt in the early morning and at dusk, when we saw ours.

I thought of all the miles and miles of walking I'd done on our land over the years, confident that I was safe in a landscape I'd described in print as "benign," that with the extirpation of bears in the nineteenth century and wolves in the early twentieth, I had nothing to fear from the animal kingdom. And so I'd blithely wandered and climbed where there was something to climb, and then descended again, happy as a lark and innocent as the proverbial lamb.

But I remembered now that there had always been places that gave me the willies. Climbing a cliffside once, I'd come to what I thought must be a bobcat den, with its giveaway pad out front; I could smell cat and scrambled away pretty fast. Now I asked myself, how did I know it wasn't a mountain lion den? Well, I didn't. It hadn't occurred to me because I didn't know then that they lived here, much less that although nursing mothers may den, as a rule cougars don't.

I remembered too that more than once, glancing out the window above the kitchen sink, I'd seen the cattle start to run, going all in one direction and then swerving to run as fast as they could in a different direction and, afraid they'd go right through the fences and, knowing something was out there, I'd run to warn Peter.

On another occasion, I was walking down a road near our house, really just a truck-wide dirt trail in the grass. I had the dog with me, nosing around, then trotting to catch up with me, and there was a strong wind blowing—I mean, a very strong wind, not to say a howling gale. It is hard to say what happened exactly. I thought I heard something, although I actually didn't hear anything over the whoop and roar of the wind; but I got this weird feeling as if there were a ghost behind me, a kind of powerful, prickly rippling down my spine, and I stopped and looked around. On my left was a high grassy bank; on my right the field flattened out, with grass at the edge and wheat stubble behind that. Directly ahead and behind was the empty road. I saw nothing, not an animal other than my dog, nor a bird. I looked at the dog for a clue. He had stopped and was giving me a strange, sort of puzzled look: *Something weird is going on here and I don't know what it is. Do you?* I thought, there must be an unusually big coyote in the grass up in that bank. Always cautious, I turned on my heel and without changing my pace, headed straight back for our house.

I've wondered ever since what animal it was up in that tall grass, and I've wondered how I knew that it—or something—was there. Failing to find any explanation at all, I've decided it must have been some sort of atavistic alarm system at work in me (or my guardian angel on the job). And now I wonder if what I sensed was a cougar. They can weigh as much as two hundred pounds and are routinely five to seven or more feet from nose to tail tip, and, scariest of all, they attack from the rear, leaping to catch their victim at the base of its skull, breaking the neck with their powerful jaws. (Ask the people of Vancouver and the Gulf Islands: they lose more people to mountain lions than anywhere else on earth.) I'd been exactly correctly positioned and, at five feet, am small enough to be a mountain lion's kill.

I have written about the wildness of that place where in 1940 I began life: between the 53rd and 54th lines of north latitude in what was then bush country (meaning forested, and so called in South Africa, Australia, and New Zealand, too) north and west of Nipawin, Saskatchewan, at the very edge of our boreal forest—it is still the edge. I am cast back to my first memories in this world: the soul-shivering nightly howling of timber wolves, the constant fear of bears, which, despite their beguiling penchant for play, are always dangerous. And the forest too seemed full of danger that was inherent in the forest itself—fear of getting lost, I suppose, fear of the unknown, and all of the forest except its very fringes seemed unknown.

As a child I did not think of it as wild, but as part of a new green world of richness and great beauty, which was also fully peopled by family and by neighbours, including the Indian people—the men who sometimes worked for my father at his sawmill, the women and children who camped nearby and sometimes came to our door. I did not know we were pioneers; I did not know any other world.

But I was also told, once we'd left, that it was a terrible world, the end of the earth, where great hardship reigned, that it was an unwelcoming wilderness where ignorance ruled and opportunities for education and culture—which were what really mattered—were nil. And so I grew up stifling my curiosity about the place where we had spent years, doing my best to forget it had been a part of my life, and assuming that all lives were a triumphal progress out of wilderness and poverty to education, prosperity, and neatly mowed lawns. I know better now, at least about that idea of "progress." And if we soon left that wilderness I'd been born into, we did not ever learn to leave behind the idea of its existence, the notion of the wildness that we had never conquered and that waited not so far away from all of us, wherever we are in the West.

Surely Europeans have no sense of wilderness lurking all around them. Canadians certainly do. It lies out there—full of promise, full of danger, full of our original selves. From the moment of our conception it hangs there deep in our psyches. Such a shadowy, omnipresent inevitability has the power to shape the psyche of an entire nation: it sobers you up, it calms you down, it is the source of Canadians' reported modesty because we are constantly reminded of how fragile the comforts of civilization really are. In this country, sooner or later, each of us must measure ourselves in the light of that wilderness's existence.

Today Westerners are filled with nostalgia for the wilderness we imagine that was the past. We want it back (or at least some of us do), we want back the wildness, and we imagine a landscape of tall grasses waving in the wind, studded with wildflowers, or of untouched, endless, dense forests, or freely flowing, torrential, or wide and placid yet inexorable rivers. We imagine the continent as it was when our ancestors first arrived here—as it was when the explorers recorded it in their journals and as visual artists, both amateur and professional, depicted it as far back as the seventeenth century.

These early accounts constantly speak of the vastness of this place, an unimaginable vastness that was awe-inspiring in its beauty. They speak of its ability to strike terror, too, in the breast of anyone, however bold and brave, seeing it for the first time.

They record how changeable and astonishingly violent the weather: on December 10, 1797, David Thompson, travelling for the North West Company in what today is southwestern Manitoba, tells of a day that had begun clear and cold at −20°F, turned to snow, then to rain, and finally into a snowstorm so violent and blinding that he and his companions nearly lost their lives. He recorded in his journal, "In little more than twelve hours a difference of temperature of fifty-six degrees [Fahrenheit]. . . . I had weathered many a hard gale, but this was the most distressing day I had ever seen."[1]

Long before the advent of global warming, Westerners knew well the violent, changeable weather. Many of us have by now lived through single days where the temperature spread over fifty degrees, and we are both proud of our ability to survive such weather and a little amazed at ourselves. Lately, it seems that with global warming, our weather has become even more unexpected and dramatic.

These accounts of the area that became the Prairie provinces speak of the wildlife, of a world teeming with flocks of birds, of beaver by the thousands and muskrats in all the streams and rivers, of wolves and bears, of herds of deer, elk, moose, and especially of the perhaps sixty million bison that roamed here. There is no more powerful symbol of the West that once was, the Wild West, than the herds of buffalo so vast that, we are told, it would take days for them to pass, sometimes weeks.

To the First Nations of the Great Plains of North America, the buffalo was life itself, both the source of housing, food, apparel, and items for many other purposes, and the centre of spiritual life, for who could forbear to thank the Creator every day for such continued abundance? The virtual extinction of these animals happened very quickly in the nineteenth century in Canada, through Métis and Native over-hunting to satisfy the trade in buffalo robes and hides and, of course, for meat. Historian John Herd Thompson writes, "In the 1820s five million bison had migrated between the Missouri River and the Saskatchewan; by 1870 fewer than two million remained." He goes on, "In 1879, the Métis' Red River carts returned empty from the hunt: the herds that had seemed inexhaustible were gone." If there was no greater body of animals anywhere in the world at that time, there has also been no comparable, so rapid decimation of so large a body of animals.

Is there a prairie person alive, EuroCanadian or First Nations, who doesn't dream, sometimes, of seeing a thousand thousand buffalo grazing their way across the grassy fields, or who doesn't once in her or his life dream of the thunder of a million bison as they roar past the farmhouse or the apartment building, a river of animals, powerful and wild, dust roiling for miles, the music of life itself, the music of the wild West?

Although we Canadians tend—all of us whose ancestors came from Europe, that is—to think of the West as the newest part of the North American world, historian Desmond Morton, in *A Short History of Canada*, notes: "The amiable Canadian assumption that the West is somehow 'new' and the North is newer still ignores the fact that *these regions have probably known human habitation longer than any other part of the continent*" (italics mine).

The place in east-central Saskatchewan my family had come to in the late thirties of the twentieth century was not by then "wild" in the truest sense of the word. In fact, it was not wild in the truest sense—untouched by humans—even in the late-seventeenth century, when the first explorers saw it. The First Nations people of the West had already been there. According to Morton, their numbers are estimated to have been "in the 1500s . . . about a third to a half a million people living in what would later be called Canada, though the numbers soon fell rapidly," and especially in comparison to the always escalating number of Europeans. In the West at Confederation there were many more Aboriginal people than Europeans or Métis.

That the West was not "new" is an idea that would have come as a surprise to my maternal grandparents, Jane and Francis Graham, my parents, Amy and Archie Le Blanc, my mother's brother, James Donald, always called Don, her younger sisters, Helen and Jessie, and Helen's husband-to-be, Charles Finney, when they arrived as settlers in the area around Garrick and White Fox in east-central Saskatchewan in 1937.

As far as they were concerned, it was a wild place, primeval and uninhabited, solid bush that the settlers would have to clear if they planned to farm; no roads, only trails, no electricity, not even a municipal government, and the only hospital (where eventually my mother would go to have four of her five babies) thirty miles of poor roads away in Nipawin and (for the first years) run by the Red Cross and called an "outpost" hospital. Only ninety miles away was Prince Albert, a city founded seventy years earlier by the Presbyterian Reverend James Nisbet, sent to minister to the Indians, which had a population in 1937 of perhaps fifteen thousand. Although we had a few neighbours, who were also the first settlers on their nearby homesteads, my family felt itself so remote that they might as well have been the first people on the planet.

My grandmother's grandparents had come to Canada from New Glasgow, Scotland, in the early nineteenth century. Their family story began, "The Elders were shipbuilders on the River Clyde," that inversion, River Clyde, echoing a tale told a thousand times. They'd come in 1817 as one of the first families of settlers on the Trout River in southern Quebec. (At roughly the same time, 1812, the first of the Selkirk settlers, fellow Scotsmen and women, but from the Highlands as a result of the terrible land clearances there, would have barely begun their difficult lives in the Northwest at the place that eventually became Winnipeg.)

Not being Highlanders, the Elders probably did not arrive destitute. Later, perhaps twenty years on, some of their children would move on to settle at Elder Mills, Ontario, then north of Toronto (just west of the city of Vaughan). From there, their descendants trekked to homesteads in southern Manitoba in 1881 and 1883; my grandmother, Jane Elder, was born in 1883 and raised genteelly on the prosperous family farm.

My maternal grandfather, Francis Ebenezer Graham, I was told, had been born "under the wagon box" at Portage la Prairie during the Graham family's trek west from Ontario in 1880. I had heard the story so often that I'd been a child the last time I had paid any attention to it. But the more I thought about the "under the wagon box" story of my Irish grandfather, the more it began to resonate for me, to take on new meanings, to gain in importance although I wasn't entirely

sure why. I soon realized that it was not just the most significant of my personal family stories, but also in some way sym-
bolic of so many Western stories that provide foundations for
families' sense of who they are—and this was mine. I began to
understand how much the story said about what it is to be a
Westerner.

One of the greatest family achievements is the claim to be
"first": for example, to be the first white child to be born in a
newly opened area in the West. My son's paternal great-grandmother was said to be the first white woman born in her area
of southeastern Saskatchewan, or perhaps it was the first red-
headed woman. I have heard a similar assertion about my own
family. If it were possible to list all these family stories, I am
sure there would be a lineup of claimants for the "first" prize.

Because many of the first settlers in Western Canada came
from the older societies of Ontario and Quebec, being first at
anything in the West carries great significance. To be first—the
first settler, the first-born in that place, the first to plow the
land—proves something about your rights and your value, and
helps to anchor both a family and a place in a demonstrable
history.


I remember my Grandmother Graham telling us about her
older brothers, who adored her and spoiled her terribly
because her mother had died when she was only two and her
father when she was seven (in 1890), although not before he
remarried at his dying wife's request and had more children.
She sometimes spoke about her wonderful, kind stepmother,
Mary or "Molly" Noble, who raised her.[2]

Jane was educated at Brandon College, where she took a
business course and studied music, voice in particular—she
had a lovely high soprano—and played the piano well. As a

young woman she sang in church choirs and gave solo per-
formances in the school districts around her home, and during
the First World War she sang in concerts to help raise money
for the Red Cross. Her memoir, of which all her grandchildren
have a copy, repeatedly mentions how much she loved to sing
and how important music was to her.

I still see my grandmother on the Saskatchewan homestead a
mile from ours, a slim, pretty woman (our cousin Gayle looks
just like her). Even then and in that place, she always wore a
trim cotton housedress she'd made herself, a crisp apron over
it, invariably with an indulgent smile for her grandchildren, in
the kitchen of the log house patiently working the butter churn,
all of this belying a nature of the firmest determination and a
backbone made of pure steel. (In those days and earlier in the
West, no woman survived without one.) She was a famously
good shot, and even mentions self-deprecatingly in her memoir
that she was a better shot than the men because in her youth
she had had more time to practise. In any case, she wouldn't
let the men shoot the chicken for Sunday dinner because they
made such a mess of it, but did it herself.

That she was much loved by everyone in her childhood and
youth is demonstrated by the number of photographs of her—
an infant, a pensive six- or seven-year-old, a young lady in
large hat and floor-length skirts. I have no such pictures of my
Grandfather Graham, aside from a formal portrait of him
standing with his six brothers (he was the youngest), taken
before his marriage, and then one of him holding my infant
mother on his knee, probably taken no later than 1911. (There
is a second photo, this one of his four exquisitely pretty sisters;
even his brothers are handsome men, but he is the hand-
somest.) After that, all the pictures are from years later and are
with my grandmother.

I should record that his father, John Graham, seems to have

been a "remittance man," someone sent out from the Old Country (County Fermanagh in Northern Ireland, in this case) most often in disgrace or else out of an attempt to turn a reckless or lazy young fellow into a worthy family member. Such young men subsisted chiefly on stipends, or remittances, sent regularly by the family back home.[3]

The story is that our great-grandmother, Margaret Grady, had been a servant in the Graham household—a dairymaid, actually—that she was very pretty, that young John fell in love with her, wanted to marry her, and was thus sent to Canada to come to his senses. However, he took his bride-to-be with him, or she followed soon after, and in 1865 in Montreal, they were married. I have a fading photocopy of their marriage certificate. It was a civil marriage, not a church marriage, that took place on November 21, 1865. My Grandmother Graham, in the aforementioned memoir, offers a slightly different version, however:

> John ran away from college and came to Canada. He landed at Montreal and managed to get work in an office. He had a good education so office work came easy for him. Before he left Ireland he fell in love with Margaret Grady, but she was a servant in the Graham household and the Grahams were landed gentry and did not approve of their son marrying beneath him. But John worked for a year in the office and then sent for Margaret and they were married in Montreal.

There is a third version of the story, which comes from one generation earlier than my grandmother's version. This one is told by Annie Graham (who became an Elder by marriage), John and Margaret's daughter:

Father left home at the age of twenty-three. He came in a sailing vessel, to Canada in 1860, and established himself as a bookkeeper in Montreal. He was quite proficient at this work, being the son of a gentleman, he had been educated accordingly. Margaret Grady, his bride-to-be, joined him the following year and they were married by an Anglican minister.

Margaret was the daughter of decent labouring people, and we have it on good authority that she was strikingly pretty. She worked on the Graham estate (Drummack), in fact, was one of the four dairymaids.

When young John announced, nay declared, his intention of marrying the girl of his choice, it brought a storm of protest from his family. John was sent to a boarding school farther from home, but still in the County Fermanagh, and his allowance was cut. Nothing daunted, he returned to Drummack and drove off one of his father's prize cattle, and sold it in the market at Enniskillen. With the proceeds he set sail to carve his fortune in the new world.

My memories of John's son, my grandfather, are all good memories. I recall him always with horses, teams of enormous workhorses, which he named for the neighbours—another Western penchant—with Grandmother scolding him over it, laughing, but afraid, too, that the neighbours would hear and be offended.

My family stories are typical of those who have migrated west. They tell of hardships, triumphs, a life on the land, and are invested with the romance and drama of family narratives passed down from generation to generation. Still, I have to confess that even I, knowing so much better, have in these later years taken pride in the fact that my family were the first on the land that they either homesteaded or, in my father's case, squatted on in order to cut the trees to feed his sawmill. While it's true that nobody had farmed that land before, or cut the trees, we were far from the first to see it, to pass through it, or to make use of it for our livelihoods.

Archaeological digs have shown that First Nations people probably have been on the prairies at least since the end of the last ice age, twelve to fourteen thousand years ago. First Nations claim that they "have always been here," and scientists respond that North America was first colonized by people walking across a land bridge from Asia, then slowly working their way southward down an ice-free passage on the east side of the Rockies, and from there, as the ice melted, spreading out eastward and westward to people this continent, and southward, through Central and South America.

But there is another theory, accepted so far by only a few, that points to the paltry evidence supporting the first, more commonly accepted one. It counters that this continent was colonized by people coming across the Atlantic and across the Pacific to South America, from where they slowly spread northward. And that they came a very long time ago. This theory has only a tiny amount of evidence to support it, but although less accepted in the scientific community so far, it too has its passionate defenders.

Whichever theory turns out to be true, the sense our parents and grandparents had of being in a primeval wilderness, although on the day-to-day level more or less accurate, was in the timeframe of the peopling of North America clearly untrue, and untrue for every European settler who ever set plow to prairie earth. In fact, when those first settlers arrived, every stream and river, every hill and lake could already testify to its long being known by the fact that each had its First Nations' name. Sometimes, the English name known to the settlers was merely a translation of that original name.

I asked archaeologist and friend Dr. David Meyer of the University of Saskatchewan, who has made the study of certain parts of east-central Saskatchewan his life's work, for the original names of the places that were the first I knew on earth. He responded generously by giving me a copy of his 1986 monograph, from which I gleaned the following: Carrot River, *oskataskwa sipiy* (after a marsh plant, the water parsnip, which has a carrot-like root), and called the Carrot River for at least two hundred years, or *Rivier aux Carrot* [*sic*] by early traders; *namew sipiy*, applied to the Torch River, but the term *namew sipiy* translates as Sturgeon River, because sturgeon would swim up it from Cumberland Lake into Candle Lake. Candle Lake's Cree name is *namew sakahikan*, or Sturgeon Lake. But *candle* and *torch* are both English translations of a Cree word having to do with light, the reference being, it is thought, to mysterious lights sometimes seen on the water, now thought to have been caused by marsh gases; *kisisakaciwan sipiy*, Saskatchewan River, means Rapid Current River, and *mihkwaski-wahkahk* means Red Earth Locality or Place, a name of one of the nearby Indian reserves, and the last, for Nipawin, *nipowi-winihk*—"standing place"—the town in which I was born but in which I have never lived. It is called this because on the banks of the Saskatchewan River near the townsite, archaeologists tell us, there is a place where for centuries Aboriginal people had been congregating. Numerous trading posts had been built there, dating back to at least 1750.

But Dr. Meyer could not help me with the town named White Fox, where my older sister began school and to which we moved around 1944, or the Whitefox River, saying only that the Cree call the river by the name *wapakesiw sipiy*, or Sauger River, with reference to a fish of that name. (He adds that his Cree informant told him that bears used to catch sauger, a pike-perch, in the river.)

The local history book says simply that the village of White Fox is named after the Whitefox River, and no history of the river's name is given. But the range of the Arctic fox, which is white, is hundreds of miles north of the river by that name, in the subarctic woodland region in the extreme northeast of the province, and I wonder if perhaps somebody saw a white fox at the river, a most unusual sighting, perhaps a very long time ago.

Or rather, I wonder if someone had a dream of a white fox—a spirit animal—at the river, and (if a European) took the dream for reality or (if a Native person) called the river after the spirit animal that had come to him to commemorate this numinous and profoundly significant moment. (Many years later, when I had gone to the Great Plains to live, I had a dream of a wounded white coyote—a spirit animal—which now I wish I could say, in poetic completion, had been a fox.)

Long after we left the bush, I wondered about those mysterious place names. Through learning them from an archaeologist who learned them from First Nations informants of the region, I found it is indeed true that we had moved not into an empty place, but instead into a peopled and intensely known world.

I wonder how our myths of the heroism of the pioneers and our moist-eyed sympathy and love for our Western pioneer grandparents (or, in many cases, our parents) and the hardships they suffered would change if we had always thought of their efforts in Western North America in this light: that they were only a part of a vastly long and sometimes mysterious human past on the land they occupied, far from the first people

there, interlopers, not the giants of early prairie literature cast-
ing the giant's shadow across a soon to be humbled land. Or
how they themselves would have altered their perception of
what they were facing as pioneers if they'd recognized themselves as people trying something new, all right, but on land
not primeval, but instead well used and intimately familiar to
others before them—others still living on the fringes of their
small societies, and with very long memories indeed. Perhaps
then they would have questioned the rightness and the heroism
of what they were doing. Not that I would want to minimize
the difficulties of the way of life they chose, having seen their
suffering firsthand.

If the interior plains to which the settlers came was not
"new" and not "empty" of people, then just who might have
been the "first white man" to see them? In 1731, La Vérendrye,
three of his sons, and a nephew set out from Montreal to find
an overland route to the Pacific Ocean and got as far west as
what are now Saskatchewan and the Dakotas by 1738. The
explorer Anthony Henday was sent out by the Hudson's Bay
Company, in later years also known ironically as "Here Before
Christ," and in 1754–55, he went as far west as a particular hill
from which he recorded first seeing "the shining mountains."
How awestruck he was by them, even paying a special visit to
the hill in order to gaze at the Rockies one last time before he
and his companions turned back east. The high point he
climbed is now called Antler Hill, from which people driving
north from Calgary on Highway 2 will soon enter the city of
Red Deer. Unfortunately, the day in early May 2003 when I
climbed that hill, I'd been driving for six hours through a
nearly impassable spring blizzard, and risking turning my head
to the left, I saw not the shining mountains but a thick veil of
opaque, swirling snow.

Today we credit a different explorer (also travelling for HBC), Henry Kelsey, as the first to see what became the Prairie provinces on a journey he made in 1690–91, sixty years before Henday climbed Antler Hill to gaze at the Rockies. Kelsey's full report was kept away from authorities, or else they doubted its veracity; the entire text of his journal of the trip finally turned up in some archival documents in 1926, when Anthony Henday dropped to second place in the race for historical (white man) "firsts."

But actually, the Henday/Kelsey claims to be the "first white man" are most likely not true either, because long before Henday came along and even, apparently, during Kelsey's time, French traders had been travelling through the West.

W.J. Eccles, in *The Canadian Frontier: 1534–1760*, shows a map by J.B.L. Franquelin dated 1688 (two years before Kelsey's trip into the interior)

> indicating the extent of French penetration into the west in the seventeenth century. . . . Lac des Assinibouels and Lac des Christinaux represents Lakes Winnipeg, Manitoba, and Winnipegosis, drawn from reports of coureurs de bois and located some four hundred miles too far east [on the map]. From this, and other evidence, it is clear that the French had reached the northwestern plains prior to 1688.

So, in fact, we really don't know the name of the first white man to see what became Canada's Prairie provinces, only that he was most probably a French Canadian. And, as Aritha Van Herk asks in *Mavericks*, her entertaining history of Alberta, *"what were the French if not White?"*

If the West has been thought of as wilder than the rest of Canada since its settlement by EuroCanadians, it has also had the reputation of being more rural in character. Everyone knows that today far more Canadians live in cities or towns than in the countryside, that Canadians as a whole are an urban people. Despite this conviction that Westerners are a rural people—meaning, one assumes, closer to nature, but including (at least elsewhere in Canada) the negative idea that to be rural is also to be "peasant"—it is a surprise to find that Westerners too have also always been urban.

I owe this belated insight about the Prairie provinces to the Prairie historian and teacher George Melnyk, who explored the idea in an essay in *The Urban Prairie* and in *New Moon at Batoche: Reflections on the Urban Prairie*. He writes:

> I discovered that urban life went hand in hand with the development and growth of agrarian society at the end of the last [nineteenth] century. We created cities in the region at the same time that we settled it agriculturally. They were not an afterthought, a late development. They happened at the same time. They were co-inhabiters of the landscape.

I remember Saskatchewan writer, historian, and English professor Don Kerr saying something similar once at a family dinner (he's married to cousin Mildred McNamee, of the large Irish Graham clan, and a worthy recipient of the Saskatchewan Volunteer Medal), and my own mixture of surprise and doubt when he remarked that although he was a lifetime prairie person, he was city-born and bred. He said he felt there were many, many others like him—prairie people with wholly urban roots and urban lives—who were unacknowledged and without status in our prairie mythology. I was dubious only because I, too, having lived most of my life in wilderness, in small towns, and on a ranch, had failed to include any notion of the urban in my understanding of who Westerners are.

Actually, as one writer has pointed out, the fur-trading fort might be seen as the first urbanization in the West. And even before that era, First Nations people had gathering places where large numbers met seasonally year after year for thousands of years: just upriver from the modern town of Nipawin (*Nipowiwinihk*) is one example, showing periodic occupation for at least five thousand years, and another is *Pasquatinow* (meaning "high, bare ground" or "bare/bald hill") between Nipawin and the Tobin Rapids, which archaeologists date to pre-Contact times (as early as AD 500). The Forks in Winnipeg, with evidence of habitation six thousand years ago, is another of many of these sites being located by archaeologists.

Later, settlers couldn't have existed as rural people had there not been towns and villages nearby to provide the tools, machinery, and implements for farming, with house-building supplies and items they couldn't make or grow for themselves but needed, such as coffee, medicines, and dry goods and, of course, with banks to lend money. And the towns and villages needed cities to provide them with supplies.

Thus, as soon as Europeans arrived in what became Western Canada, there were cities, and those cities were full of people who may or may not have been rural in their home countries but who raised families in the New World who would experience only Western urban life, down to the present generations. A little searching of the records shows the pattern in the five contemporary Prairie cities: Winnipeg, Calgary, Edmonton, Saskatoon, and Regina.

Winnipeg (meaning "murky waters") was founded in 1738, when La Vérendrye built Fort Rouge at the confluence of the Red and Assiniboine rivers. It became a city in 1873 with fewer than four thousand inhabitants, but by 1911, with its 157,000 inhabitants, it was, astonishingly, the third largest city in Canada. Its current population is about 667,000, out of Manitoba's million and a half people.[4]

Calgary hadn't even been founded when Winnipeg first incorporated as a city, in 1873 (although earliest habitation at the confluence of the Elbow and Bow rivers dates back twelve thousand years); but two years later the North-West Mounted Police set up their permanent headquarters for "F" Troop there, at the same time as Father Doucet was establishing his mission nearby. By 1912 it was home to 63,000, and after that its population expanded exponentially until, today, with some 879,000 inhabitants, its suburbs are eating up the prairie faster than a wildfire.[5]

In 1795, Edmonton House was a Hudson's Bay Company fur-trading centre. By 1911, nearly 25,000 people called it home, and today it is nearly the size of Calgary. Collectively, Alberta's urban centres, including Lethbridge, Medicine Hat, and others, make up two million of the province's nearly three million people.[6]

Saskatoon and Regina were both founded slightly later than their companion prairie cities (in 1881 Saskatoon was too small even to be counted in the census, or didn't exist at all), and they also grew very slowly by comparison. Regina in 1881 had about 800 people, and when it became the capital was described by the *Manitoba Free Press* as "in the midst of a vast plain of inferior soil . . . with about enough water in the miserable little creek . . . to wash a sheep." The two cities have been in a steady competition for population, with sometimes one and sometimes the other getting ahead until they reached their current populations of under 200,000, Saskatoon being the larger by perhaps 20,000. This out of a Saskatchewan provincial population that hovers around one million.[7]

From the beginning of the EuroCanadian arrival on the prairies, we have been urban, but it is also true that in the early days we were indeed vastly more rural, with the populations in 1911 of the five prairie cities at only 20 percent of the total prairie population. But the trend toward a growing percentage of urban over rural people started early, accelerated during the Great Depression, and has continued, until today more than 70 percent of us—about three million out of about five million—live in our cities and towns. Surprisingly, despite thinking of ourselves as rural, as does the rest of the country, the fact is that our rural–urban ratio is about the same as the rest of the country. And sadly, with every passing year our countryside is growing emptier.[8]

Prairie people's mourning over this enforced move from the farm home to the town or city has been for seventy years a prime fact of the Prairie psyche. This flow of people off the land today is chiefly, although not exclusively, a result of the increasingly mechanized farm, in which one or two men can farm in a few days what once would have taken weeks and a crew of people. The result, not solely a prairie phenomenon, is that where once most Canadians as a whole were farmers, today, despite more rather than less land being under cultivation, only around 1 percent of Canadians are.

Those many farmers forced off their places have mostly moved, and continue to move, with their families to villages, towns, and the city. Today far more people in Western Canada have an urban background than a rural one. And yet, as George Melnyk and Don Kerr have pointed out, we remain a people whose collective memory and whose myths are strictly rural.

This is true even in my own family, for when my sisters and I were being raised rural and small-town, a whole batch of cousins was growing up in a large house in an old section of Calgary that today is only a short distance from downtown. Their maternal grandfather, Samuel Adams, had served two terms as mayor of the city during the 1920s and, among other notable endeavours, gave the first Calgary radio broadcast on May 18, 1922. Those cousins never lived outside the city and were city kids, no question about it, although their father had come from a farm in the same area south of Brandon, Manitoba, as my maternal grandparents and was my mother's first cousin. The West was never merely rural to them.

Nor were they my only urban relatives. Other cousins on the Graham side were growing up as urban people in an Anglo part of Winnipeg, even though their parents had also been raised on farms near the same one as their cousin, my mother, in the south of the province. At the same time, in Winnipeg, mostly in the area called St. Boniface, my French first cousins were also growing up urban, their family farm long lost in the past of our mutual grandparents, Edith and Oliva Le Blanc, who, after arriving from Quebec in 1911, had left their small, rich-soiled Saskatchewan farm only seven miles from the village of Batoche on the South Saskatchewan River during the Depression. They had moved to raise cattle in Manitoba, and then had given that up for a new existence as city people.

But I suspect that, as with so many prairie people, *mes tantes* and *mes oncles* never made that mental transition to being city people. For it is one thing to live in a city geographically and quite another to live in it mentally, to embrace it wholeheartedly as the best way of life, as, for example, New Yorkers seem to do, and as *boulevardiers* did in the European cities of the nineteenth century, and as the young do when they finally manage to kick off the dust of their parents' despised farm or the not-so-imaginary horrors of the small prairie town.

Nurtured by the land, as all my older relatives were, they

remembered the scent of lilacs blooming in the spring against the wall of the old log house next door to theirs; they remembered the excitement of the return of the mallards, the snow geese and Canada geese, and the wild swans in the spring, the air filled with their noise; they remembered the sound of spring itself, in the sound of running water when at long last the snow and ice began to melt. Their dreams were of the black soil of their farm, how damp and loamy it was when it was plowed and how its scent rode on the air, and the tangy smell of the nearby river where they went to cool down on an impossibly hot summer day, and of the bushes bending under the weight of the saskatoons and chokecherries they picked for pies and puddings and to be canned to brighten the winter menu.

There is a way, I think, in which the truly rural can live in the city a greater part of their lives and yet never see it. I've done it myself (now that I've been a rural person for nearly thirty years), but for those born and having spent their childhoods on the land, old habits die hard—those of watching the sky, of turning your head to look when you hear a bird, of walking through snowfall, through winter, down city streets, instead of the hurried rush from one warm building to another in an absolute denial of winter as anything but an inconvenience. It's a style of observation and, especially, a state of mind that separates the rural person from the true city person, no matter where he or she lives. To rural people, whether they have a city address or a box number and a land description as home, real life takes place only out in the country, and nearly always on a farm. Everything else is a sham of real life, a mistake, a loss, and a sorrow.

Part of this endless mourning probably stems from our continuing disapproval of cities. When I was a child, I know my sisters and I couldn't wait to shake the dust of prairie small-town from our shoes. We would hit the cities, the bigger the better, we would become fully urban, forget we'd ever known the countryside, the northern lights, outhouses, and corduroy roads, ever had farmer ancestors; we'd become sophisticated and cosmopolitan—there'd be no grass growing on us. If Calgary had been the busy metropolis then that it is today, we'd have spent all our days and nights dreaming of Calgary. As it was, the city we would go to, although bustling and glamorous, was a vague and shadowy place, somewhere near Paris or New York.

In fact, during the fifties all young Westerners dreamt of departing for Toronto, but by the sixties the dream had shifted to the growing, gorgeous, if damp and self-conscious city of Vancouver. (I actually did get there when I was twenty-four, with my first husband and new baby. My husband, however, who was a few years older than I was, as a teenager had gone straight east to Toronto, returning home because, I suspect, he felt ill at ease there.)

My sense, though, is that Central Canadians are very proud of their cities—Montreal and Toronto—an attitude that appears to me to be missing in Westerners. Today Calgary is indeed a bustling metropolis, and we all deplore it; even Calgarians deplore it. Even while they make good lives for themselves in this exciting city, they watch its suburbs eating up the countryside practically by the minute, and everyone shakes his or her head and says what an awful shame it is, and how the city is too big and the traffic is unmanageable and the crime rate is horrifying.

Rural people will tell you a dozen reasons why they dislike cities: they're unbearably noisy, disgustingly smelly and dirty, laughably expensive; their people are always in a panting hurry, without the slightest regard for any other human being; and also, they are vastly dangerous—if the gangs or street muggers don't get you, you can't cross the street without getting hit by a speeding car, its driver clearly insane, and if you're stopped at the roadside with a flat or mechanical breakdown, it is axiomatic that your car will be stripped of its wheels, door handles, seats, and radio before you can say Jack Robinson. For rural people, there is no excuse for cities and no explanation at all for their *modus operandi*.

But the disapproval *urban* people express for cities while spending their entire lives in them must surely be a holdover from the rural mindset most of us once had that can't be eradicated that says cities are bad *per se*, and today that has to be more than a bit disingenuous. Could it be mere habit? Or lip service to that disapproving giant pioneer that lurks in the back of the mind of every Westerner, the one that says the only good life is the rural life? Lip service also to the pious, church-going past that maintains in a thundering voice that cities are an abomination, Sodom and Gomorrah every one?

There are, of course, differences among the three Prairie provinces. I find Manitoba a calming place, its cities laidback and its citizens having an attitude that says, *We are what we are and that is just fine*, while Alberta bustles—it bustles everywhere, it seems to me. I have even taken to calling the fast lane of Saskatchewan highways "the Alberta lane" because Albertans, except for the occasional driver from Ontario, always drive faster than anyone else. If Manitoba is laidback and calm and Alberta sharp and fast, Saskatchewan cities always seem a bit bewildered to me—as if this wasn't quite what they had in mind, but here we are and, what the heck, we'll just have to make the best of it. And if I always see Manitoba and Saskatchewan, in my own mind, covered with a thin layer of fine dust, Alberta seems to me polished and shiny, bright as a new penny.

The differences among the provinces are mostly a result of

their settlement patterns, and in turn, this is explained, in part, by the physical nature of the landscape of each province. The most beautiful parts of Alberta, ranching country, were settled by moneyed people, many from England, sometimes even titled, while Saskatchewan was settled by farming people from all over the (Caucasian) world, a million of them—at least in the south—Americans. Manitoba, the oldest of the three provinces, had a more interesting beginning, the first people to settle being Métis and half-breeds (as they were known by everyone then, Métis being half French and half First Nations, and usually Roman Catholic, half-breeds being half British and half First Nations, and usually Protestant). The Red River or Selkirk settlers arrived next, and then the settlers followed the more usual pattern for Western Canada, with many Mennonites and a sizeable contingent of Icelanders.

All of this must have contributed to the different "feel" of the cities of the three provinces. But, beyond who the settlers were, Westerners perceive the *character* of Western cities to be different from that of Central Canadian cities, and certainly from the cities of Atlantic Canada. As others have noted, the people who laid out Western cities seemed to imagine their futures as enormous metropolises and thus made the main streets twice as wide as those of Eastern cities, lending them a permanent air of spaciousness.

Nor, for the most part, do Western cities have the winding, cobblestoned streets that Old Montreal has. (We also have a tendency to number our streets and avenues rather than naming them, Edmonton being the best example, while Saskatoon uses letters of the alphabet.) Streets were generally laid out on grids, and interesting nooks and crannies are not there, hard to find, or newly created by modern urban planners. They didn't grow naturally as in the oldest parts of the ancient cities of Europe. It is also said, although I think this is a thing of the past, that Westerners are especially bad for tearing down old buildings and replacing them with tall, shiny new ones, that we are deficient in our sense of the past, or else that we are too money-oriented and so we tear old buildings down without regard for their intrinsic value.

The sense of the presence of nature is very strong in Western cities: Winnipeg, set at the confluence of two rivers, still floods at the slightest drop of rain. Saskatoon and Edmonton have maintained extensive walking and bike-riding paths along the banks of the South and North Saskatchewan rivers (as well as leaving much of the riverbanks in a natural state), and Calgary has enormous Nose Hill Park (and Vancouver keeps Stanley Park), as well as what is probably the most extensive system of greenery in all of Canada, which runs even through the non-residential parts of the downtown area. Calgarians tell me you can ride your bike from your house to work in the downtown core without encountering four-wheeled traffic at all, surely a rare experience in a city of almost a million. Even Regina, that arid city set in the middle of the flattest plains, has a narrow little river winding through it and is dominated by a man-made lake and a very beautiful, large park right in the heart of the city. Most of this was the result of more or less careful urban planning.

And why would we choose to do this, if we wanted so desperately to be fully urban? Because it is the inherent character of the West, affecting even the most urban of us.

Even smaller cities such as Red Deer and Fort McMurray, Alberta, Prince Albert and Swift Current, Saskatchewan, and Brandon, Dauphin, Portage la Prairie, and Thompson, Manitoba, all have a slightly ragged, wild look to them, as if the residents are still fighting an uncertain fight to keep nature from pushing her way down every street and across every parking lot—uncertain because the residents aren't that sure they'd be upset if nature triumphed. Besides, five minutes in any direction and you're out in the landscape again.

Mountain lions still (occasionally) stalk the streets of Banff, Alberta, and Swift Current, Saskatchewan; bears raid garage freezers in Kitimat and West Vancouver, B.C., and Thompson and Le Pas, Manitoba; deer nibble flowerbeds and ornamental shrubs right across the Prairie provinces, and occasionally knock down and trample—yes, attack—people with small, yappy dogs (and who can blame them?)—and moose wander the fringes of communities wherever they are set in moose territory. People in Eastend, Saskatchewan, I'm told, wake up in the early morning and look out their bedroom windows to find a troupe of birdwatchers, their binoculars trained on the big tree in the backyard, and you can fish at the weir in what is practically downtown Saskatoon.

Newcomers are stunned by the enormous sky, even in the cities, where it is huge and omnipresent in a way it never is in the cities of central Canada or the Maritimes—as stunned as in the past, when, it is true, some pioneer women ran from it until their lungs burst and they died.

What a long way my Scots Grandmother Graham's family had come: from out of the bush in the early part of the nineteenth century in southern Quebec, into the Ontario bush, then to rural Manitoba, and now, a century and a half later, pioneer settlers yet again in the bush country of Saskatchewan. In every province each time, setting out to carve civilization out of intractable nature. Despite the hardship of their lives, my maternal grandparents lived to be very old, my grandmother no longer recognizing her own daughters, my grandfather at ninety still as sound of mind as ever. They died a few months apart in a nursing home in Prince Albert, Saskatchewan, when I was in my early thirties.

And while much of the large, intertwined Elder–Graham clan is, both separately and together, now urban, the farms are still there, some of them still occupied by the descendants of the original Grahams and Elders. We are perhaps not the most certain of urban-dwellers, still able to imagine the wilderness life that beckons to us at once so sweetly and so frighteningly at the edge of every prairie city, town, or village. A number of my city-raised cousins have retired to rural acreages, where they happily bird-watch, sing the praises of deer, fox, and coyote sightings, tramp the countryside for hours, and dream, I am sure, of how they might live—hunting and fishing for their food, taking shelter in teepees and crude bush shelters—as our unnamed ancestors did, thus becoming one with the true West.

# CHAPTER THREE

# Shadows and Stars

*What makes a Westerner?*
*Our uncertain relationship with the Aboriginal population.*

RECENTLY, in Vancouver's West End early one Sunday morning, I stopped to give money to an Amerindian man. He was perhaps forty to fifty years old, squatting on the sidewalk with his back against a cement foundation, grinning stupidly (I thought, if not sycophantically) up at me, and reeking of alcohol. I gave him two 2-dollar coins.

He straightened then, his grin had vanished, and he stood. He was surprisingly tall, and I saw he was both a handsome and an intelligent man—above all a man, with all that that designation implies in selfhood. Mumbling that he would get some breakfast, without once glancing back at me, he strode across the street to a fast-food outlet. I saw that he had less use for me than I for him, and I felt oddly humiliated by our encounter, although I wasn't sure just why. I wandered off, my eyes on the sidewalk in front of me, to ponder this meeting.

His dignity, his selfhood, had turned out to be stronger than mine—I, the endower, he, the beggar. Why was such a man as he there on that sidewalk waiting for someone like me to give him money? How had he come to be there? *Who was he?* I wondered, and the question has stayed with me to this moment, because it was not an ordinary encounter; it was an extraordinary encounter.

I have been trying to deconstruct that occasion the way a modern critic might read a text: he needed money; he asked me for it; I gave it to him. I was, of course, at bottom quite pleased with myself. He had no need for that. He had been playing a game, one not of his own choosing, and he did not want to hang around chatting with a middle-aged white lady who was apparently asking for more of him than the game required—that wasn't part of the deal. He had behaved appropriately (by mainstream society's lights—made himself small, behaved as a sycophant). I had responded, I thought, with kindness, generosity (how many people give beggars four dollars? Isn't a quarter more usual?), and friendliness. I would have stayed and chatted with him out of curiosity, out of some need I have that I can't (or won't) define but that many of us non-Aboriginal people have to know something more about the nature of Aboriginalness. He merely wanted breakfast, and he let me know that my four dollars gave me no right to anything else. What I wanted would cost a lot more than four dollars, and I would most likely not be willing to give it. Few are willing to give it.

In fact, late the night before my encounter with that shapeshifting Aboriginal man, I had fallen into a cab, drunk on wine, and was certainly not the only EuroCanadian in Vancouver to have done so. Not to mention that my wide and various family has included among its number more than one alcoholic. Is there anyone who has not sometimes thought, *There but for the grace of God go I*?

Further, I suspect, and have for some time, that if I could only unearth the evidence, I would discover that I myself have some Amerindian blood in my veins. This I postulate simply on the grounds that on my father's side we have been on this continent—indeed, in this country—since 1647, and it is hard to imagine that no one in that long lineage, not one person, intermingled blood with any Aboriginal people. It has been said that most Quebec people have some Amerindian blood, and we were once Quebeckers, and before that, Acadians.

Indeed, my maiden name was Le Blanc, and it turns out that one of Louis Riel's great-grandmothers, Marie-Joseph Le Blanc (married name: Boucher), of Île-à-la-Crosse (now in Saskatchewan), who would have been born in the latter half of the eighteenth century, was a Chipewyan–French woman, that is, Dene. Given that all Canadian Le Blancs are thought to be descendants of the one family who came to Acadia from France, perhaps it is not stretching the bounds of credibility too far to suggest the possibility of a distant relationship with the most famous man the West has ever produced.

Now that the incident with the Aboriginal man on that street in Vancouver has receded into the past, I wonder if my desire to assist him, to know him a little, didn't stem from the kind of incident Westerners have seen at least once: It was about 1961, on a weekend trip to a lake north of Prince Albert, Saskatchewan. We were two young couples, and one evening we were spending a few hours at the local bar when suddenly we saw an Aboriginal man dragged from his table by the bouncer and physically tossed out the door. Sitting only a few tables away, we had seen and heard absolutely nothing to explain this action: no rowdiness, no loud drunkenness, nothing. But nobody in the bar, including us, moved to help or to protest. We all just sat there, in our case in pain and embarrassment, even shame, because we'd done nothing to stop the violence. And you may rest assured that none of the other Aboriginal people at the table where he'd been sitting moved or said a word in protest either, lest they get the same treatment.

I remember that it was shadowy in the bar, that I could not see the faces of the people involved in this drama. The memory has always been accompanied by my sense of a kind of gleefulness on the part of the bouncer, that he was enjoying this, and at the same time of an almost total self-effacement on the part of the table of Aboriginal people, something I've seen only once since then. On this occasion I was volunteering at Okimaw Ohci Healing Lodge (an institution for federally sentenced Aboriginal women on the Nekaneet Reserve in the Cypress Hills) and I was standing with the top official—in English, the matron—of the facility at the door to the room where I was conducting my workshop, chatting with her. One of my students—she had already survived ten years in the notorious Kingston Penitentiary for Women—came around the corner and, seeing she would have to pass by the matron to enter the room, seemed simply to pull in some human aura I did not even know until that moment humans have, so that she was barely a shadow; she practically vanished—knowing, I suppose, that to be noticed in the prison system is to be in danger of being hurt, humiliated, punished. In any case, there was nothing but shadow at that table of Aboriginal people when the bouncer had done his work.

This was a commonplace incident; it was just that I had never before been witness to it. I can only think now that somehow I'd been traumatized enough by such a sight that when I saw the man begging on the street, I'd wanted to say to him implicitly, *I am not one of your oppressors.* Although, of course, by virtue of my very existence here on this continent, I am.

My own earliest memories include the First Nations people of the area where I was born and lived the first half-dozen years of my life. My memories are steeped in difference. My first glimpse of Indians as I recall it was filled only with curiosity; later, I remember, as a small child, I saw them clearly as alien and frightening. In-between the two I must have heard them spoken of over and over again as "not like us," "not up to our standards," and, at least among the women of our family, pitiable. That others saw them as dirty, disgusting, stupid, I have no doubt, although I have no memory from that time of anyone saying anything at all about them.

But even though I don't remember hearing this myself, I do remember my mother speaking with someone, probably her sister, about their father, our Irish grandfather, Francis Graham, who, despite being in most ways a kind man and a very good husband and father, was raised from an early age, apparently, to be a bigot. Our mother said, "He says these terrible things about them, but if an Indian came to the door in need, Dad would give him the shirt off his back." I wonder if she truly believed this—I hope it is true—or if this was only the self-reassurance of a daughter who loved her father deeply and needed to find a way to reconcile this apparent barbarity in him so that she would not have to question loving him.

Francis Graham was also the man who said that he was born "under the wagon box" at Portage la Prairie in 1880. Just south of Portage la Prairie is a cairn commemorating Fort la Reine, built by La Vérendrye in 1738. It is also roughly the site of the first homestead in the West, dated July 2, 1872—which must mean the first under the Dominion Lands Act of 1872, since there had been farms in the Red River area long before that. Grandfather Graham was a true Western pioneer, born five years before the second Riel Rebellion and raised in the area where the first Riel Rebellion had taken place in 1869 (resulting in the provisional government of the Red River Settlement, run by the young Louis Riel).

Despite its name, Portage la Prairie was an English stronghold where the most virulent detractors of Riel lived, where Riel and the Métis were regarded as murderers at best because of their execution of the incorrigible troublemaker Thomas Scott. (Interestingly, Portage la Prairie today holds an event called the Gathering of the Orange, which turns out to be a celebration of the orange-coloured, defunct Allis Chalmer tractor, for which there is a huge museum there—a peculiar, if not ominous, choice of name, given that Portage la Prairie was historically a stronghold of supporters of the Loyal Order of Orange.)

My Irish great-grandparents, John Graham and Margaret Grady, must have heard much about what had happened not so long before, and would soon happen in Saskatchewan, and they must have had their heads filled with the notion of Métis and Indians as people they should hold in contempt—although who knows what notions they'd brought with them from Ireland (a country that is not free of racism itself) and then acquired on their homestead in Ontario. Whatever they had heard, they passed that particular bigotry on to my grandfather. Happily, at least in that branch of the family, it skipped the next generation. Perhaps there were no longer Amerindian people living in the area of southern Manitoba where my mother's generation was raised. More likely, racism was still there but had simply evolved into a less obviously brutal form.

But there certainly was still racism where I was raised, and it is true to say that by six years old I was a full-blown racist, a condition escaped by few of my generation (and for the most part kept well hidden)—the generation that has been running Western Canada for the last thirty years. I was, though, at the same time ashamed of myself, as if I also knew that this was wrong (but how?) and having no understanding as to *why* it was considered inferior to have dark skin and straight black hair.

If it had been pointed out to me that my own father had black hair and very dark eyes, I think I would still have known that these weren't the criteria in question, even if I didn't quite know what the criteria were. Of what an *Indian* actually was, what the essence of the definition might be of the people I'd been seeing since before I could talk, I had no notion at all, and I don't think that anyone, not even my level-headed and intelligent mother, had attempted to explain this to me. In the absence of any clear, simple explanation that I could understand as to who these people were, it is no wonder that, as with many North Americans, I grew fascinated with them, and slowly, over the years and without any conscious realization of it, I endowed them with an aura of mystery. It would be many years before I came to understand that this, too, is racism.

Despite the many decent, genuinely well-meaning, non-racist EuroCanadians living in the Prairie provinces, racism has been around here for a very long time and is well entrenched. You have only to look at the record, where you will find that in the West, generally, Aboriginal lives have been cheap. Today, June 8, 2003, I have seen just how staggeringly cheap: I have just watched footage on our national television broadcaster, the CBC, that hasn't been shown before. From the safety and comfort of my living room, I watched as police officers turned, in one case, and, in the other, picked up stiff, iced slabs that were the frozen bodies of young Aboriginal men. Like everyone else, I have seen appalling footage on television of the carnage in Rwanda, the atrocity victims in Congo, Bosnia, and elsewhere, but I have not before burst into tears out of sheer fury and disgust at any other of these atrocities, as I did this morning. To its credit, the provincial government subsequently called an inquiry into the death of seventeen-year-old Neil Stonechild, whose body I had seen on television.[1]

Some people believed men like these were driven out of the city by the police who took their jackets and sometimes their shoes, and, on unimaginably cold nights of our northern winters, left them there to freeze to death. How could this have happened?

Days have passed, and my initial shock at such terrible deaths has calmed somewhat. If it is true that this sometimes happens—and there was no proof at the Stonechild inquiry that it did in that case—then it shames Canadians. Surely such brutality stems from something more than any perceived danger from these particular men. Surely it comes out of the dark—the shadow—side of the EuroCanadian psyche, out of a fear and a hatred, stemming from an ancient, profound uneasiness at the presence of *the other*, a perception deeply ingrained against Aboriginal people since the first moment of Contact.

This perception goes back to the arrival of the Spaniards on the shores of the New World in the fifteenth and sixteenth centuries, when the Spaniards immediately identified the inhabitants as "savages." My favourite historian, the wonderful Olive Dickason, herself originally a prairie woman (and a Métis) from southern Manitoba, has studied the subject of "the savage" scrupulously and extensively in her book *The Myth of the Savage: And the Beginnings of French Colonialism in the Americas*. In her introduction Dickason remarks:

> When members of the two worlds came into contact, first impressions set the patterns by which they saw and evaluated each other. Amerindians were quick to modify initial reactions as they sought for more adequate response; they were not immediately successful. Europeans, on the other hand, were able to establish their hegemony over the New World, making it unnecessary to alter initial assumptions; only recently have these seen signs of changing. These assumptions were not substantially modified by subsequent firsthand relationships, such as occurred when Amerindians visited Europe or when the

Europeans went to the New World. The fact that such views had little to do with reality did not mitigate their fundamental importance in colonization. By classifying Amerindians as savages, Europeans were able to create the ideology that helped to make it possible to launch one of the great movements in the history of western civilization: the colonization of overseas empires.

In other words, to conquer the Americas it was necessary, despite all evidence to the contrary, to believe that Amerindians were savages.

The term *sauvage* (savage) meant, variously: to be living in a manner closer to animals than humans; to be "solitary, uncivilized, ferocious, demented, and foreign"; to be "without regular habitation, without religion, law, or civility" (or "agreeable conversation"); it meant to suffer from "sudden fear"; to live "without knowledge of God and without use of reason"; to eat (to the Europeans) disgusting things, sometimes bloody, raw and alive, to have poor manners at table—or no table—and to eat irregularly; to fail to cover one's genitals; to lack writing and to have "defective language structures," or to speak "gibberish." All these definitions are from Dickason, who goes on to say that cannibalism, dirtiness—although at that time Europeans had extremely spotty sanitary habits—and cruelty (amazing when one considers the appalling cruelty of at least the Spaniards)—were also considered to be characteristic of the savage. (She also points out that to be defeated is considered to be another proof of one's inferiority.) Today we know clearly that this list is calumny, that to have a different culture is not to be inferior *per se*. Amerindians always had habitation, government, and law, as well as religion, language, and social customs and mores.

But these ideas gave rise to a converse, yet equally dangerous, idea: that of the *noble savage*, meaning, according to Daniel Francis in his well-received 1993 book *The Imaginary Indian*, "innocent, virtuous, and peace-loving, free of the guile and vanity that came from living in contemporary society. . . . [The term attributes to the Indian] an innate nobility of character which somehow derives from their long connection with the American continent and their innocence of industrial society." Dickason describes the idea of the noble savage as one which, devastatingly, "deprived him [the Amerindian] of his position as a fellow human, both as an individual and as a social being."

Historically, it has long been recorded that different attitudes toward the indigenous people of the Northwest (which eventually became Manitoba, Alberta, and Saskatchewan) were held by English explorers and traders and by French ones. Historians point to different trading patterns in Hudson's Bay Company records and in logbook and diary accounts of the traders and adventurers themselves during the eighteenth and nineteenth centuries.

For something like eighty years after the inception of the Hudson's Bay Company in 1670, the English had done what they could to induce the Indians of the Northwest to trap and hunt for them and then to carry their furs to forts established by the HBC, usually some distance from the hinterland in which the furs were obtained. The English thought of themselves as "traders" and distinguished themselves from the Canadians (Quebeckers for the most part), whom they referred to contemptuously as "pedlars," whose practice it was to go directly to the Native people and to trade with them wherever they found them. At first the English refused to do this, but eventually, seeing that the Canadians were so much more successful than they were, the HBC men were forced into the same kind of trading.

Certainly, part of this contempt for the Canadians stemmed

from their closeness to the First Nations people, living and working with them, taking First Nations wives and having mixed-blood children (although it wasn't long, once again, before the HBC people were doing the same).

Historian Sylvia Van Kirk, however, in her groundbreaking book *Many Tender Ties*, writes that at the beginning of the fur trade, because European women were not allowed in the Hudson's Bay Company forts of Rupert's Land, the taking of Indian wives was a common practice. The need for the comforts of home was as great in the fur traders as in any man, and Amerindian wives knew very well how to make that home. Moreover, they knew how to survive in their home country, which the traders initially did not. They could speak at least their own language and often more than one Native language, and they understood the cultures in which the traders were trying to work. They were indispensable. The European fur traders appeared to have overcome the prejudices of their home countries in that these marriages were said to be often happy and long-standing and produced many children. And more than once a trader was reported as saying that when he arrived in *le pays d'en haut*, he planned to take a Native wife for the sake of convenience and to discard her on returning home, only to find when the time of his departure came that he could not abandon her, and either stayed with her until he died or took her with him back to Britain.

Soon, however, as many mixed-blood children were born and grew to young adulthood, the preference of many fur-trading men was for mixed-blood rather than Indian wives. The last stage occurred when married or marriageable European women began to arrive in the Canadian West, and these women—despite not speaking Native languages, understanding the local cultures, or knowing anything about survival in this country, nonetheless became the most desirable wives. By the time of the enactment of the Manitoba Act in 1870—the act by which Manitoba became a province in Confederation—prejudice against mixed marriages had become a significant element in that small Western society.

That society—the first major settlement in what became the Prairie provinces—grew out of the Red River Colony: 116,000 square miles in Rupert's Land that today would include part of the United States and Saskatchewan, established under the philanthropy of the Scottish Lord Selkirk in territory he had bought in 1811 from the Hudson's Bay Company. (By this time he was a major shareholder in the HBC.) The land was in the midst of the established fur-trading area, the problem this would pose apparently escaping the lord.

Just as the enormous land grant to the Hudson's Bay Company in 1670 had ignored the Amerindian people whose land it was, the purchase by Selkirk of this large tract from the Hudson's Bay Company, while acknowledging the rights of the Amerindian people, paid no attention at all to the rights of the new people of mixed blood who had been born there and knew no other country. They were the provisioners for the fur traders, buffalo hunters, pemmican-makers, and reliable workers for the North West Company. It is apparently not possible to fully separate or understand Lord Selkirk's motives—whether he hoped to bring about the demise of the North West Company by filling the territory with people loyal to the HBC, or whether the reality of the mixed-blood people (their existence in history, their habits, their rights) was simply not something he comprehended fully. One would think, though, that had they been wholly European he would not have so readily ignored the fact of their existence.

The story of the events leading up to the establishment of Manitoba in 1870 is more complicated than the simplified version most Westerners are taught in school. For anyone who wants to follow it in all its complexity, I recommend J.M. Bumsted's *Trials & Tribulations: The Red River Settlement and the Emergence of Manitoba, 1811–1870*, which renders the confusing events of those nearly sixty years intelligible.

The first of the men recruited by Selkirk began to arrive in 1812: "six Scots, four Orkneymen, and eight Irishmen," according to Bumsted, and not settlers, but HBC "servants." They were followed the same year by another party, also mainly servants rather than settlers. It wasn't until June 1814 that the first real Selkirk settlers arrived. They were neither explorers, who by definition pass through once and not usually again, nor fur traders, who by the very nature of their work do not change the land and for the most part leave the area forever at retirement.

They came, instead, to settle as farmers in the vast territory of today's West and were, in a sense, the forefathers and mothers of all Western farmers—whether Ukrainian, German, Slovak, English, or other—who settled or, in Western parlance, "opened" this land. But the mixed-blood people already there saw that settlers would disrupt the fur trade, ruin their part in it, and destroy the world they had created for themselves. They could, therefore, hardly be expected to welcome farmers in their midst.

The resulting conflict was inevitable: farmers against half-breeds (Bumsted says that at this moment in history, "these people were not yet known as Métis or even mixed-bloods, but usually were called half-breeds or *bois-brulés*"). Very soon, in June 1815, nearly all the settlers were forced to leave the colony, some under the escort of friendlier mixed-blood people and the remainder led out by the kindly Chief Peguis of the Saulteaux people. In fact, the evening after the battle he actually rescued Marie-Anne Lagimodière—the first white woman in the Northwest, who was to become Riel's maternal grand-mother—and her children himself.

Interestingly, in terms of what it is to be a Westerner, a good friend from the Peguis Reserve tells me that in 1914, about one hundred years later, these same Saulteaux people were rewarded for their service by being arbitrarily moved by the government from the area that had long been their home to a reserve between Lakes Winnipeg and Winnipegosis. Today they have ongoing land claims to return to the Netly Creek area at Selkirk, where they came from. My friend says his grandmother was part of, and often spoke of, that enforced move by boxcar.

In August 1815, the settlement was restarted when some of the farmers doggedly returned. However, matters between the settlers and the mixed-bloods (also between the HBC and the North West Company) did not improve, and on June 19, 1816, in a bloody confrontation near the settlement, twenty-one set-tlers and one half-breed were killed. This was the Seven Oaks Massacre, and none of the perpetrators was ever brought to justice. Once again the settlers felt, for safety's sake, that they had to leave their settlement.

In the meantime Lord Selkirk had mustered a private army made up mostly of Swiss soldiers, the de Meurons, and step by step he slowly retook the West from the North West Company. In July 1817, the settlers once again returned to their land. After that they had to contend merely with grasshoppers, early severe frosts, the most terrible winters in local memory, fires, and floods. The settlement grew slowly, and when adversity destroyed their crops or illness killed family members, people stayed if they possibly could, rather than returning, penniless, to Upper or Lower Canada or to Europe.

The long truce-like interlude seems to have been an uneasy one, and more than fifty years after the Seven Oaks incident, the first Riel Rebellion took place. By then, there were perhaps 10,000 to 12,000 Métis, barely 2,000 whites, and perhaps— across the West—as many as 35,000 Amerindians. (That same year, 1869, farther west, in present-day Alberta, the Cree and Blackfoot met in Blackfoot territory in a battle for access to land where there were still buffalo, and the Cree leader Maskepetoon was killed.) At this time the government of Canada had acquired all the Hudson's Bay Company's land for 300,000 pounds sterling and one-twentieth of the Fertile Belt, and made provisions for its new governance without even telling the people of the Red River Settlement. Not even the whites knew about it ahead of time. (This might be described as one of the first instances of the Central Canadian authority failing to recognize those in the West as equals.)

When land surveyors were sent into the area to begin legally dividing it to prepare for the expected new settlers, often or sometimes (historians disagree on this) disregarding the long-held property of the current residents, it was no wonder that the Métis objected strenuously. When no recourse was found against what looked like injustice, rebellion ensued. Louis Riel emerged as leader, and a provisional government was established. Had someone less focused and less intelligent been chosen, things might have been much worse than they were.

It was a rebellion (though historians tell me that "resistance" is more politically correct if you side with the resisters) in which the people native to the Red River area were easily defeated once the government of Upper Canada had the presence of mind to send out 1,200 soldiers under Colonel Wolseley. Arriving at Fort Garry on a late-summer night in 1870, he forced Riel to flee for his life (Wolseley didn't see Riel, although it is said that Riel watched Wolseley and realized his only choice was to run) and established Canadian rule pretty much without firing a shot.

In Portage la Prairie there could only have been triumph. By this time, factions within the settlement were clear: many of the Protestant Anglophones and half-breeds sided with those who thought of Queen and Country; and the French Catholic Métis believed themselves to be an independent people in their own country and were not interested, to put it mildly, in being ruled by Canada, the British Empire, or Anglophone Protestants. Wolseley's soldiers had been mustered in Canada West (Ontario) and were so anti-French Catholic that it was not safe for any French Catholic to set foot within miles of where they were ensconced in Fort Garry. Beatings and near-murders became the order of the day, including the near-killing of a Catholic priest. It was not until someone died that the soldiers were reined in.

Over the next few years something like two-thirds of the mixed-blood people in the Red River area left the region to make lives elsewhere. Historians also disagree as to the correct interpretation of this dispersal. Some believe that a secret campaign against the Métis by the Canadian government—to deliberately dispossess them of their land—explains the departure. Others agree that prejudice and discrimination against the mixed-blood people did take place, but disagree as to how deliberate it was.

In reading historians' varying accounts and explanations of this very bitter time in Western Canadian history, I sense a time of great prejudice: that to have Indian blood was to be a savage, incapable of much improvement and fit only for serfdom. Added to this was the virulent prejudice against the French and the Roman Catholic. Had the Métis been white, Anglophone, Protestant farmers from Ontario, it seems unlikely that any dispossession would have occurred at all—that there would have been any need for a rebellion to ensure the landowners' rights.

Public opinion in what became Ontario shifted over the

years leading up to the rebellion from a lack of interest in the vast, thoroughly inhospitable Western lands to the conviction that the open, unsettled West was fertile and an opportunity waiting to be seized. Further, the belief grew that the West belonged to Ontario, that Ontario would determine its destiny, and that its destiny was to be populated by people moving out from English-speaking Canada, bringing British ideas of society, customs, and laws with them to "civilize" it. There were already such people present in the area, but after Wolseley broke and scattered the provisional government and established Canadian rule, the settlers who began to come into the area, many of them taking over Métis land (whether legally or not), were not only English-speaking Protestants, but were often members of the Loyal Order of the Orange Lodge.

This infamous organization began in 1795 in Ireland as a secret society. Its purpose was, and seems to have remained, to uphold the Protestant religion, the notion of Protestant supremacy, and Protestant ideals against Irish nationalism in Ireland and against Roman Catholicism everywhere. It spread to other countries of the British Empire and was by this time well established in parts of Canada West. (As my older sister once remarked jokingly on being introduced to a descendant of one of the Irish families who brought the Orange Lodge to Canada, "Thanks a heckuva lot.")

I have trouble remembering this myself, or imagining it, so I emphasize this for readers: in 1870 there were no other settlers in all this huge land. The Métis had home, land, whether farms or not, and a way of life when Canada bought the West and began to administer it. The contempt with which the Métis were treated by the new settlers from Canada West, who came rapidly after the provisional government had been broken, drove many of them away. Their inability to prove ownership of their river lots so that these same lots were given to the immigrants drove others away. The desire not to be ruled by Canada, a horror of finding themselves swamped in numbers in their own country by hostile Anglophone Protestants, and the concern that the buffalo had all but vanished from their area pushed others to go farther west.

And so many of the Métis left, some south into the United States, some west to Lac la Biche and St. Albert and St. Paul des Métis near Edmonton, Alberta, and others into the Fort Carleton area of Saskatchewan and to the communities of Duck Lake, Batoche, St. Laurent, and St. Louis. (I began school at a convent in St. Louis and then took grade two in the one-room, eight-grade public school there.) The anger, the disenchantment with and suspicion of the Canadian government, spread across the land with them—not a happy way for the settlement of Western Canada to begin. Nor was it a happy thing to have the arrival of large numbers of immigrants who believed in the absolute rightness and supremacy of British culture.

It was then, as the agricultural frontier advanced west, that those who have "always been here"—the First Nations people—and those who founded the contemporary West—the Métis—discovered themselves without agency in a West they could no longer recognize. By 1883, Dickason says, the Amerindian population had declined, the result of an earlier smallpox epidemic that had killed many Cree, while the European population was rising due to immigration. Before long, only fifteen years, the second Riel Rebellion was taking place, this time farther west, beginning in northeastern Alberta and moving east into the territory of the Saskatchewan Rivers—the places where the Métis had gone to establish new homes.

The Métis, again under Louis Riel, with the able lieutenantship of Gabriel Dumont, rebelled for much the same reasons they had the first time—the unexplained surveying of their river lots, which meant, they thought, that they were about to lose their land. The rebellion ended with Dumont fleeing for the United States and Riel's execution. The prejudice the Métis had been subjected to so far with regard to the causes of the rebellion then shifted to the First Nations people. According to historians Blair Stonechild and Bill Waiser, in *Loyal Till Death: Indians and the North-West Rebellion*, "Most [Indians] had tried to avoid the conflict or worked actively to prevent an escalation of the unrest. Others had been forced to participate under compulsion or fought in self-defence. . . . Over fifty Indians [were] sentenced for various offences, more than twice the number of Métis convictions."

In her memoir, my Grandmother Graham tells about a house on a farm they rented near Macdowell, Saskatchewan, in 1927. It was owned by the Cameron family:

> Angus Cameron Sr. came overland from Winnipeg by oxcart. One of his daughters . . . told us she walked from Winnipeg behind the oxcart. . . . When we moved into the house on the Cameron farm, we didn't realize we were moving into an historic place. Mr. Cameron Sr. built the house in the 1850s or earlier and when the Indians went on the rampage during the Riel rebellion, he moved his family into Prince Albert . . . about twenty miles from Macdowell. The Indians rampaged through the house but did not take a thing. All the damage, they butchered a steer and ate it.

It was not until the publication of the Stonechild and Waiser book in 1997 that the public became aware of another disgraceful and tragic injustice, of Commissioner Edgar Dewdney's "campaign against the Indians." It was this campaign that culminated in the trials of eight warriors in late 1885, trials that were brief and whose adherence to strict standards of justice were slight. "A

travesty," say the authors, from English-language court proce-
dure to lack of legal representation, from juries of "White,
Protestant settlers" (the very people terrified of Indians in the first
place) to prime ministerial interference in the judicial process.

At one point, court-appointed defence lawyer Beverly Robertson said this to the jury: "I have felt that it is almost a hopeless
task to obtain from a jury in Regina a fair consideration of the
case of an Indian. It has seemed to me it is only necessary to say
in this town to a jury, there is an Indian, and we will put him in
the dock to convict him." Eleven days after Louis Riel's infamous and much-debated execution in November 1885, eight
First Nations warriors were hanged at Fort Battleford. According to Stonechild and Waiser, they mounted the scaffold singing
their death songs:

> Miserable Man was the first to ascend the stairs. He had
> decided at the last moment against fleeing to the United
> States with Imases and turned himself in at Battleford
> hoping that the white man's justice system would treat
> him leniently; now, he was facing death for killing car-
> penter Charles Gouin at Frog Lake. Next came Bad
> Arrow, Gouin's other convicted murderer, and Round
> the Sky, who had finished off an already dying Father
> Fafard. They were followed by Wandering Spirit, the
> man who had started the bloody carnage that fateful
> April morning when subagent Tom Quinn refused one
> request too many. . . . Iron Body and Little Bear came
> next. Both had been convicted of killing trader George
> Dill, as he tried to escape the melee. The question of who
> fired the fatal shot was secondary to punishing those who
> were there during the carnage, especially when several
> other participants were beyond the reach of the law in

American territory. The Assiniboines came last: the older Itka, who had settled a personal grudge with farm instructor James Payne, and Man Without Blood, who could not back down from a dare from his warrior friends and killed an unpopular local rancher.

After their deaths, relatives were refused possession of the bodies, which were placed in a mass grave in unconsecrated ground on the nearby bank of the North Saskatchewan River.

Every summer for the past forty years, a play called *The Trial of Louis Riel* has been enacted for tourists in Regina. Everyone has an opinion about Riel, as to whether he was a madman, a traitor, or a patriot, and about the justice of his execution. But there is no play about the trial of the eight Indian men: Miserable Man, Bad Arrow, Round the Sky, Wandering Spirit, Iron Body, Little Bear, Itka, and Man Without Blood.

After the taking of their land, the signing of the treaties, the bewildering "coercive tutelage" of the Indian Act, we have also this bitter story, not even remembered by the EuroCanadians of the Prairie provinces. It is, though, one of the stories on which our present relationship with the Aboriginal people of the plains is founded.

This doesn't mean that I think the rest of the country is free of racism. But I suspect that Western Canada is particularly afflicted with regard to the First Nations people. Remembering those terrible pictures on television of the frozen bodies of the young Aboriginal men, I am reminded that I do not recall reading or hearing about the freezing deaths of any drunken or rowdy or repeatedly troublesome white youths. Although the public inquiry into Neil Stonechild's death could find no evidence of this being the result of action by the specific police officers who (the inquiry concluded) had had him in custody, the death remains unexplained. An editorial in the Toronto *Globe and Mail*, dated October 28, 2004, states, "[Neil Stonechild's] death was a Canadian tragedy. He was not just anyone's son but the child of a troubled aboriginal community. He died because there are far too many Neil Stonechilds on the streets of Western Canada, and because police—some of them—did not see him as human. A 17-year-old who could have been anyone's son was not seen as human because he was native and drunk and raising hell."

If, at the time of settlement by EuroCanadians of the Prairie provinces, those very settlers and those white people who exercised power exercised it with great injustice toward the Métis and then the Amerindians, this was the foundation on which today's attitudes toward the First Nations people of the plains are built.

If, in general, Aboriginal lives in the West continue to be cheap, this is especially true of Aboriginal women. In 1973 a Saskatchewan Métis woman, Maria Campbell, published a memoir that shocked Canada. Called *Halfbreed*, it told the story of her life growing up within a community that, although once prosperous and powerful, since the two Riel Rebellions had become outcast. Maria Campbell is the same age as I am—born in 1940—and we were growing up not only at the same time, but in roughly the same place. Her memoir gave her readers an insight into the lives of families like hers, cast out to the periphery of Western life and abandoned there by the rest of society.

Our family was poor then, too, and our lives were also difficult, but we did not routinely go without food, did not have to resort to snaring gophers to ward off starvation, and had at least decent clothing to wear. We were not forced to live on road allowances or in abandoned houses. We were not much scorned by the rest of our communities (although it was dicey being French and Roman Catholic if you didn't live in a French, Roman Catholic community). My sisters and I were not viewed by certain white men as "easy pickings" for sexual purposes, especially not when we were children, and none of us had to resort to prostitution to survive, or to drug addiction to survive the prostitution or out of general despair. In the ordinary chronology of EuroCanadian lives, we went on to high school—it was, quite simply, *unthinkable* that we might leave school without graduating from grade twelve—then to university and then into professions. For the most part, we did so without so much as missing a meal, having an unwelcome conversation with a police officer, receiving welfare, or being insulted repeatedly about things over which we had no control, such as our skin colour and our parentage.

Maria Campbell, a person of intelligence, beauty, and courage, struggled down a much harder path, experiencing truly desperate poverty. She married at fifteen, after her mother's death, in order to be able to keep her brothers and sisters together and with her; when the marriage failed, she went to Vancouver, where prostitution and drug addiction were her lot. How she struggled out of this degradation is a story of a woman of great determination with a rock-bottom sense of her own inevitable worthiness, of someone who deserved—despite being a mere "halfbreed"—a decent life. And this she achieved for herself, becoming eventually an activist in the Aboriginal peoples' rights movement and a successful writer, so successful that in 2004 she received a Canada Council for the Arts $50,000 Molson Prize for her outstanding lifetime contribution to the cultural and intellectual life of Canada. How many other Métis women growing up in the same place at the same time found no respite for their suffering, much of it born of pure racism, and died far too young? Too many.

Le Pas, Manitoba, was in 1971 the scene of another shameful murder, this one of a nineteen-year-old Aboriginal woman, Helen Betty Osborne of Norway House Reserve. According to the press, most people in the town (read, white people) had a pretty good idea who had beaten and killed her; in fact, some of them knew the identities of these men. Yet nobody seems to have gone to the police with the information. She was, after all, only an Aboriginal woman, and her suspected killers were white men.

Finally, in 1985, the RCMP placed an article in the local newspaper requesting the assistance of the public in solving the murder. Subsequently, three of the four men thought to have been involved were at last arrested. One gave evidence against the other three and was granted immunity from prosecution. The other two were put on trial; one was acquitted and one, finally, after going about freely for fourteen years after his crime, was sentenced to life imprisonment. (He has since received full parole.)

If justice is hard to come by for those who have been murdered, there is also the Alberta case of Yvonne Johnson, co-author with Rudy Wiebe and subject also of the prize-winning non-fiction book *Stolen Life: Journey of a Cree Woman*, who is thought to have been treated unjustly by the courts. Younger than both Maria Campbell and me, the tale of her life is an eye-opener for anyone who thinks that racism is not alive and well in Western Canada (and also the Western United States, since a significant part of her life was spent there). Reading her heartbreaking story, it should surprise no one that finally, as a young wife and mother, she participated with three others in a murder in 1989 in Wetaskiwin, Alberta.

It was in the same town that Yvonne was tried separately for her part; the "jury of her peers" was, astonishingly, twelve white farmers. Western Canadian male farmers generally are not entirely egalitarian when it comes to women; their world is almost exclusively patriarchal. How much more difficult, then, for them to view an Aboriginal woman as any kind of an equal. It seems laughable to have to question, too, why there were no women on her jury. But justice, I am told, does not work in so reasonable a manner. The composition of her jury is the least of the difficulties with her trial and subsequent failed appeal. (Do Aboriginal people ever appear on juries where Aboriginal people are on trial?)

Apparently not believing that she would receive justice, she refused to speak for herself at her trial. The result was that, of the four people who committed this act, she received the harshest sentence—twenty-five years to life. In fact, at the time that *Stolen Life* was published, she was the only Native woman in Canada serving this severe a sentence. She is still in prison, and waiting uneasily for her faint hope hearing; it is not called "faint hope" for no reason. In the meantime, her four children have grown up without her, her husband has served his ten-year term for his part in the same murder and has divorced her, and she has become a grandmother.

Alberta continues to investigate a number of disappearances of women from Edmonton, something like twenty out of thirty of whom are Aboriginal. And then there is the "Trail of Tears," Highway 16 in northern British Columbia, along which a half-dozen women have vanished. Some of their bodies have never been found; most of the missing are, not unexpectedly, Aboriginal women.

I have chosen a few of the more notorious individual cases to make a point that most reasonable people know anyway—that especially the lives of Aboriginal women are viewed by mainstream society as of not much value. When one is murdered or vanishes there is no great public outcry, no great play from the whole media demanding that the case be solved or the missing person found. And when a number of Aboriginal women, sometime workers in the sex trade, disappeared, white women, apparently knowing at the subconscious level that they would not be at risk, didn't start locking their doors at night or insisting on escorts wherever they went. I might go further and ask, why do men of a murderous bent choose Aboriginal women? I believe the answer is clearly that they know there is unlikely to be a public outcry, and that the investigation may very well be less rigorous—that is, that they will get away with it.

Contemporary scholars, and Native people too, seem to agree that during all this time since EuroCanadian settlement, the attitudes of both government and the populace toward those people they called "Indians" was that they were a dying people (eventually the "problem" would go away) and that the only solution for the "Indian problem," and also the natural outcome—presumably for those who hadn't "died out"—was assimilation. According to professor Noel Dyck, though, Canadian policy toward First Nations people has always been based on the assumption that they do not know themselves what is best for them, and through the Indian Act and the Department of Indian Affairs, the system has always used something Dyck calls "coercive tutelage" to try to push, pull, persuade, or order from Indians whatever behaviour the current, nearly always muddled, thinking says is needed from them—for their own good.

None of this has worked very well, and the initial assumption has certainly turned out to be wrong: Amerindian people have most assuredly not died out; in Western Canada they are reproducing at a rate higher than that of non-Amerindians.

Secondly, to the extent that any "assimilation" has taken place at all, despite the government's continuing effort to keep control of Amerindian people, it has done so for the most part on Amerindian terms.

The second basic assumption, that assimilation would follow, for the most part has also been wrong. All governments since Contact in the West that have tried to "control" the Indians have seriously underestimated the determination of their resistance, which in the past often turned underground and was not spoken of. Some First Nations people have assimilated, but to this day most have not and do not ever plan to. Others have take a middle ground, going to university, building careers, living in cities, but without giving up cultural knowledge, whether it be spiritual or practical.

In fact, distressing as it may be to Amerindians after so many years of being despised, the tide is turning slowly so that a sizeable body of EuroCanadians are adopting Amerindian views of justice and spiritual belief. Potlatches and Sun Dances were once forbidden by law: both have returned, and EuroCanadians are asking permission to attend them and take part in them. Some are adopting First Nations' spiritual practices—the talking circle, the Sun Dance, sweat lodges, and medicine wheels—as well as a sentencing circle rather than a formal court trial with judge and jury. Even indigenous plant knowledge is now considered invaluable.

Many Western EuroCanadians (myself included) are beginning to think that the indigenous people of this continent have always known things about its spiritual life that we Europeans did not know and are only now beginning to realize that we need to know. In this last I am referring to our relationship with nature. As Dickason noted, we have been so blinded by our European, Christian ideology that we could not see what was here on this continent and made little attempt to adapt ourselves to it, instead expecting it to bend to the ideas we brought with us about landscape and nature, nearly always inappropriate or just plain wrong in terms of North American climate, soils, weather, and growth patterns.

The gifts of Aboriginal people to non-Aboriginal people of the Canadian West have been great ones, which we Euro-Canadians are just now beginning to appreciate. For example, surely the North American environmental movement has grown from ideas about our relationship to land that stemmed from the attitudes of First Nations people toward it: respect for it, making use of it in sustainable ways, appreciating it for itself as nourishment for the human soul, and, especially, beginning to see it as alive and filled with spirit, and as something not apart from us, but of which we are a part. Out of this grew our understanding that we must not chop down all the trees, that damming rivers kills plant and animal life, that wilderness, in fact, has absolute value.

Their reward for all this is that our cities are full of the Indian poor, that our inner-city streets are patrolled by Native women prostitutes, many of them technically children, that alcoholism and drug addiction are rampant in these populations, that the health of Aboriginal people is poorer than that of the rest of Canadians, that they die younger and their infant mortality rate is double that of the rest of the country, that our prisons are filled with First Nations people.

Saskatchewan and Manitoba have, at 13.6 percent, the highest proportion of self-identified Métis and First Nations people. It would appear that in large Eastern cities, such as Toronto and Montreal, First Nations people simply disappear into the growing populations of visible minorities who have immigrated there. In fact, in the news from Toronto and Montreal we hear much more about cases of alleged discrimination against people from African nations, Southeast Asia, and the West Indies than we ever do about any against First Nations people. Out here in the West, with the possible exception of Vancouver, the situation is reversed.[2]

When I was telling a federal government official about this book, he said to me, albeit in a careful and thoughtful way, making no direct attribution of fault, that many billions went from the federal government to Indian people every year, yet living conditions on many reserves remained appallingly bad. He commented that often this was simply because of poor management of these substantial funds, although this was certainly not true on every reserve. I could not argue with any of this, because it is clearly true that there is mismanagement and even straightforward corruption on some reserves (as there is in non-Aboriginal jurisdictions).

Today, large areas of Western cities are occupied by First Nations families. Elementary and secondary schools have many First Nations students, as do our universities, although First Nations and Métis students often choose to enroll in special First Nations schools and colleges. In any case, my nieces, now in their early thirties, all attended school with First Nations classmates, and First Nations people play a significant part in the life of our cities.

I was once cautioned by Saskatchewan premier Lorne Calvert to remember that "good things are happening," and it seems appropriate here to try to identify some of them. The very fact that the government of Saskatchewan saw fit, at last, to call a public inquiry into the freezing death of the Aboriginal youth Neil Stonechild seems evidence to me of a—if somewhat belated—desire to find some justice for First Nations people, or at least to say, *Enough is enough.*

The premier also pointed out the stunning and expensive new college building, the First Nations University of Canada, the only Aboriginal university in North America, that opened on the summer solstice in 2003 on the University of Regina campus. It was designed by First Nations architect Douglas Cardinal (who also designed the Museum of Civilization building in Hull, Quebec, as well as other buildings in Western Canada). It is a matter of record that there are now many First Nations people in the professions, from law, medicine, and education to the judiciary, and in elected positions in provincial and federal governments.

Still, as the young Métis poet and memoirist Gregory Scofield pointed out to me when I asked him if he could list some "good things" that are happening (being unable to specify any more myself), he replied very sombrely that individual instances would not outweigh the past, the full weight of continuing injustices.

Daniel Francis has pointed out the essence of the problem: First Nations people were not seen as as people first, with all that that entails—rights to self-determination, to freedom, and to a decent standard of living. The Spaniards saw them as savages worthy of only death or slavery or else in need of an education so thorough it would turn them into Europeans; the missionaries felt they had to be converted to Christianity and thus turned into EuroCanadians; the government felt they had to be educated to forget their First Nations beliefs and turned into regular Canadians; many "ordinary" EuroCanadians saw them either as inherently noble and worthy of emulation or as inherently degraded and fit only for jails and skid rows. It appears that only the original fur traders were willing to accept them as they were, because that is how they were most useful to the Europeans. Nonetheless, there seems also to have been among the fur traders and explorers admiration for Aboriginal people's knowledge and wisdom.

I suspect that children today are being taught about the appropriation by Europeans of the Indian peoples' land. I hope this is true. But all those who are older than today's children, those who run Western Canada and those who make up the bulk of its population, need to confront this fact. Endemic poverty, a high crime rate, and a low rate of high school or university education are not inevitable among the Aboriginal population, but are the result of the muddled and conflicted attitudes of the non-Aboriginal population toward them and of a century of ill-advised and wrongheaded government policies. Until we accept this, there will never be enough social justice for Aboriginal people.

I strongly suspect that First Nations people believe that in the end they will triumph. They dream of the day when they will attain the right to be who they have always been, not savages—noble or otherwise—and not failed Europeans. This will come about through their much faster population growth, through their own unremitting and determined strength as a people, and through their renewed belief in the old spiritual and cultural systems from whence came their strength to survive the endless repression since the coming of Europeans to this continent.

In the meantime, the contemporary Prairie provinces' relationship with Aboriginal people remains conflicted and contradictory. In spite of racism, there is sometimes respect and even on occasion the wonder at living next to a completely different culture and of having this model of astonishing courage, endurance, and an awe-inspiring nature-based spirituality.

Indeed, one of the dreams of the West is to know what the West's First Nations know; to know the land and its animals as well; to be, in the same inarguable and beautiful way, as at home in the West, as much a true part of it, as they traditionally have been. More reasonably, a dream of the West is to live side by side in harmony with each other, First Nations people keeping their cultures intact while benefiting from the best of Euro-Canadian ideas, and EuroCanadians learning from the First Nations people those important matters our cultures have not taught us about how to make our lives here more appropriate to this unique continent.

# CHAPTER FOUR

# Le pays d'en haut

*What makes a Westerner?*
*Our stubborn refusal to recognize the "French fact."*

W HEN I was in grade eleven in 1956 at the old tech in
Saskatoon—the Saskatoon Technical Collegiate
Institute—our history teacher asked our class of
thirty or so sixteen-year-olds how many of us had been born in
Canada: nearly every hand went up. How many of us had both
parents born in Canada? he asked. Perhaps half the hands
went up. How many had all four grandparents born in
Canada? Mine was the sole hand that went up. It is true that
ours was the school that the economically disadvantaged children attended, many of them the offspring of immigrants who
lived in the small frame houses on the west side of the city, and
that the result might have been different across the river at
Nutana Collegiate. Nonetheless, I was both astonished, it
never having occurred to me that Canada was a country of
immigrants, and very smug about that incident, enough to still
remember it clearly almost fifty years later.

It was some years before I found out that my Grandmother
Le Blanc hadn't been born in Canada as I'd always thought,

but just over the American border in Suncook, New Hampshire. This would have completely deflated me, except that I knew she was a cousin of my grandfather's, and she was a Canadian, despite her American birth. Years later, I found out that at that time numerous Quebec families left Canada in order to find work in the American mill and factory towns, one of them being Suncook (where, I've read, the U.S. factory owners referred to the Quebec workers as "the Chinese of the East"). When exactly she was brought back to Canada to live I don't know, but her daughter, my Aunt Germaine, tells me that she could speak English and that she would not have learned that in Quebec. I tell myself that even if I had known the above facts back in 1956 in that history classroom, I would still have been justified in raising my hand.

My father, Achille Antoine Le Blanc, died at sixty-seven years of age in November 1973. He had been ill with leukemia for six years, and although my mother was not surprised at what seemed to me to be his sudden death, I was, because we'd been told he had "chronic" leukemia and might live with it for as long as twenty years. By then we'd been through a number of hospitalizations and crises, and I had chosen to believe that he would live out the full twenty. (Or maybe it was just that I was as yet unacquainted with death and couldn't take it seriously.) From my teenage years I had persisted in identifying more with my father's side of the family—French-speaking and Roman Catholic—than with my mother's. This was a surprising decision since, other than for one family, my sisters and I had never known my father's family well.

When I was a small child, my father's family spoke English only to translate for my mother's benefit, or sometimes when speaking to my sisters and me. I cannot recall this ever being a problem—children tend to simply accept things so long as they are benevolent. But it was certainly a problem for our mother, and that is why we didn't know our French family very well. I cannot recall any moment of closeness with my grandfather Oliva Rudolphe Le Blanc and only perhaps one or two with my grandmother Edith Jeanne Le Blanc. As a child, I was never sure which of *mes tantes* was which—they had moved to Manitoba around 1940, the year I was born—except for Auntie Antoinette, whom I loved and whose jawline, also my grandmother's, I believe I have inherited, and whose family we were closest to.

In any case, when my father lay dying in City Hospital in Saskatoon and our mother was told it was time to call for a clergyman, I think the priest who was the Catholic hospital chaplain was mentioned. I don't remember what attitude I struck in this matter: Did I insist? Was I very determined? I must have been at least the latter, because I can't remember anybody arguing with me, and I was not used to holding sway in family decision-making, although by this time I was teaching at the University of Saskatchewan—just a lowly sessional lecturer—and I may have been feeling unusually pleased with myself.

I said that we must find a French-speaking priest for Dad's Extreme Unction (one of the sacraments, since Vatican II more properly called "anointing of the sick," whose purpose is "to give spiritual aid and strength, including . . . the remission of sins"). I insisted on this, and then I went back to my job at the university. It turned out to be quite an assignment, scouring the city for a French-speaking priest, and it took a while, I'm told, but eventually a retired priest, a very old man, was found and came out to the hospital for our dad's sake. (I thought it was for our dad's sake, but I see now that, of course, it was all for mine.) I was astonished that it had been so hard to find a French-speaking priest; in my childhood it seemed to me they were everywhere. I knew enough prairie history to know that only seventy-five years earlier the difficulty for all the settlers flooding in from Ukraine and nearby countries where Catholicism was practised was to find a priest who was *not* solely French-speaking, but who spoke one or more of the Slavic languages.

Our father was comatose, or nearly, but he roused enough to listen a bit to the priest and to respond a little, too. He knew, I believe, that a priest had come to cleanse and bless him on his last journey and, a Roman Catholic to his last particle of being, he partly wakened. I do not know how this happened because I wasn't there, although I have imagined it enough times to feel as if I were. Our French father, who had been born in Quebec and arrived in Saskatchewan at six years of age, who did not learn to speak English until he had spent some time in school, and whose family on both sides going back into a Gallic past so distant I cannot describe it had always been French-speaking, *could not understand the priest.* The priest, I was told by my mother, had to switch to English.

No one was triumphant about this; no one said to me, "It was a silly idea, you should have left well enough alone." Perhaps they had other things on their minds, his death, for example; but just as no one had demurred at my notion, no one blamed me for its failure.

I was shocked, although I was also embarrassed at having some belief I must have been clinging to so finally destroyed. It was as if some faith and pride I'd had in our inherent Frenchness had been shaken to its roots. Subconsciously, it was probably at the time of my father's death when I was thirty-three that the seeds of my determination to recover my own French past must have been sown.

In the eighties I wrote a novel called *Upstream: le pays d'en haut*, motivated by my own mixed family background, in which I tried to tell the story of the French-speaking families who settled in Western Canada around 1900. I could attribute its roughly four rejections before it found a publisher to the fact that those publishers thought nobody was interested in French Canadians in Saskatchewan, although it was also my second novel, the one which, notoriously, evades most novelists after the first successful one. (It is now being translated into French for publication by Editions de la Nouvelle Plume in Regina.)

To some extent I used my own family history to construct it. But it was a very peripheral usage. I did, however, use our surname—Le Blanc—a fact that critics found surprising. I suppose it was an unusual thing to do, but as "Le Blanc" is the most common of surnames in this country—it was said in the fifties that there were a hundred thousand Le Blancs in North America, all descendants of one family, a number which would since have swelled considerably—I thought that doing so would be harmless. "Le Blanc" is an Acadian name, and Acadians were among the very first settlers to arrive in this country, in what became in time New Brunswick and Nova Scotia.

That first family was Daniel Le Blanc and his wife, Françoise Gaudet, who arrived at Port Royal from the area around Vienne in central France (just south of Lyons) in 1647. Even though no immediate members remain in those provinces, our roots are, nonetheless, proudly Acadian. In fact, the Rene LeBlanc of Longfellow's poem "Evangeline" is an ancestor of ours. (Recently I was invited to the Northrop Frye book festival in Moncton, New Brunswick. At one point I sat in the hotel lobby with two other writers, both local, whose surnames were Le Blanc and whose first language was French, but more significantly, at the opening reception I was startled and delighted to enter a room full of elegant, small—as I am—women all chattering away in French. Even though I couldn't speak to them in French, for the first time in my life I saw where my blood was; I saw where I had come from. It was a good feeling, and I felt also a rightness—my size, which always before had seemed simply an anomaly, now made sense, located me, as it were.)

I've said that I hardly knew my French grandparents—my grandmother, born November 11, 1885, and my grandfather, born on May 22, 1882, in Ste Catherine-de-Hatley, province of Quebec. I have only two memories of actual conversations with my grandmother, and in one of them I was merely present and it was my mother she was speaking to in her halting but clear English.

She was telling my mother about the expulsion of the Acadians by the British (which took place from 1755 to about 1763), which accounted for our branch of the Le Blancs not being born in Acadia. It was clear, even to me, who could not have been more than six or seven, that she was explaining to my Irish-Scots mother about the injustice the "English" (read, my mother's people) had done to the French, her people. I remember also that once she was gone, my mother was indignant about what she felt to be an accusation, at the same time as she was adamant on the point that she had not one drop of English blood in her veins. But for my grandparents, that expulsion was not mere history; it was visceral; it was what had happened to *them*.

My other memory was of my questioning her—I wasn't more than eight years old and probably younger—about how many children she'd had. She told me twelve, but four of them had died. "What were their names?" I asked. She told me, "Willis, Lucienne, Bernadette, and Violette," but her lips trembled and tears welled in her eyes. Now I see by the family genealogy that she lost two of them the same year, 1917; one, her first-born, would have been fourteen years old; the other was ten. It was only a fairy tale to me then, but today I can scarcely grasp the sorrow of it. All of them are buried in Saskatchewan, three of them at Domremy—named after Joan of Arc's birthplace in France.

When my paternal grandparents died, my grandfather in May 1971 and my grandmother at ninety-five in September

1981, I did not attend either funeral, and I don't remember even hearing about their deaths until after they'd been buried, although I'm sure I did. Now, years later, I wonder why I couldn't simply have seen that they were my grandparents even if I didn't know them and that I should have been at their funerals. In fact, now, the whole sorry history of my own relationship (I am not impertinent enough to speak for anyone else in my family) to that half of our family seems to me strange and sad and, in the end, a great loss. Is there anyone not weighed down by ideology, history, parental strictures, priest-or-pastor edicts beyond which they haven't yet been able to see?

In any case, when my paternal grandparents left their farm near Magog, Quebec, in 1911 for Saskatchewan, my grandfather's brother, Henri, with his wife, Elodina Dupuis, and their family had already been at St. Isidore de Bellevue, called simply "Bellevue," since 1906, and a second brother, Moise, and his wife, Josephine Langlois, and their family since 1909. (I remember Auntie Josephine as an old lady in black, a deeply mysterious presence to me, as I wasn't very clear as to whose aunt she was or how she fit into the family constellation or, especially, why she was treated with such gentle respect bordering on reverence by the grownups.)

By this time, Saskatchewan and Alberta were no longer simply the North-West Territories, but had been actual provinces in the Canadian confederation since 1905, and the Dominion Lands Act (whereby a settler, for a ten-dollar fee, could obtain 160 acres and then, by fulfilling certain conditions, another 160) had been in force since 1872. Why my father's family came is unclear, as might be expected, although I remember my father telling us that it was because they hadn't enough land in Quebec to support their families—the best reason most settlers came west, or north from the United States, or from across the ocean, at that time in history.

They came to Bellevue, an area of great beauty in what is called the "parklands"—originally meadows dotted with clumps called, in a uniquely prairie usage, "bluffs" of trees—only seven miles from Batoche, where Riel, Dumont, and the Métis had fought their last, losing battle in 1885, and whose small church is still riddled with bullet-holes. In fact, the trenches the Métis dug are still there, now only depressions in the grass. In 1911 they must have been much more obviously genuine battle trenches. I remember our father saying, "They used to say that Gabriel Dumont was buried on our land, before they moved his grave to Batoche," and there was a certain melancholy pride in his voice. My aunt tells me that the story was also that Dumont was hidden on what became the Le Blanc farm, in a log cabin: "the foundation was still standing when we were growing up." So it is certain that the family—the community—knew very well who Dumont was and all about the second Riel Rebellion.

When I was doing research for my novel *Upstream: le pays d'en haut*, my husband and I stayed a week in that area so I could revisit childhood memories and see again the historical territory. Aunt Antoinette and Cousin Émile and his wife, Sylvia, spent a couple of days showing us the sights, including the land to which my grandparents had come in 1911, long since owned by someone else, and the now tumbling-down old farmhouse where my father and his siblings had been raised and, I suppose, where the four children died. A mauve lilac bush bloomed against the part that Aunt Antoinette said her father had added to make a bigger kitchen. Almost certainly, as a child I'd seen that farmstead, although I've no memory of it. As I stood there with my aunt, cousins, and husband, gazing at it, the mix of emotions most adult children of settler-families must feel at such a juncture swept through me: pleasure at "fixing" a part of the past, and thus who one is, and intense sadness at all the family dead and that the way of life was all gone before one was even born, and can never be recovered.

The history of the French in the West begins in mystery. We don't know when they first travelled to what then was Rupert's Land and later the North-West Territories, only that one map in French exists, dated 1688; it must have been made not very long after the first explorer arrived. Historian W.J. Eccles notes that until 1681, for *coureurs de bois* to go off into the woods to trade with the Indians on their own was, in fact, illegal (*coureurs de bois* was a term used in the seventeenth century to refer to independents, while *voyageurs* was used in the eighteenth century to refer to employees of the large fur-trading companies). However, it would seem that a few did anyway, but how far west they went is not something I'm able to determine apart from the 1688 map by J.B.L. Franquelin. The first French-speaking people in the West were the offspring of those men and their Amerindian wives, and of those who followed them year after year in increasing numbers.

In 1766, a "Canadian" (meaning he was from Quebec) named François Le Blanc (the one called "Franceways" by the English and "Saswe" or "Shash" by the First Nations people, translated as "Yellowlegs" for the colour of his stockings), a man I choose to think of as an ancestor, was seen on the North Saskatchewan River by HBC trader William Tomison. Tomison (as quoted in *The Saskatchewan*, the Governor General's Award–winning book by Marjorie Wilkins Campbell) described Le Blanc thus:

> His dress was a ruffled Shirt, a Blanket Jacket, a pair of Long trousers without stockings or Shoes, his own hair with a hatt bound about with green beinding, a poor

looking Small man about fifty years of age; he Seemed to have great Command over the men; he lay in the Middle of the Canoe with his wife and Son.

He had been in the Northwest often before this time, suggests Daniel Francis in *Battle for the West*, probably with La Vérendrye, was very familiar with the lakes and rivers of the Northwest, and was clearly at home in this wilderness world. This scene would have taken place nearly fifty years before the first farmers in Western Canada, the Selkirk settlers, arrived (in 1812–14) in the Red River region of Manitoba. Even though my own grandfather took another hundred years to come west, there have been Le Blancs here since the eighteenth century.

It was in the year 1818 that the first French-speaking Roman Catholic missionaries arrived from Quebec—the first missionaries, as far as we know. Saskatchewan historian John Archer says, "The Roman Catholic Church had followed La Vérendrye into the West as early as 1743" (Jesuit Father Merenerie), but the first mission in Saskatchewan wasn't established until 1846, at Île à la Crosse, and only in 1852 did the famous Father Lacombe arrive at Fort Edmonton in what would become Alberta. Those first missionaries at the Red River Settlement were soon joined by a group of French-Canadian settlers "to form the nucleus of the first French-speaking agricultural colony" in the West. But conditions were so adverse that by 1826 most had returned to Quebec. That would have left, as French speakers, for the most part those same Métis hunters and farmers and their families.

In 1870, when the province of Manitoba was formed after the first Riel Rebellion, at that time a territory of only about one thousand square miles, much negotiation by the representatives of the French and Roman Catholic residents gained bilingual services throughout the new province, meaning, also, bilingual schools. Separate schools for Roman Catholic children were to be allowed as well. In law, at least, the Métis would be guaranteed protection for their language and their religion.

But things were not to be that simple. Once the province was formed, Anglophone Protestant settlers flooded in, isolating the French, and as the new settlers were extremely, vociferously hostile to the French, most of the Métis were driven out or left their homes to go farther west, where Anglophone, Protestant settlers had not yet come. So, as I've noted in the previous chapter, they started over again, on river lots around Batoche, St. Louis, and St. Laurent, and in places such as Lac la Biche, St. Albert, and St. Paul des Métis in Alberta, while others went into the United States to live.

In fact, when Manitoba first became a province it had a population of 11,400 out of whom 60 percent were French-speaking. By 1890 the province's population was over 150,000 but only slightly more than 7 percent were French speakers. A few Quebeckers did emigrate, but they were far fewer than the Anglophones from Ontario. This was because for some time Ontario had seen the Northwest as belonging to it, while comparable sentiment in Quebec seemed to have accepted Ontario's judgement, making French Catholics reluctant to leave their own province. And French-Catholic Quebec leaders did not want to see their own province weakened by an outmigration of French-speaking, Catholic families. Nor had potential settlers in Quebec been subjected to the same glowing reports of life in the North-West Territories as those from Ontario had been. Priests resident in the Northwest had repeatedly warned Quebeckers that life was difficult in the West, and the result was that many who might otherwise have emigrated thought twice about it, and stayed home. Thus, French speakers went from being 60 percent of the population to a mere 7 percent.[1]

By this time, the once French-Catholic Red River area was now "a little Ontario," according to historian Desmond Morton, that is, Anglophone and Protestant, and determined to turn Manitoba into a "British" province. The rights of French-speaking Catholics written in the Manitoba Act were immediately threatened and soon removed. Separate schools were replaced by the right to a half-hour per day of religious instruction in areas where most people were Roman Catholics, which might be conducted in French if parents so requested.

In 1905, when Alberta and Saskatchewan came into being, the same legislation was set in place, but separate schools were allowed, although placed under the control of the Departments of Education. This was a compromise, in both cases, between the clamorous objections of the Anglophone Protestants to the fact of separate schools and of the French Catholics to no religious nor bilingual education at all.

As educator John Sokolowski has noted,[2]

> In 1912, the teaching in French in Ontario was severely limited. In 1915, the Alberta Legislature unanimously condemned bilingualism in any form in the schools of Alberta. In 1916, Manitoba banned bilingual education at a time when about 1/6 of Manitoba students were enrolled in German, French, Ukrainian, Polish and other bilingual schools. In 1919, Saskatchewan banned teaching languages other than English and French, and severely restricted the use of French. And it was only the Canadian Federal Government's official policies of Bilingualism and Multiculturalism, and the proclamation of the Charter of Rights and Freedoms in the 1960s and 1970s, which reversed many of these drastic decisions.

This 1919 law had real effects in the schools in French-speaking communities in my own province. As a child, I remember our father telling us how, when he was a child in Bellevue, they had had to take down the crucifix and other religious items from the schoolroom and how the language of instruction shifted, also by law, from French to English. Another woman born about the same time tells how her teacher would keep one of her pupils out as a scout so that if a school inspector was seen approaching, her students could hide their French books. For reasons which certainly are not clear to me—having to do, I think, with Quebec's objection to the war conscription first proclaimed in 1917—but which I wrote about in my novel *Upstream: le pays d'en haut*, anti-French attitudes, in this province, at least, were especially virulent around the time of the First World War. Quebec was entirely anti-conscription, so much so that on Easter weekend 1918, there were anti-conscription riots in Quebec City. The riots ended when soldiers arrived from Toronto and shot and killed four people in the crowd.

My mother, the daughter of the "born under the wagon box" grandfather and of the grandmother who sang so sweetly, married my father, the son of two Le Blancs with a long—indeed, among the very longest—history as French-speaking Roman Catholics in Canada, whose history began in persecution in Acadia and returned to it in Prince Albert, Saskatchewan, in 1935. I had always thought that neither set of parents attended the wedding. (When I sent this manuscript to one of my French aunts for confirmation of this chapter, she wrote back that she "remembered vividly" the car trip to the wedding and was quite certain that all of her family attended. Then I thought I remembered Mother saying that although no parents had been at the wedding, they had all attended the reception at my mother's parents' home in Prince Albert, this last with which my aunt concurs.)

On hearing this when I was perhaps ten or twelve years old, I asked our mother, *But why?* At first she refused to answer, then she said that our French grandparents did not condone their son marrying a non-French-speaking, non-Catholic girl (although she converted on her marriage). As for the non-attendance of her own parents at the ceremony, as nearly as I can remember, it had to do with not being outdone socially by the French parents—which indicates to me, rightly or wrongly, a complete failure to understand the cultural world of my French grandparents. At the same time, I am sure that my Grandfather Graham was probably horrified and angered at his eldest child's marriage to a French Catholic and that he might well have refused to attend the wedding. Not surprising, considering that my grandfather was an Orangeman and my great-grandfather was also one.

I still have our mother's father's now-fading orange-coloured moire-silk chest ribbon with its purple binding, two rows of tarnished gold fringe, attached purple badges, and darkened brass sequins, which he wore to Lodge meetings. Impressed into the faded purple badge is the date, 1918. I can remember viewing it as a child in our mother's presence with a mixture of emotion which I think now can only have been conveyed to us by her. I knew somehow that the Orange Lodge was not, somehow, *right*, and that despite the fact that this item belonged to my very own much-loved grandfather, it also represented something that I knew despised *me* personally. Because I was French (although only half, and although I couldn't speak the language) and because I was Roman Catholic. And I felt a helplessness, because I had not chosen either, nor did I understand why these were not good things to be.

At the same time that my sisters and I examined his Lodge

ribbon, we would carefully unfold a nine-by-fourteen-inch piece of pale blue paper and stare with held breath at the date on it: June 18, 1861. Across the top, *Loyal Orange Institution,* under it, *1690,* and below this, a strange diagram with its enigmatic symbols (meant to keep out the uninitiated) of a star, a fish-shaped or sheaf-shaped item, a crescent moon, six odd figures carrying on a shoulder pole something that might be the Ark of the Covenant, and below that, among other puzzling hiero-glyphs, a pair of scissors, three items that look like tents, an anchor, a ladder, a star, all encompassed within the suggestion of an ornate temple. Below this, the slogan *"Fear God, Honor the King, and Love the Brotherhood."*

The location of the ceremony conferring this document is *County of Ontario, District of Whitby, at Oshawa,* and the name written in the blank space in the elegant yet readable script of the day is *James Elder.* This would be our great-grandfather, James Tully Elder, father of our mother's beloved mother, Jane Taylor Elder, and probably born in Quebec (or possibly in Scotland). At the bottom it says, *"Joined this Lodge the April 1, 1857"* [sic]. It was not until the writing of this book that I finally sorted out the irony that the sash and the document did not belong to the same man, that, in fact, on the other side of the family we come from not one, but *several* members of the Orange Lodge.

I've been looking through the boxes of photos, too, that I became keeper of by default after our mother's death in 1987. The photos I've seen a million times, but now that both parents are gone—my father for thirty years, my mother for sixteen years—I find myself studying them as I never did before. Especially my father's old snapshots taken in the twenties or earlier, before he'd even met my mother. I see a small, trim, handsome man—it surprises me to see how much my older sister looks like him, something I'd never seen before—always nattily dressed in a white shirt and a three-piece suit, with a watch-chain across the vest's front. In one snapshot he is in the act of placing on his own head the chic felt cloche worn by a girl in another photo. There is something in his face that suggests a great capacity for tenderness, a gentle centre, someone who has known pain. Despite a family story I once heard telling a different provenance for their relationship, it is easy to see why our mother fell for him.

I wish I could go on to say that none of this clash of histories made any difference in the end to their great love for each other, but sadly, that would be untrue. Instead, over the years, and despite five children and much shared hard times and difficulties, they became more embattled than adoring, until, as grandparents, and before my father's too early death, they settled into harmony. The two families were closest through my father's sister, now deceased, Aunt Antoinette and her husband, George Phaneuf, who must have been one of the most likeable people on earth. (I once asked my aunt, when I was an adult, about that name, *Phaneuf*, as it was in my experience an uncommon one. An embarrassed look crossed her face and she said to me in a whisper and with a self-deprecating laugh, as if she were about to tell me some awful family scandal, *"They say it was once English."* She was also the aunt who told me in a faintly injured tone and with a lift of her head that said more than she meant to tell me, *"T'was your mother who taught me English."*) To his dying day, our father called our mother, named Margaret Amy Alexis but called Amy, "Aimée."

After around 1910 or so, when the huge numbers of settlers flooded the Canadian West mostly from the United States and Central Europe, it was not easy in the West to be French and

Catholic. My father grew up in Saskatchewan in almost wholly French-Catholic communities, but my sisters and I did not. We spent two years going to school in St. Louis, Saskatchewan, a historic community on the banks of the South Saskatchewan River only a few miles out of Prince Albert. Although we were surrounded there by our French-speaking relatives, we did not learn the language because we did not speak it at home. After that, from late 1947 through most of 1953, we lived in predominantly English-speaking towns. Any other language was, inevitably, Ukrainian (or Polish or Russian, but it was all the same to us), a language which discrimination taught one to be ashamed of, and rarely German, not a good idea to be speaking during and after World War II.

We also felt ourselves to be outsiders because we were Roman Catholics where everybody else seemed to be Protestant—the leading families certainly were—and someone with a French name (invariably unpronounceable by nearly everybody) could expect to be called "Frenchy," as my father was. Even then it didn't quite sink in that I wasn't supposed to be proud of my French name and heritage or that I was a Roman Catholic, that these, the latter especially, were something I would simply have to endure until I was old enough to shed them on my own. (A friend, a Saskatchewan boy, the bilingual son of a highly cultivated Francophone mother and an English-speaking father with a German surname, tells me about riding in the back seat of a car as a child to a school event in a nearby town and listening in bemusement all the way to the adults in the front seat insulting French speakers.)

But, despite the long and noble history of the French in Western Canada, it is easy to see why so many Westerners simply can't understand all this fuss about French. They cannot accept the idea of two founding nations because in their experience, French is merely one of a dozen competing potential second languages. Their own choice would be the language of their parents or grandparents, and that, most likely, would be German, or perhaps Russian, or Ukrainian, or Latvian, or, in the area where I live now, Norwegian. None of these people ever saw any evidence of that other founding nation our leaders keep telling them about, and insistence on the superior rights of the French only baffles and then angers them. That they are wrong is simply too bad; nobody will ever succeed in convincing them of it.

They came to Canada, or their grandparents or parents did, for free land and the promise of a society where they could at last make their own choices about religion and language, where there was neither czar nor king nor, in my husband's father's case, emperor. That English was the language in common usage and that they spoke not one word of it was acceptable. English would do; English they would learn. That was the practical reality of life in Western Canada around the turn of the nineteenth century into the twentieth, when between two and three million settlers poured in from the United States, the British Isles, and Europe.

For example, my husband's father escaped from Slovakia in 1913, came to the New World via the United States, and then went north to Fernie, at that time a mining community, in southern British Columbia. He wound up eventually in Saskatchewan, no doubt having rarely if ever run into a single French speaker in Western Canada. It is not unexpected that he and thousands of others like him who were not educated in this country found the idea of the "French fact" merely baffling, and unreasonable.

It was not until the seventies, when our country became officially bilingual, that French as the official second language became the cause of some very loud objections in Western Canada. It simply did not fit with the practical realities of daily life in the West, where the population of native French speakers had dropped from something like 100 percent in the seventeenth century to closer to 3 percent today.[3]

At the same time, an average of 16 percent of prairie people give another (non-official) language as their mother tongue, including every language from Arabic to Punjabi to Tagalog to Cree—in Saskatchewan alone more than 22,000 people list Cree as their mother tongue, several thousand more than list French.[4] I should note, too, that a few years ago, for the first time, English became a minority language in Vancouver because of the huge number of Chinese-speaking immigrants.

Nonetheless, I support the learning of French as a second language over all other languages (except Cree or other mother-tongue Native languages) and I continue to insist on the historical rights of the French language as one of the two founding languages—actually, the first founding language. Given my own family history, that it seemed a soul-saving act to me to learn at last to speak French should not surprise you.

At fifty-eight years of age, I decided I wanted to die bilingual. I live in the extreme southwest corner of Saskatchewan, a massive land area with a tiny, scattered population. Swift Current is the nearest large town (a two-hundred-mile round trip for me), and it has a population of only 15,000 people, of whom, judging by the pages of the phone book, not many have French as a mother tongue. Although there it is possible to go from kindergarten through grade twelve in French immersion (in 2002–3 nearly two hundred children were), it is another thing if you are not in the school system. Gravelbourg, a Francophone town with the only French-language boarding high school in the province, Collège Mathieu, is farther away than Swift Current. Our regional college (headquartered in Swift Current) rarely offers French classes because not enough people want to take them. Or else, once in a long while, there are the required eight or so eager students, but no teacher can be found for them.

I resorted to Athabasca University, where I audited three French classes by correspondence, bolstered by audio- and videotapes, plus telephone conversations with a tutor. Then the regional college in Swift Current ran a semester of conversational French, and so, from mid-September to mid-December, through rain and mud, blizzards and howling gales, icy roads and just plain winter, I drove a total of two thousand miles, so that I could learn to actually speak the language. Then there were no more courses to be had. After a year had passed, I went to Calgary for ten days, two hours a day, of one-on-one French instruction from a professional language teacher. I came away able to carry on a conversation in French, not quickly, not entirely fluently, but I was, at long last, speaking French.

Once I'd returned home, however, there was only French-language radio and television and the occasional brief conversation with French speakers (nearly all old people) I met on the post office steps in town. Past sixty now, I was faltering, and began to ask myself why was I doing this. So I could speak French possibly two weeks out of every other year when I was in Europe? So I could engage in a rare conversation with my French aunts in French? Even my stubbornly repeated *Parce que c'est mon droit de naissance*—"because it is my birthright"— began to seem less important to me in the face of my geographic reality.

How did my relatives maintain their identity as French Canadians and Roman Catholics? The older generation did this by spending their lives in Western Canadian French enclaves, mostly in St. Boniface, Manitoba, which is today a part—the older part—of the city of Winnipeg. Gabrielle Roy (born in 1909) wrote in *Enchantment and Sorrow*, her memoir about her youth, that crossing the bridge to go to Eaton's on a shopping expedition into the English-language part of the city was for her and her family a little like going into another country, that they felt themselves entering a strange place. But even today, as I write, it is possible to live "in French" in St. Boniface, and for the most part my aunts and one remaining uncle do. Even though older people still speak French routinely, they tell me it is a struggle to keep the younger generations fluent in French and wanting to speak it.

After such struggles on the part of those who wanted an "English-only" West, how very strange that today so many people with names indicating roots in countries from Poland to England are now determined not only to have their children grow up bilingual, but also that the two languages in question be French and English. The tide has turned in that, although there are still plenty of people in the West who are angry about what they would say was "having French shoved down our throats," this is an opinion that can be safely, if not ignored, then recognized for its weakness in a West that for the most part understands the pleasure and the naturalness too, in today's world, of speaking more than one language, and perhaps even the inevitability, for a Canadian, of French.

Alberta is getting ready to begin in 2006–7 implementing into their education legislation a mandatory second-language clause that is expected to be fully integrated by 2012. Right now, at least one-quarter of all Albertan kindergarten-to-grade-twelve students are studying French at some level. In Manitoba, a brave one child in every two is learning French, and in Saskatchewan during the 2002–3 school year, 45 percent of children were studying French.[5]

It is true that in the early eighties the number in French immersion programs was higher and that it has since fallen to stabilize at the preceding numbers. This seems to me to be more a consequence of the failure of Quebec in its three referendums to achieve a separate status (even the best intentioned felt the pressure relieved) than of a falling-away of interest in learning the French language among Western Canadians. Also, those high enrolments took place during the time when Pierre Trudeau was actively working toward achieving stronger status for the language outside of Quebec, and many Westerners were responding, just like other Canadians.

Louis Riel is buried in St. Boniface, where, on December 11, 1885, a Mass for the repose of his soul was held in St. Boniface Cathedral. Archbishop Taché presided, in itself an eloquent statement of how Riel was viewed by his own people. The church was packed, and according to contemporary accounts, many people were weeping. He was forty-one years old, and to this day, whether French-speaking or Métis or not, whether seeing him as a patriot, a madman, or a traitor, we in Western Canada have not been able to forget Louis Riel. Curious that one of the few names instantly recognizable in the West by anybody not currently in a coma should be not only French, but belonging to a Métis man.

I have felt that we had stolen our father's Frenchness from him, that if we had spoken French we might have helped him keep his; for a long time after his death I thought that he died so young because we had not loved that part of him well enough, that with a family who couldn't speak his mother tongue we turned him into an exile. It was not until a few years ago that I realized he had spent nearly all his adult life working with machinery or in garages in a time when no one knew that breathing in exhaust all day or immersing your hands over and over again in buckets of gasoline (to wash parts), and who knows what other contaminants he'd dealt with routinely, would eventually kill you. He was also a lifelong heavy cigarette smoker. He died of leukemia, I realized, most likely because of the way he'd earned his living and because of his smoking, and a weight lifted off my shoulders. But the weight of his lost Frenchness I still carry.

And so, I tell myself, I am learning French for my father, although, six years since I began the struggle, I often think that, despite the Official Languages Act, for an adult living where I do to master—and maintain—French-language fluency borders on the impossible.

To acknowledge that the French are a founding people is not to denigrate or demote any other of the many ethnic/cultural groups who were part of the settlement of the prairie West and who today make it the vibrant place that it is. In fact, if the history of the French in the West goes from being the first here to being only one of many, the French are still not only a founding people of this country, they are a founding people even in the West itself. And I know I speak for a lot of Westerners when I say that one dream of the West is to have the French language once again not only commonly spoken, but also fully honoured as it should be, given the dramatic contribution the French have made to the West, so that French speakers feel completely at home here, whether once Quebeckers, Acadians, or Métis, while speaking their own proud language.

# CHAPTER FIVE

# A Loaf of Bread,
# a Piece of Sausage

*What makes a Westerner?*
*Our excessive reverence for our pioneers and our pioneering past.*

IN AUGUST 2002, just in time for the historic floods, Peter and I went to the Czech and Slovak republics. We spent the first week in Prague. It was wonderful to see that ancient, beautiful city, to walk the Charles Bridge, to tour Kafka's castle and the Jewish quarter, to float down the Vlatava, attend *Don Giovanni* in the very theatre in which Mozart had premiered it in 1787 (although reconstructed after a fire), and go on a pub crawl led by a pretty, outspoken female student; but none of this was the reason we had come to Europe.

We had come, in fact, so that Peter might see his ancestral village. We knew it was to be found near the city of Kosice (pronounced *koe-shi-tza*) in the eastern Slovak Republic, from which, in the spring of 1913 at nineteen years of age, with only his passage money and the clothes on his back, in the dead of night, his father had walked away.

When the subject turned to the breakup of Czechoslovakia

(formed only in 1918), the young student guide remarked to those of us who'd paid our fees in order to have a tour of some historic Prague pubs that the Slovak Republic was "a peasant society." I was torn between believing her—realizing that, having grown up on the Canadian prairies, I'd been led to believe that myself—and feeling a touch of anger at her casual stereotyping of an entire nation, especially by one so young. Nobody else (a Swedish couple, some Americans) seemed even to have noticed the remark, but it stuck with me enough so that eventually, after we'd spent time in the Slovak Republic, and after I began to think about writing this book, at last I began to understand why.

We took the train from Prague, a ten-hour trip, to Kosice in the far east of the Slovak Republic. Neophytes to Central Europe, we lucked into a trans-European train, bought first-class tickets, and rode all the way in high comfort—there were even computer ports at the seats—in a virtually empty car. For a "peasant society" this wasn't half bad.

Images from that memorable trip remain with me: the English family, that of a former diplomat to the Slovak Republic, going to a wedding in a small village near the end of the line who were playing card games together and apologizing profusely for the noise they'd made, which, in fact, had barely risen above a whisper; the three thin, dark-eyed gypsy men the dining-car staff ignored until one by one they left, one of them barely containing his rage, all of them having entered the car with expressions and demeanour that said to me they fully expected this to happen. (As I watched, I was unable to contain my mounting curiosity and dread.) And then, oddly, hours later, when there was almost no one left on the train but us and the gypsies, the staff—two young men, one very large, with a bleached yellow brushcut and earrings—not only served them, but sat chatting amiably, quietly, with them.

At least three times we passed clumps of three or four concrete nuclear reactors, their unique shapes unmistakable, and
we ran beside or crossed, one after the other, rushing, swollen
brown rivers and streams. Nearing nightfall, the two young
men who worked the dining car pointed out in the distance
Slovakia's vacation area, the snow-capped High Tatras. And,
well after dark, when we finally arrived in Kosice, they insisted
it was too dangerous for us to walk across the unlit park from
the station to our hotel, but crowded our luggage into the tiny
trunk of a Skoda and drove us there, firmly refusing any compensation. (After costly Prague with its generally rip-off cab
drivers, we were stunned by this generosity.)

Kosice has about 300,000 inhabitants, but few of them are
English speakers. We were told that most could speak Russian but refused to, and that, as in most of Europe, people routinely spoke several languages—Czech, Polish, Ukrainian,
Russian, or Hungarian—German being the only non-Slavic
language many people could speak. We had to buy children's
school dictionaries—readily available in the local Tesco (a
department store chain), so clearly children *are* now learning
English—in order to buy water, *voda*, stamps, *marke* ("*stampskis*,"
an old lady at a kiosk called them for our benefit, we supposed thinking she was speaking English), or bread, *chlieb*, the
"ch" sounding like a throat-hacking minor explosion ("ch"
had a separate listing in our Slovak dictionaries).

Going clockwise from the Czech Republic on the west, the
Slovak Republic (our tourist brochures routinely referred to it
by its old name, Slovakia) is bordered on the north and east by
Poland, also on the east by Ukraine, on the south by Hungary,
and then, to complete the circle, by Austria. Slovakia, a land-
locked, small country compared to these neighbours, is
nonetheless very old. It first appears in history in 1230, giving it
lots of time in which to have been dominated in turn by each

of its neighbours. Its recent history is, of course, Communist.

We knew, from one of Peter's cousins, now ninety years old but, although born in Canada, still speaking fluent Slovak (and who turned out to be a slender, elegant gentleman who had spent his life as a musician), that since he had visited the village in the sixties, the Communists had moved out a number of villages, each of about fifty people, buildings and all, in order to build a dam for a water reservoir. Nonetheless, we planned to go there to see the area Peter's father had come from, even if only the water covering it. The Butalas, in fact, had not been landless people in 1913; it was only that with each generation the land had to be further subdivided until, in George Butala's generation, no one had enough to raise a family on.

Slovakia wasn't even on my list of places I want to see before I die. It spoke to me only of drab Communism and of war and poverty. And besides that, I've never gotten over being surprised to find myself bearing a Slavic last name. Growing up in Saskatchewan, home to a very large influx of Slavic people around the turn of the twentieth century, I went to school with kids whose last names ended in "ski" or "chuk" and who were known collectively—whether Polish, Russian, Czech, or whatever—as "Ukrainians." In fact, the word was usually pronounced as "*You-KER-ain-ian*" (when it was not simply "bohunk" and applied indiscriminately to any Slavic person). In all the years I'd lived with people of Slavic background, had them for neighbours, met them at parties, dated them (being thrilled—so hungry was I for a different world—to find my dates' real names were Stanislaus and Vladimir, not Stanley and John), I never dreamt I'd wind up with one of their names myself. There had been much prejudice against people with those names when I was growing up; I would not be surprised to find, unknowingly and despite my conscious efforts not to be, that I'd been influenced by all the derogatory remarks and name-calling I'd lived with.

So I knew nothing about the Slovak Republic and had no curiosity about it. Further, the tourist brochures I managed to acquire ahead of time in English emphasized things in which I had little interest: hiking trails, mountain climbing, skiing, and so on. Ancient, sophisticated cities weren't even mentioned. But I felt that my husband had gone where I asked him to go, uncomplainingly for the most part, and that it behooved me to be as generous toward his desires as he had been to mine. So I shut my mouth and played travel agent for a trip so major in his life.

By the time we'd been two days in Kosice, we'd given up hope of ever finding George Butala's village because it was no longer on any maps and thus we couldn't simply take a local train or a bus to it. In fact, we didn't know where it was, other than east of Kosice, and that it was not the two other villages still extant with the same name, to which people kept trying to send us. So few people spoke any English that detailed enquiries varied from difficult to impossible; there were no cars with drivers for hire. (Too late, we realized we should have hired a car and driver out of perhaps Austria.)

Then, with only a couple of days left, we finally found what in our sightseeing I'd been half-heartedly searching for since our arrival: the Dolna Brana (Lower Gate) archaeology complex on the main street—actually a long oval-shaped "square"— Hlavna Ulica ("main street"). We are always interested in archaeology, but Peter leaves such local map searches to me. I don't know why because I, map-challenged, invariably go in the opposite direction to the one I should. Besides, the complex was hidden behind the enormous St. Elisabeth of Hungary's Cathedral (begun at the end of fourteenth century and finished in 1508) in the square's centre, which had so many interesting sites and wonderfully beautiful old buildings around it that every time we set out for the archaeology site, we'd get side-tracked by other, ancient churches, a frightening plague column, a fountain, the vast, ornate state opera house that seems to exist in every European city.

Finally, we came upon it: a low iron railing in the middle of the cobblestoned square with a few low, wide steps leading down into the exposed brick and stone arches of the once-fortified city. When the two male guides waiting there for a paltry handful of daily tourists recognized that we were speaking English, the younger—at last, a speaker of fluent, correct English—became our guide. He was named Andraj, and something like six-foot-four or so, taller than my usually biggest-man-in-the-room husband, though still with a boy's awkward skinniness. In fact, we'd noticed how big Eastern Slovak men were—at least those in downtown Kosice—well over six feet and thick and strong-looking, next to whom my husband was, for the first time in his adulthood, generally smaller.

Our young guide was delighted for the chance to practise his English, and during our tour he asked us what we were doing in, of all places, Kosice. We told him we'd hoped to find my husband's father's village, but that it had seemed impossible and we'd given up. In a couple of days we'd leave for Zellina to the northwest, from where we thought we might take a bus or train into the High Tatras.

Andraj was, surprisingly, interested and said that he knew some old people and would ask them if they remembered where the village was, and that he could also look it up on old maps in the archives. We should return the next day and he would tell us what he'd found. Our tour ended, we shook hands and departed. I, for one, was extremely dubious that any of this would actually happen.

The following afternoon, though, we made our way back to the archaeology complex. Andraj, seeing us, came bounding up the steps. "I have found the village!" he told us, "and the water reservoir is called Starina. It is this one"—we had our maps out now—"right here, not this one or this one!" And he wasn't finished: "Tomorrow is my day off," he declared. "I have a car, and I will take you there." When we'd recovered from our shock, we offered payment, which he refused absolutely—he never did take a penny from us, only allowed us to buy a few dollars worth of gas—and we made arrangements to meet in the same spot at 8:30 the next morning.

We were the first, and then Andraj arrived with a student from England he'd met in a bar the night before. She was small, dark (as was Andraj), very slender, and lugging a backpack almost as big as she was. We piled into his car, men in front, women in the back, which caused Nikki, probably forty years younger than me, and I to mutter some sarcastic witticisms to each other. We resigned ourselves to the apparently unavoidable, and began to chat. She was on her third and last summer of travelling. She'd done South America the previous year and Asia the year before that—all of this solo. Now she was out of money and needed to finish her degree. "People are always asking me how I manage alone," she said in an exasperated tone. "I don't know why they think there's something special about it." It seemed pointless to respond, but I spared a moment's thought for her mother. Already I was beginning to suspect that Nikki, at home, might be just a touch—well—*difficult*.

The reservoir we were using as our destination was only about fifty miles from Kosice, but the roads were narrow, winding, and poorly marked. The result was that we missed our best turn-off and took a longer route on a busy main road, passing through a couple of towns. Eventually, Andraj having stopped a couple of times to ask directions, we began to drive up a long, curving hill with a lake far below on our left. At the far end of the lake, we turned off on a narrow side road that took us up hill and down dale for maybe half a dozen miles until we came to a dead stop at a barrier, of the kind one finds at a parkade exit, attached to a low concrete-block building. To our right was a steep drop, perhaps two thousand feet, and to the left was thick forest. We appeared to be in genuine wilderness.

A scruffy young soldier came out, unarmed, wearing camouflage pants and boots and an olive-drab T-shirt. Andraj got his identification out of his pack in the trunk and disappeared inside the guardhouse with the soldier. Moments later he came out and jumped back into the car, the soldier lifted the barrier, and off we bumped, down a narrow, unpaved trail. In only a few miles we saw, even farther below us and to our right, the famous reservoir we'd been hearing about in Canada for the last twenty or more years. It was tiny, we thought, and we were surprised that the Communists had deemed it necessary to move out the people who'd lived here for who knows how many hundreds of years for this little bit of water.

Andraj told us that this was done in order to maintain a pristine water supply, but I wondered (since we were only a few miles from the Polish and Ukrainian borders) if this was code for reducing the risk of sabotage. It was a heartless thing to do, in any case, and this, my first visit to Central Europe, gave me a truly visceral understanding of the magnitude, the determination, and the sheer hubris of the Communist vision. Never again would it be just a movement in history that I'd read about in books or seen on television and in movies. And in my admittedly very small experience, it is still hated more deeply than I could comprehend. I saw another way in which we Western Canadians are infinitely lucky to live so freely.

On we went, bumping along in our tiny car on a narrow trail thickly wooded on each side, winding along mostly downhill for perhaps twelve miles in total, until we came to another barrier and had to stop. This one, we recognized: a barbed-wire gate. We stopped the car and piled out. To the right was a

handmade sign with a homely drawing of a cow and the word
*Zlata* above it.

"What!" Andraj exclaimed. "Are we in Ukraine? That is not
a Slovak word!"

Nikki was unbothered, Peter considered the situation, and I
looked around nervously, expecting at any moment soldiers
armed with machine guns to appear threateningly on the nearest hilltop. We climbed through the makeshift gate anyway,
and began to walk down the road, Andraj having decided, on
consultation with the guard miles back, that this road would
eventually lead us to the site of the former village. We walked
and walked, but no soldiers appeared; there were no more
signs, no buildings except a dilapidated cowherd's shelter, and
not a single, solitary soul.

We were delighted to be in the Slovak countryside: Andraj
exclaimed and exclaimed how he hadn't realized such wilderness was so near at hand to Kosice and declared that he would
get together with his friends to go backpacking here. (The soldier had told him that no overnight visits were allowed, but
hiking was. He also warned us to watch out for logging trucks.)
Nikki was pleased to be able to chalk up yet another adventure
in yet another country; Peter and I were holding our breath,
expecting at any second to come upon the ancestral village,
which had by now grown in our minds to mythic proportions.

The terrain here was hilly—we were in the Carpathians—
leaving space only for small flat fields; all the others had a
marked slope to them. We walked and walked through this
lovely, humid countryside, the grasses and bush along the
roadsides dense and intensely green. Wildflowers bloomed
everywhere, and we paused often to eat fruit from apple and
pear trees and berry bushes growing wild and untended within
easy reach. Peter and I thought it a kind of Eden, and we grew
more and more awestruck, wondering aloud how a man could

bear to exchange these wonders for the wide, empty, and both frigid and roasting grasslands of southern Saskatchewan. And never look back, as his father never had.

Andraj told us there were still wild boars in these hills, and also bears. At one point, I caught a glimpse of something brilliant yellow on my shoulder and brushed it off with a loud exclamation. It was a very large spider.

Nikki picked up the poor, maligned creature from the ground and deposited it gently on a blade of grass while making not-quite-cooing sounds to it.

We had gone perhaps one mile, had met a herd of Simmontal cattle contentedly grazing on a green hillside, and were beginning to feel we must be on the wrong road. As we stood discussing what to do next—I began to realize I'd never expected to find the village anyway—suddenly coming up the track we'd just traversed was a woman wobbling along on a rickety, misshapen bicycle. She was probably in her forties, with a weathered, hearty face, and, when she reached us, a shyness to her manner.

She told Andraj that no, we weren't in Ukraine, that *Zlata* was the name of the village that had once been there, and that at the separation of roads a few miles back, we'd taken the wrong branch. She wobbled away on the bumpy road, on her way, probably, to check her cattle.

We got back in the car, laughing at how just at the moment of our giving up we'd turned around in the middle of nowhere, to find a woman appearing out of nowhere, as in a fairy tale, riding a rickety bicycle toward us. Soon we were back on the right road, and before we knew it, there was a newly erected sign with a little roof over it for protection from the rain. The sign named the village we were looking for.

We stopped again, all of us got out, and I took pictures of Peter standing beneath the sign, although, with its little roof and the angle of the sun, in all the pictures the sign is cast in shadow and you have to peer hard to make out the word. We drove on a few more feet and parked again. High on the hillside above us we could see a roofed platform, the wood still appearing fresh. And there were glassed-in signs on legs just above the roadside.

If Peter and I had exclaimed with excitement at finding the sign telling us we had at last come to the right place, now our silence held a kind of superstitious awe. Out we got once again, and while I took pictures, the three others went to the signs and studied them. Two of them held the list of the names of all the inhabitants who'd been moved out and the third held coloured photos of a commemorative ceremony held in the early eighties by those who'd been displaced. The photos showed dignitaries making speeches from the roofed platform on the hillside above the signs.

We went up the hill and saw that we had found the cemetery. In all directions there was not a house to be seen, not a building. Nothing but wooded hill after wooded hill, the trees, mostly coniferous, a dark blue-green, and where there were no trees, there were yellow patches where crops were ripening, or sloping fields of intense green. The sun had come out, the air practically steamed with moisture, the sky was very blue, the place silent. Once there'd been people all around, tiny village after tiny village, and cattle and horses, and fences too, one presumes. Now there was no one, and virtually no sign that anyone had ever lived there.

Here my description grows less certain. I saw the immense emotion my husband was not showing—odd as that seems. He held his face differently, his mouth was different, his eyes different. We've been married a long time; he is not a man to show his emotion, and when he is ill or filled with emotion, he grows silent; he likes best to just go away. While I'd been thinking these thoughts, he had gone into the graveyard and begun searching out, among the wildflowers and tall grasses and under the shade of deciduous trees, the graves of his ancestors.

After a moment, not really sure what my wifely role should be, I followed him, and began to read the headstones that hadn't fallen down. Many were iron crosses, the engraving too badly rusted ever to read again; one had been painted with a silver rust-retarding paint and it said "Peter Butala, 1904–1967" (Peter's grandparents had died in about 1900 and 1904). Others, made of stones, said, "Michal Butala, 1897–1962," "Andraj Butala." The headstones were hard to read, but we thought the latter had 1970 as the burial date. So it would have been after that when the Communists pushed everyone out. We took pictures of them, not for reasons that at that point we could have explained to anyone. It was just that we didn't know what else to do with what we'd found.

Peter moved around the graveyard quietly, by himself, pausing to kneel and dig the thick, entwined grass from around some of the fallen headstones in order to read them. He told me later that he'd been trying to find his grandfather's grave, also Peter Butala, but headstones erected in the first half of the century were either indecipherable or had fallen, and the undergrowth was so thick it would have taken hours of patient digging and cutting to reveal their remains.

When I'd seen all the standing graves and spoken with my husband about them, I walked out of the graveyard and stood on the narrow track beside it that ran up the hill. Andraj came over to me, Nikki was elsewhere, and I said, "He is very moved. I know he doesn't show it, but the fact that he is still there, kneeling among the graves, shows how moved he is." Andraj said, "I know it. Men like him who have had hard lives cannot show their emotions." I wanted to say, *But he didn't have an especially hard life*—whether this was true or not depended on your perspective—and I wanted to ask, *How do you, so young, know this?* But, I thought, everyone older than him has lived through wars. This countryside, these people, are steeped in war. Deaths, hunger, suffering.

All of us wandered around a bit more, each going our separate ways. After a while I went back to my husband, who was still studying the graves. I noticed then that the young people had climbed to the top of a grassy hill and were standing, silhouetted against the sky, talking. Then, after a moment, they lay down side by side, and began to roll down the steep hillside. Peter and I, standing far below them, began to laugh.

And then we were done, had finished with the site, because really, what was there left to do? The relatives still living had moved to nearby towns and into the city of Kosice and wouldn't speak any English and besides, we didn't know who they were. We got back in the car and began bumping down the narrow road, back the way we'd come. After a few miles we heard a loud noise and saw that a large, decrepit truck with a khaki-coloured tarpaulin enclosing the box had come up behind us. As he pulled over to let them pass, Andraj explained that the truck would be picking up loggers to take them back home after their day's work.

As it passed slowly on the narrow, muddy track, from the back of the truck, in the dark place where the tarp cover didn't meet, a face appeared. It was a man's, dark-skinned and lined and very round, staring at us open-mouthed and with profoundly curious, even amazed eyes. A small, incredulous part of me was thinking of trolls.

The quest for Peter's ancestral village satisfied, we thought the adventure was over; we thought there could only be anticlimax after this. A week or so later, after we'd spent a couple of days in the pouring rain in Zellina (the High Tatras were too rain-soaked for prairie droughters like us) and a few days in

Bratislava just as the flood emergency was declared (we'd stared at the Danube as the waters on the far shore crept up the sides of buildings there, coming within inches of the embankment top), we took the train to Vienna. It was a mere fifty or so miles but took something like two hours because of various stops and, of course, the border crossings. Vienna, as everyone knows, is an imperial city.

As with all tourists seeing Vienna for the first time, we toured the palace of the Emperor Franz Joseph and his wife, Elisabeth, the next-to-last rulers of the Austro-Hungarian Empire. We read the brochures, we chatted a little with the young attendants who were less than impressed with the splendour. Even the splendour seemed a bit shabby to me, and the royal pair faintly pathetic—of course, I told myself, that was the idea in the selection of details of their lives and their letters that are featured there.

The name Franz Joseph was familiar, not just from history classes, but also from Peter's father, who occasionally mentioned him—astonishing to me—in tones such as I might have said "Lester Pearson." And so I was more interested in this palace and artefacts than I was when I'd visited other splendid housing quarters in Europe.

I began to think of the empty, tree-lined, grassy slope where Peter's father's village had been, and of what I knew about how the family had lived in Slovakia at the end of the reign of the Emperor Franz Joseph: so badly that George Butala had escaped in the dead of night with other young men, penniless, with nothing more than the clothes on his back, in order not to serve as cannon fodder in yet another war, and in the profound hope of acquiring enough land to live.

Outside the palace in the wide, paved courtyards in the sweltering summer heat, I gazed around at the rows of magnificent buildings, at all the other tourists, at the horse-drawn carriages waiting to sell rides, and failed to connect the emperor and the peasant as they had been connected in life. But of the two places—the grassy hillside where the village had been and this shabby palace, the one speaking of vigour and courage, the other of grandiosity and failure—I found the emperor's last home the more pathetic.

George Butala made his way to Hamburg, and from there to England by ship, and from England to New York City, where he went through immigration. At the end of his examination, when he was pronounced fit, without a cent in his pocket or a word of English, he was handed a loaf of bread and a measure of thick sausage and set loose to make his way in the New World.


Every Westerner knows the facts: in 1872, two years after the first "postage stamp" province of Manitoba was created, one year after British Columbia became a province, and when the provinces of Alberta and Saskatchewan were still the vast North-West Territories (including the rest of what would become the present province of Manitoba), the federal government passed the Dominion Lands Act. By this act, the West was surveyed into townships (thirty-six sections, each section a mile by a mile), and each section divided into four "quarters" (each 160 acres). Because the act's purpose was to prepare for the orderly settlement of the West, it offered a settler, for a ten-dollar fee, 160 acres of land and, provided he—women were almost entirely excluded from this—fulfilled certain conditions of residency, building, and land-breaking in a three-year period, he could then file on an adjacent quarter section called a "pre-emption."

The major purpose behind the impetus to fill the West with settlers was that the federal government feared that the Americans, seeing all that tempting "empty" territory, would simply move in and take over. This impetus wasn't humanitarian or purely benevolent: it certainly wasn't to provide homes and a means of livelihood for millions of destitute or near-destitute Europeans. This system of land division, combined with the requirement of residency on one's quarter, guaranteed isolation and loneliness for the farm families, the women in particular, and with the pre-emption proviso, right from the start the option of getting bigger—and therefore the assumption that one would want to—was built in. It set the tone for a West made up of agricultural people who would see a nearly moral obligation in and who would place high value on the steady growth of their farms, first to establish oneself and one's family, and then to acquire more land, to clear it of trees and of stones, and to put it to the plow—that became the dream of the West.

Between 1896 and 1911 more than a million people poured into the region. Historian Douglas Hill put it this way: "In 1901 the area that became Saskatchewan held about 90,000 people; ten years later, there were more than 490,000. Alberta contained 73,000 in 1901; in 1911, 374,000." The area as a whole had a population increase between 1901 and 1931 of two million people. The settlers came from Central Europe, as did George Butala and many of his neighbours, but they also came in equal numbers from the British Isles, and even more surprisingly, as the opportunity for free land closed there in 1896, about one-third of them were Americans.

In fact, so many Americans came—chiefly to southern Saskatchewan and southern Alberta, a quarter of a million in all—that Hill says the American government, concerned that fifty million dollars of U.S. cash and goods were leaving the country, instituted a campaign to dissuade Americans from leaving, by propagandizing about the severity of our winters and the "oddities" of the British system of government. (This may well have a familiar ring today with regard to matters such as

American access to Canadian drugs via the Internet, and an American government campaign to persuade Americans that our drugs "aren't safe.")

The result was the more or less instant creation of a brand-new society. Gerald Friesen, in *The Canadian Prairies: A History*, has said it best:

> By 1920, prairie agriculture specialized in the production of wheat for export. By 1928, Canadian wheat sales constituted nearly half the world export market. An entire society was organized to facilitate this activity. It was built upon rural village and transportation networks, a grain marketing system, and a family economy attuned to the rhythms of the seasons and the demands of the work itself. In this period, at least six of every ten prairie citizens lived in rural areas, either on farms or in villages that existed to serve farms. Thus, in the course of two generations, 1880–1930, the farm had become the paramount institution in the prairie west.

That the prairie agricultural pioneers—of which my family has many, as does nearly everybody I grew up with—were doing the right, although also the hard, thing, and that they were immensely courageous and strong, is axiomatic in Western Canada. At the time they were starting their farms on the so-called bald prairie or in the parklands, every way they turned somebody was telling them how right they were, and how wonderful what they were doing was, and how by their labour and the labour of those who stayed in the villages, towns, and cities, a great new and better society was growing up, where there would be wealth for all.

Although this attitude, now called "boosterism" by historians, applied mostly to the villages, towns, and would-be cities (they all believed, or said they did, that one day they would be great cities), farmers were certainly affected by it too. It all had to do with growth, with more people coming, with growth attached to the idea of progress, and with progress and growth both attached to the idea of wealth.

Imagine a rosy cloud of optimism, a little like the shining pink cloud of light that glows over a city or town as you approach it out of the night, hanging over the entire prairie West. Knowing the "truth" about this prairie world, one doesn't know whether to laugh or cry. Boosterism it was, and it came from city fathers, bankers, and businessmen, and could be read in the newspapers and heard on the radio. It had also to do with the valorization of newcomers, whether farmers, ranchers, or townsfolk. It lasted into the forties and perhaps longer, by which time the original pioneers had been around for fifty or more years.

Dr. Grant MacEwan, born in 1902, died in 2000, is an example of someone who, in his more than fifty books about the people and events in Western Canada, never failed to support and enhance such a view of the West, that is, as the true home of giants and the best place in the world. He was the son of a Manitoba pioneer (he was partly educated in Saskatchewan) and he grew up to go to college and become an expert in animal husbandry, and to live and work in each of the three Prairie provinces. He was dean of the college of agriculture at the University of Manitoba and held the same position at the University of Saskatchewan. In Alberta he became an MLA, mayor of Calgary, lieutenant governor, and eventually a member of the Order of Canada. During most of this time he travelled widely across the West, speaking and judging animals at fairs and exhibitions. He was a true son of the West and, all his life, a genuine "booster" of it.

In 1948 he published a book called *The Sodbusters*, where he selected thirty-seven Western Canadian pioneers, all men, and wrote short biographies of each. The tone is laudatory, the sketches glowing, the same lessons hammered home over and over again: these men were brave, daring, hardworking, and undaunted by the prospect of spending their entire lives labouring on the land. They were utterly self-reliant, far-seeing, self-made men who embodied the British virtues of humility, selflessness, and quiet courage. So many of them, all having started with nothing—with less than nothing—became farmers of huge tracts of land, millionaire businessmen in agricultural enterprises, senators, or winning politicians. Or else they were famous for being tellers of tall tales and handy fighters. All were famously quick-witted.

Grant MacEwan's life spanned the West's formative century, and he saw it all and was part of it all. He was tall and lean and didn't walk, but strode, even at ninety, full of vigour and a zest for life that was extraordinary. As a much younger person and an educated woman, I viewed him with some puzzlement and skepticism; at the same time I held great respect for him, for his learning, for his dauntlessness and his undying eagerness for life and his wonderful optimism, and for holding a dream of the West in his heart and mind until the day he died.

But I could not entirely admire the men he admired and about whom he wrote in *The Sodbusters*. In the end, I did not share his idea of what the West was. His attitude tended to obscure, I thought, the actual facts that ordinary Westerners know: that our ancestors' lives were too often desperately difficult, so that they did not always share his dream of success and wanted only, finally, to survive, and that a definition of success might have more to do with home, family, and living in semi-tamed wilderness beauty. And I objected to his thoroughly patriarchal worldview.

The dream that rested in the breasts of government officials and politicians was a very different one from that which filled the heart of the ordinary settler and which kept him and his family going through crop failure after crop failure, through disease and deaths, and through years of bitter and unrelenting hard work. In fact, only when the politicians responsible for filling up the West realized that nobody would come if they didn't take some measures to persuade them that Canada was not simply "a few acres of snow" did they send agents to Europe and into the United States to paint glowing pictures of the balmy climate, wonderful soils, endless growing season, and ample rainfall. People began to come in record numbers.

When I was a young university student, eighteen or nineteen years old, I had a part-time job at the provincial archives, at that time in the basement of the University of Saskatchewan library. There I began each morning with a stack of files, each containing the original filing papers on a quarter section under the Dominion Lands Act, the pre-emption papers, and the documents of abandonment if such had occurred. The new filing papers, as well as any correspondence relative to each quarter, were included too. My job, as well as I can remember, was to condense and type on filing cards this pertinent information, one card for each sometimes very thick file. Some of the papers inside them were yellowed with age and disintegrating at their edges.

I trembled with excitement because I knew I was being handed *the truth*, about the lives of my parents and my grandparents, the truth about the very ground I walked on. Once I remember calling over Lloyd Rodwell, my boss, because I had found Peter Verigin's (also spelled Veregin) original homestead papers. Archivist Lloyd's eyes brightened on seeing it and he took the file away for safekeeping. He must have assumed that

I knew who Verigin was, but the truth was that I had only a vague notion, and when I got home I had to look him up in a history text. Verigin was the "visionary" leader of the eventually 7,400 settlers who came to what is now Saskatchewan from Russia with the help of Count Leo Tolstoy and others, including the Quakers. Here they established three colonies in the Yorkton and Prince Albert areas, basing their lives on principles of communal ownership and collectivity.

According to historian John Archer, this style of living conflicted with the homestead regulations that gave one quarter section to each family and required that the family live on it, not in villages from which they would go out each day to work the land as they had done in Europe. Nor were they supposed to work the land communally as the Doukhobors did. Besides, they were pacifists, and this didn't sit well with their neighbours either. When pressure to conform was placed on them, they left for the interior of British Columbia, where some became the Sons of Freedom (famous for protesting by parading in the nude and burning down buildings). Not to mention the extraordinary story of the group who for a short time fell under the sway of a charismatic leader and straggled off on a march in a viciously cold Saskatchewan winter, women and children too, to some sort of glory, and had to be stopped by Mounties, the children rescued and the others turned back before all of them froze to death.

Day after day in these files I would find letters written by the homesteaders to the government, or if the homesteader was illiterate, or illiterate in English, the letter might have been written by a neighbour or friend. If I began that job as a young student full of youthful *joie de vivre*, those letters sobered me. I remember mostly the ones written by homesteaders pleading for more time to meet their building or plowing or clearing requirements, and explaining that they were behind because over the winter family members had died from illness brought on by a diet solely of frozen potatoes. I remember tales of such woe—of entire families of children, four or five of them, and sometimes their mother too, dying over the winter from diphtheria and scarlet fever. I remember stories of men walking a hundred miles to try to find work in the nearest small city, finding none, walking back again.

You may wonder why people had only frozen potatoes to eat. Through inefficiency or misunderstanding, far too many settlers arrived on their new land after the growing season was over. None of them had much cash to buy food or any crop to sell, so they had to make do with what they could scrounge or beg or borrow. They wouldn't have had the time or the money to build anything to live in except a small, inadequate shelter, and thus they suffered from the full blast of winter. Many of them also did not speak English so that they could convey their situation; or they had no neighbours, or neighbours who couldn't or wouldn't help them; or they were too proud to ask for help until it was too late.

I did that job something like forty-five years ago, but I have never forgotten those files. Many years later, when I became a writer about rural, agricultural life on the prairies, I phoned the archives to find out if I could read them once more. But it turned out that they were not available separately as I'd thought, or someone subsequently had put them back into the body of the files. Since there are 180,000 homesteaders' files, it would be impossible for one person to try to find them.

In spite of my fascination with these files, in 1990 when I was hired by *West* of Vancouver, a short-lived magazine of the highest excellence that accompanied the *Globe and Mail* newspaper, to write an article about farming in the northern Great Plains, this was not the story I chose to tell. Instead, I wrote from a larger perspective but based on everything I knew from my family history and my own experience as a Westerner with roots in the pioneer days.

I chose, audaciously, to write that the whole enterprise of farming the northern Great Plains had been, for the land and for most of the original farm families, a mistake and a disaster, that while there were places where farming had worked and continued to work very well, that, on the whole, John Palliser had been right when in his report of 1859 he'd written that a vast part of the plains of Canada was "unfit for agriculture." This area became designated as the Palliser Triangle, the apex of which is at about 52 degrees latitude (at about Kindersley, Saskatchewan), its base at the 49th parallel, its eastern extreme just south of Brandon, and its western end at about Calgary. I imagined the howls of outrage I would have to listen to, especially given that millions of bushels of grain had come out of that very area over the fewer than one hundred years it had been farmed and that many people had made a decent living on it, had fed their families, and had even passed their land on to their sons, and sometimes their grandsons, who were still proudly farming it.

I set to work on the article. I had only six or seven weeks to write it, and the research to prove this contention was monumental because, as far as I knew, it was breaking new ground. I had a stack of books on the floor of my office that came up to my waist (granted, I am not very tall) and I would simply extract one from the pile, place it on top, and do my search for data.

I concluded that there had been so few profitable years since the southern prairie had been opened that with each succeeding year more people left farming or, more likely, were forced out, and the size of the average farm grew bigger and bigger, while fewer and fewer people owned the farms, lived on them, and did the work. At the same time, billions of dollars went from the governments into supporting the family farm, with no hope that in the future this might no longer be necessary. I argued that this huge amount of money might better be spent putting the land back the way it was when settlers first arrived, or spent on re-educating the displaced rural population for a different life, that we ought to rethink the uses to which we put the southern prairies. I suggested a vast national park filled with the original wildlife, one which might be used to attract tourists and scientists and to satisfy the growing yearning for wilderness in the breasts of so many people of the Western world.

My conclusions as to the failure of the original government dream of the farming West were backed with statistics, and nobody argued with them in the form of letters to the editor, other than one man, very knowledgeable in the matter, who felt my conclusion too drastic. None of my farming neighbours quibbled with me because nobody read the article, the *Globe and Mail* not being readily available around where I live. But I have no doubt that most of them would have been outraged (although probably secretly some of them would glumly agree with me), out of a sense of obligation to the hardworking and brave pioneering ancestors whose exploits gave them the very farms they were living on, and which they feel they could never live up to. In other words, they felt too strongly that any failures on their farms had to be their own fault, because they weren't courageous enough or hadn't worked hard enough, both of which were patently untrue.

Many Western historians have done thorough research and written significant books and essays about this period. The "slant" of each book is different, but certain facts are inalterable. One such fact is the difficulty in establishing a homestead, in living up to the promise offered in settlement brochures and propaganda. Gerald Friesen says that the failure rate for homesteaders was "extraordinary," at 20 percent in Manitoba, 57 percent in Saskatchewan, and 45 percent in Alberta, or an average across the prairies of more than 40 percent.[1] Professor Vernon Fowke's classic 1957 book *The National Policy and the Wheat Economy* argues that in certain areas of the Prairie provinces the number of failures was an extraordinary six out of every ten.[2]

The Butala ranch (now the Old Man On His Back Prairie and Heritage Conservation Area) is a case in point. Situated in the extreme southwest corner of Saskatchewan, originally grazing land, and today an area of just under twenty-one sections, it saw its first settlers in 1910. (In 1909 the driest area of the plains, where the ranch is, was opened for homesteading. According to Fowke, "860 miles of railway were built south of the South Saskatchewan River in the five-year period after 1910" to aid settlers in getting themselves and their possessions into the region.)

Eighteen families started homesteads during a ten- to fifteen-year period on what would become the Butala ranch. (Several of this number were on the same quarter, which was often home-steaded then abandoned and re-homesteaded by a new family.) Of those eighteen settlers, only twelve obtained title, only one family stayed twenty years, and by the late thirties, all were gone. Only three of the original families, including the Butalas, still have one or two family members elsewhere in the area.

Westerners today tend to agree with Grant MacEwan and to admire those pioneers to the point of idolatry. And it is true that except for a few brief years, things did not get easier for the average rural agricultural person. For every good year, such as 1915, there were usually three or four bad years, which is how the West went from being called "The Last Best West" and "the breadbasket of the world" to being referred to as "Next Year Country."

And of course, the truly, undeniably terrible years of the Depression are part of that same mythologizing: how the land blew away, how people had crop failures seven years in a row until they hadn't any food to eat or shoes to wear. (I've heard of a man who claims that during the Depression his family was so poor that he had only one pair of pants, and ever since, his measure of wealth is having that second pair of pants.) Every prairie family here during the Depression—every family then rural, at least—has its fund of stories about the hardship of the Depression, and about how the family survived, although left with lifelong psychological scars.

Only the other day a woman raised in southern Manitoba began to tell me the story of the boxcar full of salt fish Nova Scotians had sent out to her area as assistance to a people who were literally in danger of starving. "But nobody knew what to do with these slabs of fish and so . . . ," she began to laugh, and I joined in with her last words, "they shingled the barn roof with them." It's a hoary old (apocryphal) tale we Westerners all know—sometimes it's the outhouse and sometimes it's a granary—although nobody means to slight the generosity of those Atlantic Canadians. Surely at least the many Norwegian immigrants knew what to do with salted fish. My mother and grandmother used to tell about the time during the thirties when my pretty young aunt washed her polka-dot dance dress, hung it out on the line to dry, and the grasshoppers, very bad that year, ate all the big dark dots out of it. These stories, of which there is a plethora, are always accompanied by laughter, as if those who were there prefer to think only of the funny side.

Laughter or not, lives were changed irrevocably by the "Dirty Thirties" or the "Dust Bowl," as the Depression was called on the prairies, where it struck with a ferocity exceeded nowhere else on the continent. Many a child had to stay home from school for lack of warm clothing in our cold winters. Many a boy (and quite a few girls, too) left school before grade eight, and then his home as well, far too early, so as not to be a burden on the hopelessly hard-pressed family and to find work to help out. Farming families in droves lost their farms and never recovered them, became forever city or town people. Others to this day—sixty years later—are unable to throw away even a used light bulb, because you just never know when hard times might come again and even that used light bulb (ball of string, worn-out jacket, zipper out of worn-out jacket) might be needed. *One day you might be darn glad you have it*, our parents would remonstrate when we rolled our eyes at their foolishness. In the schoolyard we would compete: *My mother won't throw away a single old newspaper, can you imagine? My mother keeps worn-out socks, bales of them!* There is another side to the story about how many women survived, to what lengths they were forced to go, which Barry Broadfoot only hints at in his collection of memories about the thirties. But it is one that should hardly surprise us.

Men, on the other hand, have a well-written history about what they did, the On-to-Ottawa Trek being probably the most famous. This was a trainload of unemployed men that set out from Vancouver and gathered men as it crossed the prairies, with the intention to demand work from the federal government in Ottawa. In Saskatchewan, where they stopped and held a rally, the so-called Regina Riot took place, in which one policeman and, according to new information discovered by historian Bill Waiser, not one but two rioters were killed and many trekkers went to jail. (I say "so-called" because it seems pretty clear that the police caused the riot.) I heard the story of those who went to jail from an old man who, on the night in June 1935 when the Regina jail became jammed with so-called rioters, had a ringside seat because he was serving a two-year sentence for horse-rustling (which to the day of his death he swore he wasn't guilty of, at least not that time).

As if the great movements of European and EuroCanadian history were not enough to make for difficult lives for these immigrants, there was also the harshness of our weather: the winter blizzards (some five days long), the two-week stretches at −50°F, the killing lightning storms of great ferocity and splendour, the constant wind revving up to gale force and blowing away everything that wasn't nailed down—including soil—and sometimes nailed-down things too, the tornadoes, and summers when the baking heat rolls up off the ground in wave after wave. (One woman, now deceased, who lived through many years on a prairie farm, used to say that she always did her ironing—irons heated on the stove, etc.—on the hottest days because she couldn't get any hotter anyway, an example of proud hardiness having turned into masochism—a protest, perhaps, against the unreasonableness of her life.) Add them all together, and you get a people cohesive in that shared mythology of tremendous hardship and in their resulting proud sense of there being no tougher people anywhere on earth.

My own mother suffered two miscarriages while we were on the homestead in the bush and our father was away, leaving her alone with two or three toddlers. She took an old bedsheet and wrapped it around herself and waited for the bleeding to stop, and in the morning, burned the sheet in the trash barrel before anyone saw it. You may be sure my mother's story, and countless others much like it, would never even be spoken of above a whisper.

Although farmers shared many of their stories of hardships with ranchers, the mythology of the rancher was and has always been different from that of the farmer. When I was growing up I thought the antagonism between ranchers and farmers told in the wildly popular 1943 Rodgers and Hammerstein musical

*Oklahoma!*, with its echoes of the Montagues and Capulets from *Romeo and Juliet*, was either a fabrication or true only in the American West. Imagine my surprise when after about thirty minutes on the Butala ranch I discovered that not only was it true in the Canadian West as well, but it also continues, although politely, to this day.

Although the definition of "farm" on the prairie West once always included animals, and that of "ranch" also included some farming, this is much less true today, and the essential way of life of each is different. On a farm, people plow all the available land to grow crops. On a ranch, as much of the land as possible is left in its natural state for cattle to graze. The landscape is different, the work is different, the daily life is different, the subjects constantly discussed about the work and its prospects are different. Even the clothing is different— although farmers, truck drivers, and even Bay Street financiers persist in wearing cowboy gear, or at least the boots. The reason for this must be not because they are so comfortable, as people keep insisting to me, but that those boots, that hat, those tight riding jeans, represent a vision of the male dream of freedom and "real" masculinity that no other available wardrobe can say. It is a rare thing to see an urban male dressing like a farmer ("farmer" being an adolescent epithet for clueless and tasteless—at least it was in my day) in—well, what is farmer dress? Ball cap, T-shirt, jeans, steel-capped workmen's boots, running shoes? Sometimes, but just as often it's cowboy gear or simply whatever comes to hand in the way of work clothes.

So the cowboy world is admired in ways that for many are not even conscious, and while farmers may be admired as well, the reasons for the admiration are very different, and have to do with the intrinsic value of the work farmers do—raising food—and with the values that were once thought to be inherent in the life: honesty, hard labour, decency, a kind of primal innocence growing out of an acceptance of nature and her vagaries. Is it any wonder that there has been conflict between ranchers and farmers?

We all know about American range wars from cowboy movies, when farmers moved into range land and a struggle ensued. Our sympathies were usually with the ranchers—that is, the cowboys—the farmers not being so romantic a lot, with the exception of the classic Western *Shane*.

At first, most of the southern Canadian prairie was range land, unfenced and used freely for grazing; apparently, American cattle grazed along the border too. Next was the more organized ranching stage; in Alberta quite enormous grazing leases were given very cheaply to a few wealthy cattlemen. David Breen says, in *The Canadian Prairie West and the Ranching Frontier: 1874–1924*, that "grazing regulations were ill defined" before 1881. For one thing, lessees weren't forced to settle on their land as homesteader-farmers were, and such land could be given to companies and also to non-residents. This left the way open to absentee landlords, usually wealthy owners from Central Canada and England. Farmers, of course, had to be resident, and homesteads were given only to individuals. And where farmers paid ten dollars for 160 acres, ranchers could lease up to 100,000 acres for as long as twenty years for one cent an acre per year, and settlement by anybody else on that land was prohibited. The lease system was designed, whether purposely or not, to exclude the small farmer and to privilege the large company. If you had the capital to pay the fee and to stock that much land with cattle, how could you miss?

Breen mentions the famous Cochrane Ranch, owned by Senator Matthew Cochrane, a wealthy businessman and farmer from Compton County, Quebec. At one time, he points out, "Cochrane and his associates controlled and excluded all others from a fifty-mile stretch of the river valley from Calgary to the mountains to the west." Breen points out, though, that in the United States it was the case that the first rancher to arrive with his cattle had the rights to that land (although often someone arriving at a new area would simply drive out cattle that were already there), whereas in Canada all public land had to be applied for and conditions met in order for it to be under the exclusive use of one individual or company. Range wars thus were common in the United States, but although they occurred in Canada, they weren't usual and were small in scale by comparison. (Although guns may have been drawn in southern Alberta, apparently none were ever fired.)

Immigrants from the United States, England, and Central Europe were rarely people with a lot of capital, and so they couldn't acquire the large grazing leases. For the most part, these went to people who already had money, and thus class bias was introduced. As well, it is no secret that influence with the federal (Conservative) government could guarantee a lease. Breen notes that "the Canadian cattlemen of the period were representatives of the metropolitan culture of the east and of the stratified society of rural Britain." With such huge differences in the backgrounds of the two sets of people, it was no wonder there was often trouble, especially when squatters made homes on the leased land of the large, powerful, and influential ranchers.

In the early 1890s, would-be homesteaders, feeling the injustice, as they saw it, of these wealthy men occupying thousands of acres of land, began to agitate for the right to farm on small portions of the large leases. Ranchers responded by taking the law into their own hands and evicting any squatters they found—in one famous case, a legitimate homesteader—and then pulling down their houses. The settlers were, of course, poor people, so this was disastrous, especially when, as in at least one case, the destruction of the house took place in winter. In return, the settlers were accused of responding by burning many tons of the ranchers' hay. Breen describes public opinion as being in favour of the homesteaders, not the wealthy ranchers, and public feeling about this matter in Alberta was very strong: "a vicious range feud or even an armed outbreak in the southwest was a distinct possibility."

In 1892, prominent Eastern businessmen, powerful representatives of the cattle companies, and a few Westerners met with the federal government to try to resolve the conflict between ranchers and homesteaders. In the end, new lease legislation was drawn up that put an end to the "no settlement" leases and that, while giving the ranchers some plums, mostly served the need for settlement. It wasn't the end of the great cattle companies in Western Canada, but it did put an end to the growing number of disputes between ranchers and farmers. (The Medicine Hat Ranch still controlled 270,000 acres in 1956!)

If the government had clearly favoured the ranchers up until the 1880s, this didn't last. Eventually, the government, seeing that the West would not be settled by ranchers who continued to occupy huge chunks of land, began to make it more difficult for them. Ranchers believe that the federal government has favoured farmers for the past fifty or more years through programs involving payments to farmers that ranchers couldn't get, such as subsidies and supports of various kinds, from the Crow Rate (the farmer bore only a small portion of the cost to ship grain to port, while the rancher still paid every cent of the cost to ship cattle) to forgiveness of debts during the Depression.[3] A rivalry between the two camps, built on the very nature of the two ways of life, continues: the independent, stern, and free rancher-cowboy (the terms *rancher* and *cowboy* not necessarily synonymous) and the humble yeoman farmer (although there never were yeoman farmers in most of the West, and *farmer* and *humble* are not synonymous). Although farmer and rancher still aren't friends, they continue to exist side by side as equal but virtually opposing dreams of the real West.

Now that we have so many historians of Western history, revisionists and all, and now that I have lived the agricultural life myself for nearly twenty-eight years, I look over that past of ours with a more skeptical eye than I did when I was growing up. And I wonder if just maybe we haven't overestimated the horrors of the settlement years and the virtue of our pioneer ancestors.

On one occasion I wanted to write the story of the pioneer women on the southern prairie, where the world is seven-eighths sky and one-eighth land. Homesick, lonely, and made desperate by their living conditions, they tried to run out from under the omnipresent, overwhelming sky, and ran and ran until "their lungs burst and they died." (Even now, in considering the most effective way to tell this, I am forced to think of how it must have been and I get a powerful sense of the mythic, of the West as a place of mystery and power, a place where, as those poor women must have known, the gods dwell.)

But, always on the lookout for the apocryphal tales of which the West is full, I asked a writer friend who was born here and spent her early years on the open prairie. She was astonished I would question the story and responded vehemently, "It happened right here!" (referring to the community adjacent to her ranch). If I wanted to search it out, it appears that I just might even be able to give the name of one of these mad, desperate women.

The surprised indignation with which my questioning was greeted was not merely that of someone whose veracity had been doubted. I think it was, although at an unconscious level, saying, *Don't tamper with my beliefs, on which my whole sense of who I am is based. Of who Westerners are.* Even though I was pleased to know that the story was the truth, I confess that the reaction made me falter.

Having a German brother-in-law, I once tried out, on his visiting relatives as we toured Fort Walsh and its cemetery, a version suggesting that life for the settlers of Western Canada was perhaps as difficult in its own way as it had been for certain Europeans during the Second World War. He listened carefully, attentively, and then explained how war changed not merely one's circumstances for the time being, but altered one's life forever—in his family's case, losing an estate that had been their home for several hundred years, along with the status and wealth they had expected would be theirs forever, and forcing them, despite their distinguished lineage and connections, to rethink their entire lives, to begin all over again without an asset to their names. His tone of voice conveyed to me in some measure the effect such a shocking, sudden, unthinkable loss would have on the psyche. What it would be like to have to reinvent oneself from the ground up, as it were. Perhaps it is harder to have much and to have it all torn away in one desperate night of war, to escape with only one's life, than to have little one's entire, hardworking life.


The first fact that the EuroCanadian version of history has obscured for a hundred years is the terrible hardship our arrival inflicted on the Amerindian people of the West. Having devoted a chapter to this already, I will not repeat it here. I have also talked about the Métis and what they lost, and how they were driven from their homes and land not once, but twice as a result of our coming. These are both, surely, historical wrongs of no small magnitude. But at the same time, we virtually wiped out French influence and language that had been so important to this area before the arrival of huge numbers of non-French-speaking settlers. This last strikes me as an important piece of history, too, which we must never forget.

And it is axiomatic that we changed the character of the land itself drastically, cutting down the trees for farms, thus changing the watershed, and plowing up millions of acres of prairie—eventually also levelling rises, draining sloughs, and, increasingly, driving off and/or killing the wildlife. All of this was done before most immigrants had time to acquire any sense of place. Certainly, no one was encouraged to discover a sense of place; for the most part they arrived with heads full of lies and exaggerations about what they were coming to. And on the very day of arrival on their homesteads, their heads full of government propaganda and their own dreams, many settlers set their plows to work.

Imagine the beauty of this land once, as Westerners often do, the dense, seemingly endless forests, the wide-open grass-covered plains gleaming in the high, hot sun, or snow-covered and glistening like fields of blue-shadowed diamonds; imagine the flocks of birds, the great herds of animals, the perhaps sixty million bison in particular. It is hard to believe that probably six million bison were virtually exterminated in a few short years (granted, before the settlers arrived). And since then, the extirpation of the prairie wolf and the bear, the swift fox, the black-footed ferret, and other species. Imagine the bitterness and sorrow of the Aboriginal people of the West, watching their beloved earth fill with strangers who did not know it and certainly did not love it or believe in, much less hold any respect for, its ruling spirits.

Those early Westerners had no chance to grow into this place, to test it, to find what they might learn to love about it. Has there ever been such an influx of settlers in such numbers in so few years in a "new" land anywhere else on earth? I look back on that time with great regret and wonder, imagining that if the threat of an American takeover of the West hadn't been there, the government might have populated the area more slowly and thoughtfully. If there had been no checkerboard system laid on the land along with residency requirements, perhaps immigrants would have adopted a more European style of living. As in George Butala's Slovakia, they would have lived together in villages, the men going out to the land to work each day, so that women would not have been so lonely or have had to work so hard (they'd have had each other for help), and children would have been better educated.

Many rural Western schools shut down from January through March because children couldn't get to them and because they couldn't be kept warm enough. My husband, Peter, who in the forties rode a horse five miles across uncharted rolling prairie to school each day and then back again, tells the same stories my mother did about her tiny school in southern Manitoba from 1916 to 1924. If you sat near the heater, sweat poured off you, and if you sat far away, you had to keep your mitts on. Your lunch, kept in the cloakroom, was always frozen.

Even the places where people lived on their homesteads might have been different; perhaps these would have been attractive, hospitable places beside streams, in the shadow of hills, where trees would grow and wildlife could survive. If it hadn't been for the conditions set down for the settlers, nobody in his or her right mind would have chosen to live in some of the places they did—barren and unattractive in appearance, wide open to the worst weather. In winter blizzards and summer heat, they were shelterless. With no natural water supply, they needed to dig deep wells. The railways determined where villages would be, and when the branch lines were closed, the small wooden elevators began to shut down and the countryside to empty out, and dozens of prairie villages, the meaning of "home" to thousands of Westerners, emptied out too because, often, set as they were on the open prairie, there was no other reason for them to exist.

More to the point, the prairie would not have been opened to homesteaders wholesale as it was, because time might have been taken to find out what was suitable for farming and what was not, instead of having settlers find out the hard way— through starvation.

The West indeed promised freedom and dignity and hope, and it promised it not only to poor, oppressed European peasants, but also to people from Ontario and Quebec and to Americans. But, as historian Douglas Owram writes in his 1980 classic, *The Promise of Eden*, "The character of the society which it was hoped would develop in the North West . . . had Britain as its model," and also, "It was Canada's 'noble task to fill the still untrodden plains' and eventually to assume the mantle of 'the Britain of the West.'" Historian Walter Hildebrandt, in *Views from Fort Battleford: Constructed Visions of an Anglo-Canadian West*, begins by pointing out: "the political and social culture was imported from Europe. It shared the same ideology that produced an industrialized Europe, including the Christian values that accompanied capitalist culture. Introduced along with these values were concepts of liberty and private property."

Attitudes toward nature also were European, that is, to conquer it rather than to adapt to it; the Mounties themselves were mostly from the upper classes of Anglo Canadian or British culture, and many retired to settle in the West, continuing to promulgate their ideas of law, order, and culture; even the early government buildings were designed by British architects, with their Christian, empire-building, Victorian backgrounds and ideas.

Niall Ferguson, in his bestseller *Empire: The Rise and Demise of the British World Order and the Lessons for Global Power*, concludes that in balance the British Empire did more good than harm. Many would disagree, although I doubt in Canada. But I wonder what kind of society we might have had in the West if we had not had the English, with their notion of "the white man's burden" and their unwavering certainty of the superiority of their ways, as the basic structure behind the new Western society. I believe that we would be a good deal more French, and if we were more French, we might also have had a less superior attitude toward the Métis and Aboriginal people of the West. As for the many Slavic people who came to settle here, I can only guess as to whether they would have found less prejudice against them foreign if British influence had been weaker. Also, we might have fallen more under the sway of the attitudes and style of the thousands of American immigrants, with the result, perhaps, that we would have a more American-style egalitarian society, for example, more elected than appointed officials.

I doubt that every European or American who came here during the period of greatest influx of settlers believed that he would become wealthy, or even dreamt, first and foremost, of wealth. And if something like six out of ten farmers of that period failed entirely and had to abandon their homesteads, those who managed to hang on must have slowly seen that true wealth did not come from the kind of hard labour they and their families were doing every day, year after year, on their 160 acres. For the most part, the fortunes that were eventually acquired in the West were made, as elsewhere, in the cities, and there, in business: the Richardsons of Manitoba, who according to Peter C. Newman have "one of Canada's great fortunes" (and who "had all of Canada for a playground"), acquired wealth in the grain markets, not by farming; the Lougheeds of Alberta, from land speculation and oil shares; the Dunsmuirs of British Columbia, from coal, and that wealth extended into real estate (Robert Dunsmuir built the rail link in 1883 from Nanaimo to Victoria for a federal subsidy of $750,000 and one-fifth of Vancouver Island).

To name a few other of the best-known families: the Rogers family of Vancouver, who had already become rich in sugar in the United States, enhanced their wealth in the same endeavour in British Columbia; in Saskatchewan, the Mendels/ Mitchells became wealthy from meat-packing, the Hills from insurance and real estate, and Morris Shumiatcher from his extensive law practice. Despite the marvellous promise of the West as farm and ranchland, its great fortunes have not come directly from farming or ranching.

The claim of a superior degree of egalitarianism in the West is often made. As most Western women know all too well, egalitarianism rarely extends equally to them. Nor, as we know, has egalitarianism been extended to Aboriginal people. As for visible minorities, the territorial and federal governments certainly didn't advertise for immigrants in Asia or Africa (or even South America) a century ago. Some visible minorities did manage to enter the West, though. For example, during settlement days nearly every small community had its Chinese café, and the discriminatory treatment to which its proprietors were subjected is well documented. (Read Wallace Stegner's *Wolf Willow*, a memoir of one small Western town from 1914 to 1920, for a lurid but typical example.) And, of course, the notorious head tax on Chinese immigrants is well known, an astonishing $500 by 1903, as is the work done by Chinese immigrants building the CPR for small recompense in terrible living conditions and in the face of extreme discrimination. Alberta had some small black communities and Saskatchewan a few tiny, now defunct, Jewish farming communities, but besides the Chinese, there were no visible minority immigrants in groups large enough to be worth mentioning.

All the bad old attitudes were as evident in the West as they were anywhere else; in fact, not only were these views promulgated by the government in Central Canada, but they also came to Western Canada with the settlers. And discrimination didn't end then. Only today on CBC Radio I heard that a study of the city of Swift Current, Saskatchewan, concludes that it does not welcome minorities.


I suppose we ought to be angry, and some of us probably are, about what a few Eastern plutocrats and boosters did to our ancestors, some of whom are still alive in nursing homes. And yet the fact is that many Westerners were eternally grateful to escape the fate of many Europeans of that period—war, pogroms, displacement, and life as desperately poor exiles. Most of us survived to grow a lot of grain and a lot of cattle, and to build universities and art galleries and research institutions and concert halls. We had babies, and our babies grew up and had babies and life hasn't been that difficult for nearly all of us since the Second World War.

What virtues might I have preferred over those so valorized in the ideal pioneer? Generosity, open-heartedness, love of learning, gentleness, respect and admiration for women, good fathering and husbanding, having and expressing a genuine love of nature. Courage, hardiness, and determination are and have always been admirable, but the one set of virtues need not preclude the other. From the stereotype of the hardy and suffering prairie farm woman, old while still in her thirties or forties, to the powerful figure of the dauntless male, his eyes always set on the distant horizon, we have tended to forget that there might have been other, kinder, more nurturing and respectful ways to found a country.

Although George, John, and Charles Butala came from a gentler climate and an established, Old World, easier way of life, if they were alive today, like many thousands of others like them, I know that they would say that the Canadian West they came to was—eventually—plenty good enough for them, that it fulfilled their dream of the West.

But, I wonder, what would their wives have said?

# CHAPTER SIX

# Tough Stock

*What makes a Westerner?*
*Our profoundly patriarchal world and our gritty, resolute women.*

T HE WEST has always been about land, by which I mean
that land ownership has always been the measure of
wealth, of respectability, of class and status. From the
time of the settlers, we have used the British system of primogeniture, the practice of passing on property to the eldest son.
This is an ancient system, introduced into England at the time
of the Norman Conquest, but it is not practised in all cultures
and countries. Its advantage is that wealth is kept together. A
more egalitarian system, where each child, regardless of gender
or position, inherits an equal share, forces the breakup of
wealth, and thus diminishes it. Primogeniture is still viewed on
the Western prairie as the standard system of inheritance;
other ways of providing for inheritance are common but
viewed as deviations, although reasonable.

As for daughters, for the most part the attitude has been that
they will marry land and that is how they will survive. Or they
will receive their inheritance by having their higher education
paid for and this will enable them to make a living, although

not on the land. Occasionally, a father wills a certain amount of land to his daughters and the sons farm or ranch it for them; the sons are supposed to make annual payments to their sisters from the income off that land. Although there is no discrimination anymore *in law*, women still do not have equal rights when it comes to the ownership of land.

The West was opened to become the region that it is today by the 1872 Dominion Lands Act; the comparable act in the United States was called, less ponderously, the Homestead Act. By the Dominion Lands Act (as noted earlier, homesteaders received 160 acres for ten dollars and a three-year residency requirement, plus some breaking of land) men could become landowners. Women were specifically excluded by that same act. Unless they were widows, divorcées, or deserted wives *and* had dependent children under eighteen (rules that were stringently applied), they could not file for a homestead.

I would perhaps be less critical of this unfair law, seeing it simply as a product of the times, if it were not the case that in the United States the Homestead Act of 1862 allowed "spinsters, widows, and female heads of households to claim homesteads on the same terms it extended to men." Historian Paula Bagman concluded, in *The Female Frontier: A Comparative View of Women on the Prairie and the Plains*, that this was "one of the great democratic measures of world history, in that it allowed women the right to own land by homesteading."

Readers should know that, for example, in Ethiopia, the new government that followed the terrible Mengistu period enacted a law giving women rights to land ownership. Before that time, if a husband died and his brother wouldn't marry the widow, "they would drive you away like a dog," one woman told me. There remains, I am told, a huge gap between the law and actual practice on the land. My point, though, is that we are talking about a continuum in the story of women's rights, and that is why I believe Bagman to be absolutely correct.

Despite protests and even a petition to Ottawa, Saskatchewan and Manitoba never did allow women equal rights under the Dominion Lands Act (they eventually dissolved the act so no one could homestead anymore) and Alberta didn't do so until 1930, fifty-eight years later, when the best land was long gone. In this one, extremely important way—for what is land owner-ship but power?—women certainly got off to a less than equal start in the new, so-called egalitarian societies of Western Canada.

Even today, only about 4 percent of the farms in the Prairie provinces are owned solely by women. Roughly 24 percent are jointly operated by a husband and wife, with Alberta having the second highest number in the country, and British Columbia, at more than a third couple-operated, the highest.[1] It's interesting to note, too, that although women-operated farms are increasing in number, very often (over 10 percent of the time) they are small goat- or horse-raising farms or greenhouse operations rather than the standard grain or grain-and-cattle operations. The census also reports that while 50 percent of Canadian farms earn under $50,000 per year, *80 percent* of farms operated *solely by women* are in the under-$50,000 category.

Because women don't often inherit the family operation, they must buy, and because they don't have the same access to credit as men, they cannot raise enough money for the larger operations. It is also possible that some women may want to do hands-on farming, where they actually know their animals individually and/or grow things that they handle on a daily basis. Or perhaps most are just not interested in the massive tractors and $350,000 combines that male farmers seem to get such pride and delight out of owning and operating.

Just because rural women rarely own and operate their own farms or share the direct farm work equally with their husbands certainly doesn't mean they aren't doing at least as much work as their husbands. When I first entered the agricultural world by marrying into a ranching family (although I'd always known this simply by virtue of being prairie born and bred), I saw at once that the stories I'd been hearing my entire life about how hard women work on farms and ranches were true. The work was mostly split by gender, so that the women did the child-rearing, looked after the house and all the endless work that entailed, without running water or electricity. They tended the garden, from seeding through hoeing, weeding, and watering to harvesting and preserving the crop. They also helped out with the farming chores, which meant that they were at work before their husbands began their day and were still at it when their husbands were sitting in the living room reading the newspaper before going to bed.

Children on farms began doing their share of the daily "chores" (chasing the milk cow in or out, gathering the eggs, penning up the chickens at night and letting them out in the morning, weeding in the garden, carrying water to the chickens, geese, and pigs) the moment they were old enough, often as young as four or five years. As they grew, they graduated to helping with the actual farming or ranching, getting on their first horse at seven or eight (or much younger) to help "chase" cows and to stook or tramp hay in the fields. Nowadays, they learn to drive a tractor to summerfallow and a truck to carry messages, parts, and people long before the legal driving age. No wonder a lot of children left home as soon as they were old enough. To them the farm meant only constant, unrelenting work.

Today, with so much mechanization, hard physical labour is mostly a thing of the past, but roughly half the adults on prairie farms have off-farm jobs too.[2] The consequence is, for women, that the long days of work haven't ended, they have simply changed in nature.

All of this adds up to a rather dim prospect for rural prairie women, who appear to have tremendous and unending responsibility but virtually no power, so it is ironic that Western Canadian women have led the country in attaining certain other rights. For example, British Columbians were, in 1873, the first women in Canada to receive the franchise, in that female property holders could vote municipally.

Western women were the first in the country to get the right to vote in provincial elections, with Manitoba leading the way in January 1916, followed closely by Saskatchewan and then Alberta.[3] At the same time, women were given the right to run for and hold provincial office. None of this came without a fight, however, and it was prairie women who led the battle.

How this came about is well-documented historically, but the Manitoba story is particularly interesting in that Icelandic women, having come from a society that has the world's oldest parliament (AD 930), the highest literacy rate, and the most magazines, newspapers, and books published per capita in the world, were agitating as early as 1870 for the vote (although it was 1915 before they received it in Iceland).

Icelanders have a long history in the New World: an Icelander was thought to be the first European to see the Canadian coast, and although there were earlier, smaller settlements in Quebec, Ontario, and Nova Scotia, in 1875 Manitoba received a contingent of 250 Icelanders and another 1,200 the next year, to form virtually self-governing "New Iceland" on the shore of Lake Winnipeg. In the years that followed from this high point, disaster, of course, ensued—floods, small pox—and many departed for more hospitable places. By 1881 there were only about 250 left; the main settlement, Gimli, is still a stronghold of Icelanders today.

But it was an Icelandic woman, Margret J. Benedictsson (also spelled Margaret Benedictson), founder and editor of *Freyja* magazine, which existed from 1898 to 1910, who in 1908 formed the first women's suffrage organization in Winnipeg. She is one of those, along with Mrs. A.V. Thomas, Dr. Amelia Yeomans, and Mrs. J.A. McClung (famous writer and political activist Nellie McClung's mother-in-law), credited with persuading the government that women should have equal rights at the polling booth and also the right to stand for election provincially.

Sir Rodmond Roblin, premier of Manitoba from 1900 to 1915, vehemently opposed women's suffrage in his province, thus bestirring everyone in favour of it to fight harder than he or she might have otherwise. (In Saskatchewan, Premier Scott waffled, saying soothingly that the time wasn't ripe just yet and that women would have to unite and show legislators that all of them wanted the vote. So women waited, uncertain, rather than rising up in a fury of fiery debate as they did in Manitoba in response to Roblin's insufferable attitude.)

In January 1914, Nellie McClung wrote and performed a hilarious and widely reported play called *The Women's Parliament*, a mock legislative session in which men appeal to women legislators for the right to vote. They are subjected to the same rhetoric as in Roblin's legislature, only this time it applies to men. The absurdity of the arguments was clear. McClung imitated Roblin's demeanour and gestures (as well as his condescending and dismissive tone), causing the sold-out house—in Winnipeg's largest theatre—to roll in the aisles with laughter.

Although this was a jocular high point in Canadian women's history, it was the many hours of paper-shuffling and visiting in homes, of organizing and campaigning and canvassing and speech-making, that were the solid framework of the movement for female suffrage. Two years later Manitoba women achieved the right to vote in provincial elections.

It must have been an exciting time to be alive and a woman in the West, because around this time nearly all Western women—at least English-speaking ones from the British Isles—were members of one women's organization or another: the Woman's Christian Temperance Union (also called by men "Women Continually Torment Us"), the Women's Institute, the National Council of Women, and/or the women's branches most farm organizations had. Historian Veronica Strong-Boag says that all these organizations appeared between 1913 and 1919: "The Women's Section of the United Farmers of Manitoba, The Women's Section of the Saskatchewan Grain Growers, the first women's local of the United Farmers of Alberta, the UFWA [United Farm Women's Association] itself, and the Interprovincial Council of Farm Women."

It was through these women's organizations that the movement for women's suffrage came to life, but as early as 1912 the Saskatchewan Grain Growers Association formally stated its support of female suffrage, indicating that a large number of prairie men also supported it—whether because this would increase the farm lobby, as some have argued, or quite altruistically doesn't really matter. Doubtless it was a little of both.

Interestingly, the fight for the vote for women was never a wholly separate issue within women's groups, but was part and parcel of the strong social conscience of these same organizations. Their leaders were appalled by what they knew of how most Western Canadian women—most were on farms—were forced to live.[4] They argued that if women could vote, they would change society, that women's ideals and their great strengths of gentleness and a compassionate morality would then have some sway in the places where power was held. They saw, too, the injustice of a society that held women to a different, more stringent standard of behaviour than the men of the time were held to and that rendered them helpless in the world.

If women activists wanted the right to vote for all women, they wanted equally to stop violence against women, especially in the home, and, seeing alcohol as the villain behind much of such violence, they were thus usually strong supporters of the temperance movement. Many of them also, especially around the First World War, advocated pacifism, two attitudes that, sadly, tended to split or, at least, weaken the women's rights' movement itself.

Besides suffrage, temperance, pacifism, and other concerns, reform of the Dower Act was an important goal of these same organizations. British common law allowed for dower rights: that is, if a man died his wife had an "interest" in his estate. Such was the case in Britain, of course, and in the United States, Ontario, and the Maritimes. But, shockingly, in the "egalitarian" Canadian West dower rights were eliminated in 1886. The government apparently did this so as not to "impede land registration." The stories heard and retold by these early fighters for women's justice concerning abandoned farm women, with their many small children, whose husbands sold their homes and farms out from under them and vanished with the proceeds, were beyond disgraceful; they encouraged a vigorous fight for property rights for women in Western Canada. In 1910, the Married Women's Relief Act was passed in Alberta; it made it possible for a widow to receive part of her husband's estate through the courts, if unprovided for by him. As historian Alison Prentice reports, "Between 1910 and 1919, all three prairie provinces passed legislation guaranteeing wives' inheritance rights and restricting a husband's ability to sell or mortgage property without his wife's consent."

In the midst of attaining the right to vote provincially, on May 24, 1918, women attained the right to vote federally, and a year later the right to be elected federally (confirmed by the Dominion Elections Act of 1920). This put some women in the odd position for a number of years of being able to vote federally but not provincially; on the prairies, for two years, they could vote provincially but not federally. And yet, despite being able to vote in provincial and/or federal elections, no woman in Canada during these years was legally a "person."

In a prominent position in downtown Calgary stands a circle of five larger-than-life women cast in bronze. (There is another on Parliament Hill in Ottawa.) They are not young women. At least one of them wields, triumphantly, a teacup. They are Emily Murphy, Nellie McClung, Henrietta Muir Edwards, Irene Parlby, and Louise McKinney, collectively known as "The Famous Five." Although none had been born in the Canadian West, this was not unusual; in the mid-nineteenth century virtually all Westerners who were not Aboriginal people, Métis, or descendants of the Selkirk settlers had been born elsewhere.

It was Emily Murphy (1868–1933) who led the fight to eliminate what might be seen as the last governmental male bastion, the fact that women could not be appointed to the Senate. The story of the Famous Five has been told often, and I will not repeat it here. In response to the Famous Five's petition, the Supreme Court of Canada decided that Section 24 of the British North America (BNA) Act did *not* mean to include women in the term "persons." When the women appealed immediately, the case was sent on to the then final court of appeal, the Privy Council in England. On October 18, 1929, the Privy Council declared that the BNA Act had indeed meant to include women as persons and that therefore they were eligible to become senators. Nellie McClung was heard to declare that she'd always suspected she was a person.

Since that victory, according to historian Strong-Boag, certain feminist researchers have been critical of these women on the grounds that they were not truly interested in universal rights for women, but merely in preserving their privileged positions. (They were all English-speaking, white, middle-class, and subjects of the British Empire; they lived and worked in a West that was ruled by British traditions and law and whose culture was clearly privileged over all others.) Even if these women also represented a minority of Western women, they knew, as Strong-Boag says, "that the crux of women's oppression lay in their heavy responsibilities for work in the private sphere." As stateswomen, understanding that they were privileged, they knew that they had a duty to the majority of Western women of the time.

Westerners believe that urban women did not work as hard as rural women, and that they largely worked only in the home—even if it was somebody else's home. Mary Kinnear, who has studied the world of women's work in Manitoba, in particular in *A Female Economy: Women's Work in a Prairie Province 1870–1970*, points out that the notion that all women in the Canadian West at the turn of the century were workers in the home has always been false. From 1880 on, women made up from 10 to 20 percent of Manitoba's workforce. Steadily increasing, the percentage began to really move up in the fifties (to 24 percent) and by 1971 it was 42 percent.

However, none of this was easy. As well as the limited work opportunities for women, the poor pay, and long hours, there was also agitation by other women and by men to keep women from taking men's jobs, as well as simple mistrust of women entering the workplace. None of this, of course, was unique to prairie women, although in Manitoba there were more factory and sweatshop-style jobs available to them by far than in the other Prairie provinces. (Manitoba started out with hunting and trapping as its major industry, but it wasn't very long before manufacturing became very important, and today it leads the list, ahead even of agriculture.)

Very early, Winnipeg was the largest city on the plains (by 1911 it was the third biggest in the country). Although it was run by a British elite, whether directly from the British Isles or from Ontario, it had many more inhabitants who were Slavic and/or Jewish immigrants from Europe. They came to Winnipeg because there were jobs, but they suffered severe discrimination regarding where they could live and what jobs they would be hired for, and faced overt name-calling and property destruction. Working conditions at the time were simply appalling by any standards, pay was poor (the country was suffering from postwar inflation), and there was extreme opposition to the principle of collective organizing and bargaining on the part of the factory- and business-owning elite, who were definitely not Slavs or Jews. (One of the best novels ever written in this country is about the immigrant community and life in North End Winnipeg: *The Sacrifice*, by Adele Wiseman, was published in 1956 and won the Governor General's Award. Wiseman was the Canadian-born daughter of Jewish Ukrainian immigrants to North End Winnipeg.)

When at last the unions organized sufficiently to call a strike, thirty thousand workers walked away from their jobs and for six weeks shut down the entire city in what is the biggest strike in Canadian history, if not one of the biggest ever in the Western world. But few people know that when the Winnipeg General Strike began on May 15, 1919, the first to walk off their jobs were women: telephone operators, and then confectionery workers and sales clerks. In fact, women made up a hefty 13 percent of the strikers. Besides this, they provided meals for strikers and gave them money to pay their rent.[5]

In fact, certain militant women actually destroyed three delivery wagons belonging to men who were still working and assaulted their drivers, causing a detective to warn men not to go into that district. Part of the same initiative, the general strike in Vancouver, was also supported by women workers. Kinnear notes, however, that union membership wasn't popular among women, who didn't begin to join unions in large numbers in Western Canada until the sixties.

Far too many women in both city and country were also victims of spousal abuse. As Strong-Boag points out, all the Famous Five and their hardworking, determined, even passionate colleagues were strongly motivated by the desire to end violence against women. All wanted to gain high office in order to be a voice for women (among so many male voices) in such matters. McClung and McKinney, especially, believed alcohol was the root cause of most of this violence and were determined to stop its sale. (They apparently didn't know, as I heard on the radio the other day, that only two societies in the world have never had alcohol.)

Despite Prohibition, there was still violence against women, and today, despite women having both the provincial and federal votes, and being officially declared persons, violence against us has not stopped. In fact, the federal government's 1999 General Social Survey, which included physical, sexual, financial, and emotional abuse, found that 25 percent of Canadian women are abused; Alberta has the highest rate.[6] The figure for Western Canadian Aboriginal women is an appalling 57 percent.

These are shocking enough statistics, but the West also has the distinction of having the highest rate of spousal homicide in the entire country—the rate of homicides of women is double that of men. Manitoba has the highest rate for the ten provinces (but the rates for the Northwest Territories and Yukon are well above Manitoba's).[7] It is depressing to note that Aboriginal women are murdered by their spouses at eight times the rate of non-Aboriginal women. The only hopeful statistic here is that spousal homicide rates have been declining across the country generally since 1993.[8]

I had the good fortune to take part in a Prairie*action* Foundation Research Day in Saskatoon in November 2003. The Prairie*action* Foundation is a relatively new initiative (1992), brought to life in response to the 1989 Montreal massacre of fourteen women students. It is an alliance of five regional research centres "devoted to finding the cause of family violence and violence in general against women," and covering the three Prairie provinces.

There I found out, to my surprise, that once again the West—Saskatchewan—led the country in enacting legislation regarding family violence: the Victims of Domestic Violence Act, of February 1995. Prince Edward Island introduced a similar act in 1996, and Alberta and Manitoba followed suit four years later, Manitoba broadening its act to include stalking and emotional abuse. Sadly, a number of provinces still don't have such legislation.

In the nineteenth century, women could not vote, did not have legal authority over their own children, had virtually no dower rights, and had a much harder time divorcing their husbands than their husbands did them. Historian Alison Prentice says that if they left a husband after being beaten once or twice, they were told by a judge that they hadn't sufficient patience, and if they stayed longer and then left, they were viewed to have condoned the husband's actions by not leaving sooner.

Since settlement times, women have gained many rights and received protection under the law. As well, women have acted to help themselves when the governments would not, or would do so only minimally, by setting up transition houses for battered women, rape crisis centres, and reproductive counselling, not only across the Prairie provinces, but elsewhere too. But the worst statistic of all is that the highest rate of violence against women is against those who are disabled.

The intrepid Violet McNaughton (1879–1968), a former teacher and social worker came from Kent, England, in the early 1900s to a farm near Harris, Saskatchewan. From 1925 to 1951 she was the editor of the women's page in the *Western Producer*, a farm newspaper she helped start that to this day is distributed right across the Prairie provinces.

She was an early advocate for the vote for women, and to this end organized the Women's Grain Growers' Association, becoming its president. Under her leadership it became the leading force for women's suffrage in Saskatchewan, although all the well-known suffragettes on the prairies exchanged ideas, gave each other support, and attended one another's rallies and meetings. Nellie McClung, especially, often spoke in Saskatchewan. Once suffrage was finally achieved, McNaughton did not rest on her laurels, but went on to work for women's right to control conception, and for adequate medical care. She is also credited with bringing prairie women into the Women's International League for Peace and Freedom in the twenties and into the League for Social Reconstruction in the thirties.

McNaughton is even credited with helping the women of Ontario. In the summer of 1918, those in the United Farmers of Ontario who wanted women to be allowed to join their organization invited her to speak at a meeting in Toronto. She is said to have so stirred those in attendance that day that they immediately formed the United Farm Women of Ontario.

One day a few years ago I received a call from a friend, University of Saskatchewan historian Georgina Taylor. In her search

of the provincial archives for material for her doctoral disserta-
tion on Violet McNaughton, she had come upon a bundle of
letters exchanged between McNaughton, women's page editor
of the *Western Producer*, and my husband's mother, Alice Butala.
Georgina thought the family should know about them.

These few letters began in late 1937 and ended in 1944. They
revealed Alice's extraordinary character, which I had ample
time to discover between my marriage in 1976 to her son and
her death in 1984 at seventy-seven. Born in 1907, she was
raised as a hardworking helper for her mother, who had eight
living children (out of ten, of whom Alice was fifth) and as a
mere child was sent to be a helper to her pious maternal great-
aunt. This, apparently, among other experiences, left her with
an undying dislike of religion of any sort. She graduated from
grade twelve and attended normal school, eventually teaching
for perhaps eight or so years in the ubiquitous one-room
schoolhouses set out on the bald prairie.

In these letters she describes herself with pride as coming
"from tough stock," referring to her mother in particular. Like
so many women of her period on the prairies, she was too
smart for the life she found herself leading; but unlike most
women, rather than choosing to keep quiet, she occasionally
got herself into trouble as a result of thinking too much and
daring to say what she thought.

She was made desperate by the long years of the dirty thirties, desperate in the sense that she could hardly bear to see the
growing hopelessness of her friends and neighbours, the
lengths to which they were driven for mere survival. She was
appalled by what she saw as the corruption and the life-and-
death power mere "relief" agents and inspectors had, and her
rage at what she saw as the terrible injustices of the period, not
only in southwest Saskatchewan but in the wider world, drove
her to heights of exasperation and anger. Violet McNaughton,

often called "V.M." by Alice in these letters, saw this too, and responded gently, indicating concern for Alice's health, by which she seems to have meant her mental health.

This was after McNaughton had published Alice's letter in the *Western Producer* about people in the southwest reduced by the drought to picking up "cow chips" (dried manure) from the prairie to use as fuel because they had no money to buy coal or firewood in a region where there are no trees. Alice signs herself, "Alice Butala C.C.P., being of the ancient and honourable order of Cow Chip Pickers." This letter created quite a stir. Alice was "bawled out" by neighbours or snubbed by them, and her husband, George, was told by a government official on the street of a nearby town to keep his wife quiet!

McNaughton apparently challenged her to suggest what might be done to improve things for the rural people of her area, and Alice replied, in a long, handwritten letter dated August 1938, with the list of things she herself had done:

> written letters and articles attempting to portray some of the common wretchedness, distributing books, papers, magazines, holding meetings in an effort to arouse people to a sense of their own tragedy (not that they starve, but that they starve so dreamlessly)—joining UFC (United Farmers of Canada) and Homemakers Clubs, attending political meetings and trying to obtain an intelligent grasp of current affairs (It is difficult to do that at the average political meeting) talking to people.

Sitting quietly at my desk, reading photocopies of the originals, I tried to place all of this. In late 1938, Alice Butala would have been thirty-one years old, the mother of a four-year-old boy and pregnant with her first daughter. Though the prairies were much more heavily populated in those days, she lived on a very large piece of land, which put her far from her neighbours, and she was many, many miles from a city. By temperament, too, she seemed an outsider even in her own community—that intelligence again, plus a remarkable verbal ability, despite being, as she once said, "as rural as you can get."

Not only was she an inveterate reader from childhood, she had a million questions about politics, government, and philosophy, to which she wanted answers. McNaughton sent her books and magazines, and Alice wrote for and received magazines and books from wherever they were available, especially the Wheat Pool Library, but also from the Association for Adult Education and from the director of women's work at the university: "Every time I see a chance for free literature . . . I send away and get it." She had always wanted to write, and even with her heavy responsibilities on the ranch she wrote story after story as well as poems. She had a few published, not only in the *Producer*, but apparently also in the *Forum* (I presume *Canadian Forum*) and in the *Clarion*, and at one point told McNaughton that she is ashamed of her writing efforts, "But someday I'll write something I won't be ashamed of."

She said too, with regard to the conditions about which she wrote and the people living them, "Someday some one will write a story about us like Stow [*sic*] wrote about the negro slaves." In May 1944 she asked Mrs. McNaughton for a reference to apply to the Banff School of Fine Arts for a writing class, because she couldn't get ten minutes to herself at home: "It would ease the fever in me just to get a few articles and stories off my chest."

McNaughton was kind enough and interested enough in Alice herself and her writing to actually type her stories for her, so that she might submit them elsewhere. She told her, too, that she had lived "sixteen years in a sod house," and Alice at one point expressed her surprise at finding out that V.M. had an OBE (she was an officer of the Order of the British Empire, awarded her in 1934 for her efforts among rural women).

I am struck by this warm epistolary relationship, that McNaughton was so generous in her replies and truly interested in Alice's life, and that Alice seemed to have found in McNaughton the listening ear she needed so desperately: "But just to let off steam by writing to someone you don't know—that is a real safety valve."

Although I suspect she was a feminist of sorts from childhood (as was my mother), it was only after her husband's death in early 1977, when the second wave of feminism was well established, that she began to travel to feminist gatherings. Sometime between 1981 and 1984, she made a special trip to Calgary to see, with her daughter, Judy Chicago's feminist installation *The Dinner Party*, and she came back eager to talk about it. I do not think many of the women of the community were interested, but her daughters were, and I certainly was.

Once, she invited the local member of Parliament to come to her house in Eastend on a Saturday morning to speak to the group of women, including me, she'd gathered there. There had recently been some new legislation regarding women, and she wanted him to answer our questions. We gathered, and waited, and drank tea or coffee, but the MP did not show up. I remember that she seemed neither disappointed nor particularly upset about it. By this time, there wasn't much left that could surprise her, and it had been many years since she'd had any faith in politicians. Alice Butala did not lack courage; I think her a truly remarkable Western woman.

Prairie women—at least rural prairie women—have always believed that they are a tough breed. It's one of the prairie myths, that we stand second to nobody in our ability to work, to survive the most difficult conditions, to be inventive and ingenious problem-solvers, to make something out of nothing, both in the kitchen and in providing necessary clothing or equipment. All of my family history leads me to believe this firmly, and to try never to fail when I'm put to the test, because my mother didn't fail, nor did my aunts, nor my grandmothers. And I am immensely proud to be part of such a tradition.

The concept of going to a wild, empty place to start an entire new life, of winning out over the elements and besting nature to wrest a living, is pretty much a man's dream, not a woman's. After all, the settling of the West had been a male initiative, the myth of the West was a male myth, and the qualities required to settle the West—courage, endurance, innovativeness, independence, strength of character, physical strength—although women might also have them, were viewed as male qualities. Women had little choice but to follow their husbands and to subdue their own dreams in favour of their husbands'.

My grandfather, the one who was "born under the wagon box," dreamt of being a true child of the West and one of the first (European) people in the wilderness, my grandmother was certainly dreaming a different dream, in which being a true child of the West could not have figured very large.

As for my great-grandmother, the one who in my grandfather's story gave birth on the hard ground with only a wagon box for shelter on a freezing, late November night, far from doctors, midwives, hospitals, and the comfort of women of her family, I doubt very much that she lay awake nights dreaming of the prestige of such a birth. Such women as my great-grandmothers and my grandmothers—and, indeed, most female settlers—came West because they hoped and prayed that their husbands were right, that here they would be able to establish a "decent" home for their families, be free of want, perhaps rise a little in society's ranks, or at least make it possible for their children to do so. I do not think they were dreaming of glory as they packed their belongings, said good-bye to their parents and siblings, took their children by their hands, and turned their faces to the West.

CHAPTER SEVEN

# The West Wants In—or Out

*What makes a Westerner?*
*Our constant dissatisfaction.*

A N OFTEN-TOLD JOKE about Western farmers is this one:
A farmer returns home from selling a load of wheat in
town to find his cattle are dead from drinking bad
water, his crop has frozen in the ground, and his wife has run
off with the neighbour. He raises his fist to the sky, shakes it,
and shouts, "God damn the CPR!" People used to laugh their
heads off at this joke, but today it is more likely to produce
baffled stares.

The Canadian Pacific Railway was much hated by Western
farmers, mostly because the original arrangement was that the
CPR owned sixteen sections in a checkerboard pattern on
each side of the railroad bed, out of every township of thirty-
six sections. (The Hudson's Bay Company owned a further
two sections, and two sections were reserved for schools.) This
was often the most fertile land, and because it was the CPR's,
it was not open for homesteading.

As well, it was the CPR that determined where townsites
would be. The scramble to persuade the CPR to put its railway

through an existing town is well documented. If the railway missed a town, that town was pretty much finished, and everyone knew it. The CPR czars apparently had little hesitation to pass well away from an existing town if the town fathers appeared uncooperative in giving the CPR what it wanted, an attitude not likely to win friends.

Besides that, except for cereal grain shipments, which under the Crow Rate received special treatment, freight rates were set so that it was half the cost to ship something east as the same distance west. This injustice clearly—or so Westerners have always believed—had no other purpose than to favour Eastern interests over Western, and Westerners have to this day not forgotten it.

I was present at the rally in Saskatoon at Saskatchewan Place in January 1993 when thirteen thousand farmers came by bus from all over the province to protest the Mulroney government's agricultural policies in the face of the drought. Part of this policy was to stop the Canadian Wheat Board from being the only seller of cereal crops. The Wheat Board was a product of farmer dissatisfaction with a system where each farmer sold his own product and was therefore at the mercy of buyers. It was established in 1935 as voluntary, but in 1943 became compulsory for the sale of all wheat, and in 1949 for barley and oats.

I was close enough to the stage to see the then agriculture minister, Charles Maier, lower his head in what looked to me like stubborn embarrassment as all thirteen thousand farmers roared their disapproval at the deregulation of the sale of oats, which farmers saw as the thin edge of the wedge that would end in the destruction of the Canadian Wheat Board. Oats had been deregulated in 1989, and since that day the board has been more or less democratized with the farmer-election of ten of its members, but pressure continues from a vocal minority to toss all farmers into the every-man-for-himself chaos of the "free" market. The Crow Rate would soon go, too, on August 1, 1995, despite the loudest protests of farmers.

Included in Western farmers' eternal discontent with the CPR was their anger at never being able to get enough cars to ship their grain to ports during the harvest season. Contemporary research has revealed that this was not entirely the fault of the railways, although Western farmers could never be convinced of this. Railways, of course, tried to make enough money on the profitable sections of their lines to make up for the unprofitable ones, and farmers saw this practice as simply unfair. As historian Doug Owram notes in *Western Separatism: The Myths, Realities & Dangers*, "the whole Western concern with freight rates [is] a subject so complex that the mythology is practically impossible to sort from the facts." But political scientist John Richards has written, "Via land grants and other subsidies to business, the National Policy undeniably directed far too much of the benefits of Western development to the merchants and industrialists of central Canada."

It was out of this kind of dispute that Western grain farmers acquired the reputation of being never satisfied, a reputation they haven't been able to shake to this day. Western discontent stemmed from suspicion of the East always preserving its own interests first at the expense of Westerners; over and over again, Westerners believe, they were made to feel they were not in any way equal partners in Confederation.

I would be remiss not to mention that a new generation of cultural historians has challenged this sense of the unfairness of our treatment by Central Canada, which is so deeply embedded in Western Canadian life. Kenneth Norrie, in a 1992 paper, argues: "The basic economic structure of the western economies is effectively explained by geography, history and market forces. . . . Federal economic policies, with the possible exception of the Crow rate distortion, have played little or no role in determining this structure." He goes on to say, "The cause of good policy analysis would be well served if western spokesmen were to begin with a more rigorous appreciation of the binding constraints" (*The Prairie West*). I am inclined to think that this is a minority position.

On my cluttered desk are stacked no fewer than five books about prairie radicalism by more than five different authors, with publication dates from 1981 to 1995, and I know there are a lot more out there that I haven't yet found. And on the floor behind me is another, a thick leather-bound book, this one a master's thesis, The Paradox of Prairie Radicalism, written at the University of Saskatchewan in 1974 in the department of economics and political science. The author is a friend, Dr. Gerald Schmitz, originally a farm boy from Englefeld, Saskatchewan, and now a multilingual international affairs principal analyst in Ottawa. His thesis explained what I couldn't put my finger on precisely.

I live in an area that has an Alliance MP (now a member of the Conservative Party of Canada) and a Saskatchewan Party MLA (conservative with a small *c* and, at least partly, also with a large *c*, as in Progressive Conservative); they now must be talking to each other as a result of "uniting the right" to create the new Conservative Party. The people in this area have been here since about 1911 and thus lived through the creation of the CCF (Co-operative Commonwealth Federation), precursor to the New Democratic Party, and yet this important ideology seems almost entirely not to have influenced them. How did such a historically left-wing province wind up with a large part containing some of the most right-wing people in the country? (This may be a good place to point out that the Ku Klux Klan was a significant force in Saskatchewan for a short period during the late twenties; it spread like wildfire only to die out in the thirties.)

And what about Alberta, probably the most entirely right-wing province in the country, coming into existence next door—separated only by an entirely arbitrary and imaginary line—to left-leaning Saskatchewan? And Manitoba, the oldest province in the West, seeming to have avoided both extremes and yet, as early as 1919, staging the biggest labour strike ever in Canada, possibly even in North America?

Settlers came by the millions to Western Canada mainly to get free land and then to be free to use that land as they chose—that is, they wanted free land in a free country—they wanted democracy. The difficulty is that democracy requires co-operation, and the powerfully individualistic ethic required by the nature of the countryside, the distances, the lack of services, from medical help to terrible or non-existent roads, and the vagaries of the Dominion Lands Act were at odds with the need for co-operation. One had to be at once absolutely self-sufficient and king of one's own land, and at the same time willing to co-operate with other people in the same situation in order to attain some of the much-needed services. As well, immigrant farmers soon discovered that they needed to present a united front in opposition to the perceived cheating of grain and cattle buyers, against which one individual was helpless. Most very quickly owed too much money to lending institutions (who make their own laws, as Westerners know all too well) and to town merchants.[1]

Thus, a lot of individualists were forced into an uneasy alliance. They created marketing and retail co-operatives, where they were owners as well as members, and credit unions, where they loaned small amounts of money to each other without high interest rates, arbitrary administrative charges, or onerous repayment terms. As Gerald Schmitz points out, the result was a remarkably skittish kind of dedication to various kinds of political action from people who wanted practical results without a commitment to the ideology that would produce them. They were not radicals themselves, although Schmitz says their leaders often were, and the very word *Communist* was enough to make them refuse to support any agency that had the faintest whiff of that ideology.

The influx of immigrants to each Prairie province has a lot to do with the politics of each province today. Alberta had all that magnificent scenery, some of the most spectacular in the world, and it had the romance of the cowboy image to sell, with thousands and thousands of acres of grassland in the shadow of the glamorous Rockies. The result was that many of its first settlers were the wealthy and even the titled from the British Isles and Central Canada. They knew how to maintain their positions of privilege, and they established the underpinning small-*c* conservative political sentiment of that province.

Depending on the perspective, Saskatchewan was luckier or not so lucky. Many of its share of immigrants—something like 300,000 across the three provinces—came from the northwestern United States and were not wealthy. Usually they had left behind failed or poor farms, and arrived in Western Canada with the profound hope that our land would be better. Saskatchewan, as well, had a surprising number of settlers and settler colonies established under the purview of religious groups: the Doukhobors, the Hutterites, the Mennonites, and even the famed British Barr Colonists. These last were brought out by Anglican clergyman Isaac Barr (who turned out to be a bit of a rascal as well as an incompetent and was eventually replaced, although not before a song was penned about him: "Barr,

Barr, wily old Barr / He'll do you as much as he can; / You bet he will collar / Your very last dollar / In the valley of the Saskatchewan").[2] Barr's idea was that Canada would be for the British, and he tried to create a large, all-English colony. He was prevented from doing so by the government, although it did agree to introduce only English-speaking settlers in the vicinity of the Barr settlers.

There were also the many French Catholics who settled in conclaves, where they could maintain their language and their religion. Many of these places were original Métis settlements, such as St. Louis, which was founded by those Métis who were so shamefully driven out of Manitoba.

All of this provided a fertile bed for the social gospel of the early CCFers.

The "social gospel" is defined by minister and theologian Ben Smillie, in *Beyond the Social Gospel: Church Protest on the Prairies*, this way:

> Many of the early settlers on the prairies were Protestants, with strong connections to a theology based on justice and equality of opportunity. Many came from working-class backgrounds in Britain and the United States. Several ministers and lay people led protests in women's suffrage, temperance, farm and labour movements. They protested the exploitation of the Prairies on theological grounds—a theology known as the Social Gospel, which flourished in Canada from the 1890s to the 1930s. . . .
>
> The protest which developed out of the Social Gospel was motivated by the belief in the coming of God to a marginalized people. Central to Social Gospel belief is the conviction that it is impossible to love God and neighbour without developing a theology of hope. That

meant becoming immersed in political structures; it meant "building the New Jerusalem" on the streets of every city and hamlet on the prairies.

Manitoba, however, began as a Métis settlement, with deep roots in both the wholly Aboriginal and the mixed Aboriginal/French-speaking and Aboriginal/English-speaking communities. And it began in rebellion against the central government, followed by a mass exodus of the Métis people, who felt they were being driven out (and who were to be driven out yet again). As Ben Smillie put it, "they were the first group to challenge central Canada's political power in the West." When, despite the justice of their cause, they failed in the face of superior fire-power, they were instantly replaced by rabidly anti-French, anti-Catholic, Protestant, English-speaking Ontarians (some of whom, ten or so years later, were my relatives and my husband's, with ties to the Orange Lodge).

It is out of these disparate, not very coherent, beginnings that the differing political sentiments of today's Prairie provinces evolved: Alberta has tough capitalistic views, to the point of trying to break our national medicare program; Saskatchewan is still predominantly democratic socialistic, but is much less left-wing than it once was, and an increasingly vociferous right-wing element is doing its best (but so far failing) to break the pools and privatize everything in sight; Manitoba is sometimes one and sometimes the other, and pursues the most moderate, pragmatic course of the three provinces.

Of course, in Western Canada we don't any longer spend much time worrying about the English–French struggle, although I am told that it remains at the top of the list of political discussions in Central Canada. Out here, the equivalent subject for discussion is how Central Canada has all the power and has continually acted for its own best interests instead of ours (even choosing Quebec's interests over ours), and how we should try, have tried, and will try to get equality.

The most extreme manifestation of this is the various, usually short-lived and not very strong, parties that spring up demanding our separation from the rest of the country; its more usual attitude is the low-level, continual grumbling (like a case of flu that won't go away) about Toronto and Ottawa and how they think they are the centre of the universe and are always looking down their noses at us, who are the "real" people of this country, people of the land, who know what real work is, having built our country from scratch.

The West has had a long tradition of populist politics and new reform movements, from the rightist Social Credit League of Alberta (in power under William Aberhart from 1935 to 1943 and under Ernest Manning from 1943 to 1968) to the leftist CCF of Saskatchewan, formed in 1932. The earliest populist movements, of course, were agrarian organizations to protest the many perceived abuses of the Western grain farmer; these abuses were seen, at worst, as the deliberate policy of the federal government to drain Western wealth for the benefit of the East and, at best, as the illegal, malevolent tactics of grain and cattle buyers, elevator companies, and other businesspeople.

What a time it must have been to be hale and hearty in the teens and twenties of the last century out on the prairie. Everybody who could speak English, and many who could not, I gather, belonged to something to protest the difficulty and injustice of the lot of the Western settler. Farm organizations and social gospel advocates, such as J.S. Woodsworth in Manitoba, were fighting for labourers' and immigrants' rights, and a growing and powerful women's movement was fighting for suffrage and temperance. Membership in these movements overlapped; farmers could belong to the grain growers' organization and support its women members in their fight for suffrage, and the women could also be members of the temperance union, as well as churchgoers and runners for public office. By the 1930s the above-mentioned two parties had been formed, although the CCF didn't take power in Saskatchewan until the forties.

The Great Depression, the concurrent terrible drought on the prairies (whose dreadful results were at least partly the consequence of the farming practices of the period), and the truly shocking failure of governments to help Western farmers (whose desperation had radical effects on town-dwellers too) radicalized Westerners even more, if that was possible. That era changed lives forever; it altered the history of families; it taught a never-to-be-forgotten lesson to many of the people who lived through it that still echoes in my generation, a lesson that, sadly, is just about forgotten, and will soon be just a note in a history book.

If the Winnipeg General Strike of 1919 was a watershed event in Manitoba, the On-to-Ottawa trek of 1935 was the same for Saskatchewan. Many trekkers had come out of the relief camps, where they did hard physical labour for twenty cents a day and felt themselves to be merely slave labourers in slave camps. Historian Bill Waiser says that the camps were little more than jails, and eventually the men in them organized the trek for Ottawa to demand real jobs, better wages, and decent working conditions.

The trekkers were dispersed in Regina and sent home by the provincial government, which also paid for their train tickets, although a committee of them did meet in Ottawa with the prime minister, Richard Bennett, the source of the term "Bennett Buggy," a fuelless car pulled by a team of horses.

But then the Second World War started, and although there was rationing, there were at last jobs to be had. Young men could join the army, too, and now had a mission to set their eyes on. But Western discontent did not go away permanently; it merely faded in the midst of such a heroic time.

The peak of Western separatism as a movement occurred some thirty five years later and was directed largely at Prime Minister Pierre Trudeau, who was perceived to be particularly anti-Western and too pro-French. Most Westerners were not separatists, but only two Liberals were elected in all of Western Canada in February 1980, and they were in moderate Manitoba, indicating a high level of dissatisfaction with the Liberals. Much separatist sentiment, however, was also anti-immigration, anti-metrification, and anti-abortion; it supported an Anglo-Saxon, Anglophone, and Protestant West. This was not true for the Western population at large, but the more radical separatists got so much press that it is hard to blame the rest of Canada for thinking all Westerners were politically reactionary. Many Westerners who deplored the bigoted rhetoric and beliefs of some of the Western separatists nonetheless privately applauded them because they too felt anger at Central Canada for the same old, still-not-addressed reasons.

Today, Conservative Party of Canada leaders have to clamp down on yet another MP, MLA, or member espousing bigoted or racist sentiments, while former Progressive Conservative prime minister Joe Clark of High River, Alberta, is left high and dry, he says, without a party. Western politics continue to be—whether wrongheaded, too left, or too right—deeply interesting.

Westerners cannot forget: the continuing failure to develop an agricultural policy to keep farmers on the land; the wholesale abandonment of railroad branch lines and the loss of most of our VIA Rail service; the desperate and failed struggle in 1995 to hang on to the historic Crow Rate (the rest of the country having little idea even as to what the Crow Rate was); the National Energy Program of 1980, which caused Albertans to suggest that "the Eastern bastards could freeze in the dark"; the otherwise admirable Trudeau's contemptible 1968 remark, "Why should I sell your wheat?"; the favouritism shown Bombardier when tenders were called for, in that the federal government gave the contract to Quebec despite Manitoba's having the better, cheaper bid; the handing over of huge chunks of the prairie to the CPR and the Hudson's Bay Company as part payment for the purchase of the West, and to satisfy the railway barons. In all of these cases, Westerners suffered on a large scale—or believe they suffered—through decisions made by the federal government that favoured the business interests of Central Canada.

The current hot-button issue, though, that tends to set us apart from Central Canada is the struggle over gun control. Not long after the enactment of the legislation, when the entire country was agitated about it, I had a sophisticated Toronto woman friend ask me, in all seriousness, and in a voice filled with disbelief, even scorn, "People are saying that guns are a part of Western culture. That's not true, is it?"

I must begin by saying that if Westerners on the whole oppose gun control and, among other arguments, maintain that it is just another attempt by Central Canadians to homogenize the country by destroying an aspect of Western culture, this is even more true of the people of the North, so many of whom are hunters and trappers who rely on their guns for food. Nobody argues, interestingly, that Northerners don't need their guns, and nobody argues that guns are not part of the Northern culture.

I told my friend that guns definitely are a part of Western

culture, but I went on to say that, nonetheless, I supported gun control. As with many other Western, educated, leftish types, I felt then that no measure would be too strong to ensure that this peaceful country never goes the way of the United States, one of the most violent countries in the world. But a year or two later, at a reception in Regina, I asked a group of urban Western lawyers what they thought of the attempt by the federal government to register all guns. They responded that, in their informed opinions, the gun control law is written for people who work in high-rise offices in downtown Toronto, that is, that it makes no sense in Western Canada and reveals a lack of understanding by the federal government of Western life and culture.

I suddenly realized that those who made and support the gun control law were thinking of guns in terms of criminals, drunks, and dysfunctional soldiers of fortune rather than the serious family men who hunt for food, to kill hurt or ill farm or ranch animals, or keep their families and livestock safe from the dangerous predators that still stalk the rural West.

When the law was first enacted, as I've said, I was in favour of it. Like many urban Canadians, I thought that if there is no gun in the house you can't get shot by accident or by a family member who is in a rage, drunk, or addled by drugs or mental illness. Most important, I worried that if there was little to stop Canadians from buying guns, then gun ownership might escalate, and the kinds of guns routinely available might reach the insanely dangerous, as they had done in the United States.

Many gun control advocates seem to think that only the police and armies should possess firearms. Westerners were saying that the enforced registration of guns was merely a prelude to the removal of all guns from civilians. It is true, too, that the opponents of the legislation are right that gun control laws will have no effect on criminals. Reform Party MP Lee Morrison pointed out to the House of Commons on March 13, 1995, that the District of Columbia in the United States, "with the most stringent controls of any North American jurisdiction except Mexico, has the unbelievably high murder rate of 80 per 100,000 per year, the highest in the Western world." (The approximate rate in the Prairie provinces since 1978, he said, is about 3.2 per 100,000.) As Michael Moore pointed out in his documentary film *Bowling for Columbine*, we have a different society in Canada. Eventually, and much to my own surprise, I found myself reversing my first opinion, and siding with most Westerners in my opposition to the gun law, Bill C-68.

A constitutional challenge to the gun law—that Bill C-68 was outside the federal government's jurisdiction—by eight provincial and territorial governments went to the Supreme Court, where the objection was denied and the bill was declared to be within the federal government's mandate. Subsequently, the Responsible Firearms Owners Coalition of British Columbia, the same group in Alberta, plus the Recreational Firearms Community of Saskatchewan paid for Dr. F.L. (Ted) Morton, a professor of political science from the University of Calgary, to direct a study to determine whether the bill violates the Charter of Rights and Freedoms. Suffice it to say that the document asserts that "Bill C-68 contains as many as 28 distinct Charter violations." (I am told that only a court can determine this, though.) Professor Morton traces the right to carry arms back to English common law, the system on which Canadian law outside of Quebec is based, tracing this right back to the Magna Carta of 1215. It is an argument that does not impress the federal government.

Although it is true that since 1968 we have had three prime ministers from Quebec and three from the West, the fact is that Joe Clark, John Turner, and Kim Campbell together served a total of about one year and four months, while Pierre

Trudeau, Brian Mulroney, and Jean Chrétien were government leaders for a total of something like thirty-three years. And Paul Martin is not a Westerner, either. Thus, I think that Westerners as a group are a little clearer-eyed when it comes to viewing the federal government than are most other Canadians (there is plenty of agreement with the government, too). After all, it has been a long time since we last had a government we felt really represented us, since we had one that even *liked* us, much less understood us.

If I think that I understand Westerners, I continue to be somewhat baffled by the most right-wing of them. It seems to me that the only real hope for equality in Confederation will come about in a more natural way than through posturing and shouting by our politicians and the more fanatical rightists: that is, through the application of the Charter of Rights and Freedoms, through good provincial government where no lobbying element gains too much power, where the needs and the rights and the participatory ability of most Westerners are not forgotten or ignored, and through an increased emphasis on trying to maintain and enhance the truly great way of life we have—from our smaller population to our wonderful wildernesses to our long tradition of across-the-board political awareness and action.

What do Westerners want? Very few of us want *out* of Canada, but a lot of us still want *in*. We still want to feel that within Confederation we are not merely the hinterland, still *le pays d'en haut* of the *voyageurs*, a breathtaking wilderness whose sole purpose is to provide wealth for Central Canada, but that we are equal and valued partners in the enterprise of our collective nationhood. We want our unique attitudes toward living today, and our unique style, both personal and regional, and all the word implies, from dress to linguistic habits, and that which we love and that which we abhor to be respected, even admired, by the rest of Canada.

We are not bumptious, ungrateful "whiners," but a remarkably varied people who have, through much hardship and turmoil, evolved into a modern, egalitarian society of free-thinking, tough-minded, and robust Canadian citizens. Yet the early politicization (to national politics) of our populace, the style of political life in the Canadian West, with its extraordinary vehemence and vigour, not to mention its confusing polarity, have always distinguished us, in cultural terms, from the rest of Canada.

# CHAPTER EIGHT

# Visions of the Prairie West

*What makes a Westerner?*
*Our mythic view of the West.*

M ANY CULTURAL HISTORIANS, including Ronald Rees, Gerald Friesen, and Douglas Owram, have written about the changing views of the West as depicted by artists. These historians demonstrate that whatever the prevailing view of the society of their time was about the Western lands, artists tended to paint or to write about that view. R. Douglas Francis, in his influential 1989 book *Images of the West: Changing Perceptions of the Prairies, 1690–1960*, offers the most comprehensive framework, extending backwards into the mid-seventeenth century and forward to the late twentieth, and covering a range of "responses," not merely that of visual or literary artists. I recommend his book to those especially interested in this question.

In the early years, travellers into the North-West Territories saw them as infertile, harsh, and dangerous, and wrote this in their personal journals, logbooks, and reports to superiors back east or in Europe. Yet much of what they saw—the Rocky Mountains, the wide plains, and the deep forests—is what today we see as rich and beautiful, demonstrating that the pre-set ideas we carry with us about a place colour what we actually see.

Two centuries later, politicians began to see the North-West Territories as having the potential to both save and create Canada fully; they began to try to persuade others of this view of the West. Slowly, although the West itself had not changed, the *sense* of the West as hostile, dangerous, and wild began to change in the minds of ordinary people. I have already mentioned the intensive campaign of government propaganda, both through visual artists' depictions and in written and oral descriptions, designed to persuade settlers to come; it was so successful that they came in droves, believing that Western soil was uniformly fertile, the climate benign, and the countryside virtually domesticated. The countryside itself had not changed, or had changed very little from the mid-seventeenth century, but the interpretation of it had changed, and so the newcomers, in their naive hope, and having no experience to make them doubt what they were told, saw what the propaganda had told them was here—a beautiful, fertile land that would make everyone rich.

In the eyes of many Westerners, this remains the prevailing view. Not so many years ago, I had a local man say to me with some indignation that he knew of no other place on earth that held such economic opportunities as the Prairie provinces— and though most people in agriculture don't hold this view anymore, surely all those Newfoundlanders and Maritimers who uproot themselves from their ancestral homes, cross the entire country by whatever means, and head into Alberta to look for (and usually to find) work share this view. So do our many immigrants from Europe, Asia, and Africa, and, as I've said, while most farmers no longer feel this way, agribusinesses clearly do.

Even while government artists, at the beginning of this new period, were busy painting glowing pictures, both verbal and visual, of an agrarian paradise, other artists, less ingenuous, were aware of this duplicity. Before long, ordinary people began to see that the West was not the promised paradise, or any approximation of it, but instead a difficult place to live and an even more difficult place to make a living. Born in 1940 to settler parents, I can attest to the difficulty, as can many, many others of my generation, whether French Canadians, Doukhobors, Slovaks, or Scots. My family lost much in the Great Depression of the thirties, and it had a very sobering effect on them. My French grandparents moved to Manitoba in 1940 but eventually gave up farming and moved to Winnipeg, where they died, my grandfather in 1971 and my grandmother ten years later. Their children and grandchildren, my cousins, are for the most part urban people. And when my Irish-Scottish grandparents left Manitoba in the twenties, believing in the vast promise of Saskatchewan, they found themselves thoroughly enlightened. Despite more than twenty years of hard labour and deprivation, they finally had to give up their farm in the forties, moving back to the small city of Prince Albert. They both died in the early seventies, at the ages of eighty-nine and ninety-one.

If I had asked them if the promise of the West had been true for them, I think my Grandmother Graham would have laughed and made a wry joke. When she sobered, I think she would have pointed out the good times, her children and grandchildren, and the beauty of the places where she lived as compensation for the hardship and the failure in economic terms. Made wise by the long years of her life, she would have smiled at me fondly and lapsed back into a reflective, distant silence. "Sadly smiling, and emptied of desire," as John Newlove put it in his 1968 poem about the West and Westerners, "Ride off Any Horizon."

Historians have noted that from settlement up to the Second World War, Western farmers did not love the land. They struggled against it, and in time, this losing battle led many of them to hate this place, or at least to see the land as more adversary than friend. Out of this period came many of our famous depictions of the West, such as Sinclair Ross's bleak 1942 novel *As for Me and My House.*

But by the time the Depression ended, most Westerners could not leave, either because they were too poor to go anywhere or because, having struggled for a couple of generations here, they were entrenched. Like it or not, this was home, and leaving wasn't an option. Now Western artists began to respond with their own ideas of the meaning of the West and of its place in Canada than to—once again—that which constituted its reality. Here I am referring to the much-quoted concept Henry Kreisel originated in 1968 when he spoke of the prairie West as "a region of the mind" (although the phrase is sometimes attributed to poet Eli Mandel, in an essay he wrote in 1972 where he quotes Kreisel and criticizes the phrase). R. Douglas Francis explains the expression as a shift from "that of an actual physical landscape . . . to a mental landscape . . . shaped by its own mythology" and argues that Western artists have blended "fact and fiction, historical truth and literary creation, physical locale and mental perception so as to create a uniquely prairie outlook."

We have done this so well that there now exists a national stereotype of the Western literary arts, which I occasionally see or hear being criticized by (usually young) Central Canadian critics and writers. In it, we are seen as writing sentimentally only about the farm, about the past, about our legendary hard life and our endurance of it. This has become so much the stereotype that any Western writer approaching that world in an attempt to say something new and interesting about it runs the risk of being dismissed without a reading.

And yet our best-known and most gifted writers are hugely successful, both critically and commercially, in resurrecting it. Alberta writer Fred Stenson wrote about it in his novel *The Trade*, and in *The Englishman's Boy*, Guy Vanderhaeghe, from Saskatchewan, tells a well-known (at least here where it happened and where I live) true Wild West story about this part of the country, a story that had also never been told in fiction. In a masterful feat, Vanderhaeghe found a way to bring the story to life and to give it meaning, not just as part of the flow of history, but for contemporary North Americans. Though focusing on the male West, both writers have made a major contribution to our understanding of ourselves and our often heroic past; their visions of the West enlighten us all, Westerners or not, about how we once lived and about the events, people, and ideas that have made us who we are today.

Young writer Lee Gowan, from near Swift Current, was raised in the ranching tradition and shows us in his novel *The Last Cowboy* what is happening in the male, rural, agricultural West today, a subject with which he is intimately familiar. "The last cowboy," the descendant of Vanderhaeghe and Stenson's literary worlds, is an anachronism; grim, heartlessly determined to keep his eyes fixed firmly on the past, and those of anybody near him too, he is an appallingly unredeemable human being who cares only for his horse, and possibly for the calves in the spring. Here the younger generation of men wrestles with the older, struggles for a grip on the New West, trying to shake off the—in this telling—malign influence of the past in order to live in the contemporary West and to mould it to its, and their, own needs.

Jacqueline Baker published her first book in 2003, a collection of short stories, *A Hard Witching*, about the Sand Hills area where she was raised in southwestern Saskatchewan (less than a hundred miles from where Lee Gowan grew up and from where I live). She too writes about the contemporary West of unprosperous and remote farms and ranches and their hard-working inhabitants. Where Gowan focuses on the male struggle for place in the New West against the death grip of a harsh, unforgiving past, Baker, in a more feminine telling, focuses on human relationships and the dark secrets of the human heart. The ranch, the farm, are backgrounds to these stories of humans, usually women, negotiating their world. Closely examined, her Westerners are hard to tell from the small-town people in Alice Munro's southwestern Ontario. They do not look outward much, nor do they critically examine their own small worlds; they have the feel of people thoroughly settled, if not trapped, where they are.

Manitoba's current writers since Margaret Laurence and Adele Wiseman (*The Sacrifice*) have achieved less national fame than a few of those from the other two Prairie provinces. They are more experimental in their approaches, although there is also a distinct turning back to write or rewrite our fascinating past. (Margaret Sweatman, for example, recently published a successful novel about the Red River District.) Manitoban Birk Sproxton (who lives in Alberta) has written an engaging memoir, *Phantom Lake* (not yet published), about growing up in northern Manitoba, in which he mingles family issues with the literature about the landscape in a thoroughly postmodern telling. He illustrates how the literature about a place itself becomes a part of the place, influencing the local people's perception of their home. Winnipegger Miriam Toews, in her original, brilliant novel *A Complicated Kindness*, introduces us to a sixteen-year-old small-town Mennonite girl who, despite her upbringing and her surroundings, is as modern as any teenager in Toronto or New York, thoroughly critical of her world, and subject to the once-big-city vices of disaffected youth: drug and alcohol abuse.

John Newlove, a Saskatchewan poet of great gifts, wrote many Western poems, including "Ride off Any Horizon," a poem that is enshrined in prairie literature. But despite the many male poets, and excepting always Tim Lilburn, poetry has tended to belong to prairie women. Lorna Crozier's poetry springs to mind; Crozier is also from Swift Current, and even though she has lived elsewhere for many years now, her poetic sensibility remains steeped in the prairies and her small-town girlhood. Di Brandt, like Miriam Toews, is from a Mennonite community south of Winnipeg; in 1987 she published a poetry collection called *questions i asked my mother*, which had a major effect on Westerners, especially those of Mennonite background. Or perhaps I should say, especially on women. It is profoundly feminist (in a way that Crozier's work is not) and the voice is so true, so pain-filled, so powerful in its effect that once read, it cannot be forgotten.

I have touched on only a very few contemporary Western writers, selected because they are among the most successful and because I am interested in their approach to writing out of and about the West. Readers will doubtless want to think about many others: Joy Kogawa (in Central Canada now), Maggie Siggins, Anita Rau Badami, Andrew Nikiforuk, Gloria Sawai, Kristjana Gunnars, Gail Bowen, Ken Mitchell, Hiromi Gotu, Peter Oliva, and several dozen others, including the renowned Carol Shields and Albertan Aritha Van Herk, as well dozens more of a younger generation who are making their marks. All of them are rewriting the West, in very personal terms, often feminist in their outlook, loving, yet critically acute of current Western society. I doubt that Frederick Philip Grove or even Sinclair Ross would recognize this West, a much more varied, nuanced, and complex one than theirs.

But there has always been a gap, a missing element in our literature. As Henry Kreisel (1922–1991) put it in his famous essay "The Prairie: A State of Mind," published in the early 1960s,

> The conquest of territory is by definition a violent process. In the Canadian west, as elsewhere on this continent, it involved the displacement of the indigenous population by often scandalous means, and then the taming of the land itself. The displacement, the conquest, of the Indians, and later the rising of the Métis under Louis Riel, are events significantly absent from the literature I am discussing. Occasionally Riel breaks into the consciousness of an old man or an old woman remembering troubled times; occasionally the figure of an Indian appears briefly, but is soon gone. No doubt that is how things appeared to the European settlers on the prairie; no doubt our writers did not really make themselves too familiar with the indigenous people of the prairie, seeing them either as noble savages or not seeing them at all, but it is likely that a conscious or subconscious process of suppression is also at work here.

Edmontonian Rudy Wiebe, in his 1973 novel *The Temptations of Big Bear*, has probably done the best job of any non-Aboriginal Western writer of filling this gap. But, since the 1970s, First Nations people themselves have increasingly been coming forward to write their own stories. From Joan Crate to Beth Cuthand, Thomas King, Lee Maracle, and Louise Halfe, First Nations artists are writing novels, plays, and poetry in English.

Our Saskatoon high school, which I attended from 1954 to 1958, had the only art department in the city. Although our teacher was not trained as such, he was a true artist, who arrived in Canada in 1926 from Vienna speaking little English and with only five dollars in his pocket. At first, he worked as a farm labourer and was often so lonely, he told us—yes, he actually talked to us as if we were members of the same species as he—"when I worked with a six-horse team in the field, I would sing folk songs and the tears would run down my face." He became the important Saskatchewan painter Ernest Lindner. Looking back at something I could see only faintly at the time or not at all, he was one of the tiny handful of people in my entire life whom I can credit with making a significant—in a good way—difference to the person I became.

I think I knew at the time how privileged I was in the West of that era to have such an opportunity to get to know the visual arts as well as I did. Having a rural education until grade eight, in 1953, I had only had the rare opportunity to hear trained musicians playing classical music, and I do not remember ever seeing a painting—not even a reproduction in a magazine of a famous painting, or even a semi-famous one. This was hardly unusual for the time and the place, but was closer to the norm. To become acquainted with dance, classical music, the visual arts had been even harder for my mother's pioneer generation, although her parents' generation often had come from the Old World, where they had been educated to some degree in the arts. Unfortunately, despite lively and indefatigable efforts to keep that knowledge and experience alive in the "new" society of the Western plains, successes were rare.

To that end, the town nearest where I live, as early as 1914, when it was incorporated, had an organization called the

Dauntless Society. (I often think the name would still apply to our Arts Council because it remains a daunting prospect to try to provide the arts to a community generally more interested in sports.) Charming as the name is, though, it turns out that the Dauntless Society was a charitable organization. *The East End Enterprise* noted on September 24, 1914: "The ladies of East End and district have formed a society with general Charity and Benevolence as its object, and judging by the list of members which already number forty-nine, the new society promises to be an unqualified success."

The newspaper explains that the women of the society chose the name "Dauntless . . . because of its meaning which signifies Fearlessness. They will not be daunted by anything when good can come of it. They will go anywhere and at any time where charity is need and can be dispensed." Before Christmas of 1914 they held a box social and made an amazing $110 in profits. (Our Arts Council has often been pleased to make the same amount. It must have been extraordinary for the time.)

At the same time, often noted in the same local news column is the Musical and Social Club, also sponsoring dances and concerts, also extremely well attended, and apparently without much overlap of membership. There seems to have been considerable confusion about roles, though, as the Dauntless Society's first effort was to raise money to buy children's presents to put under a town Christmas tree and the Musical and Social Club's first effort was to raise money in order to pay for "nursing of an invalid."

Times were hard in 1914, when the country focused on war, and there were no government grants for the arts, no art schools or galleries or concert halls in the area. But the arts were, nonetheless—even if they consisted of home entertainment or, later, movies at the local cinema—always a part of rural and small-town life on the prairies.

Viennese immigrant writer Henry Kreisel came to Canada in 1940 (and was interned for a year and a half before he was allowed out into Canadian society). While teaching at the University of Alberta, he wrote a seminal short story, both charming and sad, called "The Travelling Nude," about the reception of the visual arts in small prairie communities. (The poor Travelling Nude usually had to cover her nakedness with a coat.) It is worth reading, and unfortunately often it still applies.

Today, children living in the town nearest me drive only twenty miles for dance lessons; music lessons are readily available for those who can pay and have an instrument; a four-concert series is also available; the library brings in writers to read from their books; and there is a gallery that hangs shows that circulate around the province. It may not be downtown Vancouver when it comes to the arts, but it is much better than forty years ago.

Our community was home to the American writer Wallace Stegner when he was a boy. Three of Stegner's books—*On a Darkling Plain*, *Wolf Willow*, and part of *Big Rock Candy Mountain*—take place there when Eastend was a pioneer community. Even his last book of essays, *Where the Bluebird Sings / To the Lemonade Springs*, published when he was eighty-four, hearkens again to his boyhood here on the Canadian plains. This place had a tremendous psychological impact on him, which he never stopped trying to understand.

I was one of those who saved the house his father built, which today is owned by the arts council and is a residence for artists. One of the reasons I wanted this to happen was so local children would have artist role models, so that they might see for themselves that it is possible to spend your life as an artist, as I, for example, had dreamt about when I was a child.

In 1994 CBC Radio invited me to be part of an on-radio phone conversation with Wallace Stegner, the great man himself, on whose behalf (partly) I'd been working for quite a few years. CBC was interested in the annual Wallace Stegner House Dinner and in Stegner's reaction to our saving his family home in Eastend. In response to a question, I told Stegner that local singers were going to perform "Big Rock Candy Mountain" at the dinner—as mentioned, the title of one of his books, a large section of which is about Eastend. Before he could stop himself he laughed, clearly dismissively. Stung, I said, "We are trying to celebrate all that is the best in rural culture." I was grateful for the reply that sprang to my lips but, frankly, if he'd questioned me as to what that best might be, I would have had to scramble for an answer.

I've had a lot more years to think about what "all that is the best in rural culture" might be, and I think the answer lies first of all in the fact that the transplantation of art is a mistake. In my experience, if high art is simply dropped into a rural environment, people stay away in droves, and if it is "dumbed down" it tends to pander to the lowest common denominator and thus loses its essential purpose. What is best about rural culture is the way that, rather than excluding the masses, as high art tends to do, it attempts to include everyone, to speak to everyone in the community—the way that it, in fact, creates community.

I have argued for years now, in essay after essay and in my books and bits of journalism, that rural people speak a different language than urban people, one full of spaces and meaningful silences, where what is not said is often what carries the point, whereas urban people seem to think that *everything* can and should be said, the more fluently and precisely, the more applauded. (I think that rural people use irony with more exactitude and more often than urban people do. It is one of their chief tools for conveying meaning.) If we do not even, in this sense, speak the same language, how could we produce or care for the same artistic worldview? And if the schools fail to do an adequate job of educating the next generation in an understanding and appreciation of at least the visual arts, how will this ever change?

Cowboy poetry is a distinct part of rural culture. It is a true folk art, with its rhythm that echoes the gait of the saddle horse. Its dry humour, its grieving at the suffering and death of animals, and its celebration of their tenacity and wisdom reflect the Western way of life. It describes the West in precise detail in the language of those who live there, and with a wry love uncommon in other poetic genres. Much of the language is so particular to the way of life that I suspect urban people would simply miss the point of any particular poem.

Cowboy poetry began as a man's art, and the Western male values of humility and self-effacement are reflected in it. I am reminded of a remark made by an old, uneducated settler-cowboy who said of a terrible winter that he could understand God making people suffer, but never that He could make animals suffer the way they were that winter, and that is why he had ceased to believe in God. (It occurs to me that it wasn't God at work there, but humans who insisted on importing to this harsh country animals that were not able to withstand the climate the way the indigenous animals—buffalo, for example—mostly were.)

It is no surprise to find that many women also became cowboy poets, and that the best of their work frequently undermines the male tradition. The best example of this I can think of is a poem by lifelong ranchwoman/poet Thelma Poirier ("Sorting Cattle," in *Grasslands: The Private Hearings*) about working with her adolescent son, which ends:

you should have known you could
not build a corral large enough
for both of you

This may not say much to urban people, but it is an eloquent statement of a major aspect of this subculture, and one that breaks hearts. That is, the woman teaches the boy how to be a cowboy, raises him to be one by valorizing the enterprise and the men who are part of it, but inevitably the day comes when he turns around and denies her—also a part of the lifestyle—as a mere woman. In this case, the poet rejects this explanation, saying instead that her dismay at his pushing her out stems instead from the pain it causes her as a mother to see his desire to take on a man's burdens far too soon. While this may well be an occasion of denial on the part of the female poet, and if such a subject might be possible for a male cowboy poet, the approach would be quite different, in that it would probably celebrate the boy's accepting the "burden" of manhood.

Recently I did a radio interview on the subject of cowboy poetry. Because I had mentioned the fact that opera was, after all, originally an Italian folk art, the interviewer asked me, finally, if I thought that cowboy poetry would ever make a transition from a folk art to high art. We both laughed. I mentioned *Oklahoma!* (Rodgers and Hammerstein), but of course that is not high art, and it was written by a pair of city slickers. Besides, instead of celebrating the Western way of life, it makes fun of it. But suddenly I remembered *Filumena*. *Filumena* is an opera written by the eminent Canadian playwright and Calgary resident John Murrell, with music by John Estacio, the composer-in-residence with the Calgary Philharmonic Orchestra and Calgary Opera, himself the son of Portuguese immigrants. Then I had to add the demurrer that *Filumena* wasn't about cowboys, but instead was about Italian immigrants to Alberta. Nonetheless, a discussion of *Filumena* certainly deserves a place in a chapter about Western cultural life.[1]

John Murrell told me that he and John Estacio had agreed at once that this opera would be accessible to everyone. Murrell wrote in the program notes:

> We wanted to create an opera which looks, sounds, feels, smells and tastes like the place we live in—this remarkable place which has maintained its own supernatural reality through the successive waves of human immigrants and their destinies, from the earliest arrivals in this corner of the earth down to the most recent. We wanted for our audience to see and understand Filumena and her world as thoroughly as if she were a neighbour, or a member of the family, even if they have no particular ties to her place or time.

Filumena Losandro, an Italian who immigrated to the Crowsnest Pass area of Alberta around 1915, was, in 1923, the last woman to be executed in the province. The story is about some immigrant people, including Filumena's husband and to some small extent Filumena herself, who are involved in the illegal sale of alcohol, or "bootlegging." Eventually a Mountie kills one of their number, and in their attempt to exact revenge, the Mountie himself is killed and Filumena and her husband both go to the gallows. It is a tragic story, quite suitable for an opera in 2003, despite there being no kings, queens, aristocrats, artists, or supernatural beings in it, and the opera was accessible, interesting, enjoyable, and moving.

Theatre companies in all three Prairie provinces have commissioned plays about the West from Western playwrights (including my own *Rodeo Life*, at Saskatoon's 25th Street Theatre; at the same theatre, the collectively written *Paper Wheat* was very successful in 1977, and its sequel, *Street Wheat*, written by Mansel Robinson, was produced at Dancing Sky Theatre in Meacham, Saskatchewan, in 2000). Thus, theatre groups inspire, nurture, and help create genuine local art, so that from now on children out here in the West need not grow up as I did, concluding that I must live in a strange and aberrant backwater because all books and plays were about landscapes, people, and problems I did not recognize.[2]

Today, the successful Saskatchewan comedian Brent Butt creates, produces, sometimes writes, and appears as the central character in a television comedy called *Corner Gas*, about a handful of Westerners living in a small prairie town. The show is really designed, I think, as a showcase for Butt's wit and talent, and as a comedian he uses his background as a Saskatchewan boy (small-town and rural) as the subject of most of his comedy, so it is no surprise that his television program does the same. And it is very funny, playing on all the stereotypes but with an unusual, dare I say *urban*, quickness, and informed by a much wider view of the world than such people had when I was growing up.

Still, when a location was chosen, it was a community set on a wide plain with not much view but sky in all directions, and every stereotypical prairie foible is put on view for humorous examination. The show is about rural and small-town prairie culture and, at last, it gives us a chance to laugh at ourselves. The last episode I saw involved the ubiquitous small-town talent show, where actual talent is, unfortunately, usually in short supply. I can imagine that there might be those prairie people who resent the show—in fact, I am told that there are those who are angry about it—thinking that it drags us backward in the view of the rest of the country, that it celebrates the urban and also Central Canadian image of our mythical (and apocryphal) "dumb cluckness." I prefer to see it in the context my

actor son, Sean Hoy, does, as a kind of consolidation and celebration of our image of who we are, in the same way, he says,
that Atlantic Canadians have been solidifying and celebrating
their culture for many years.

This program, popular culture or not, shows that today we
have an identity that we all recognize: that wry wit, the quiet
steadiness of our style, and the silences used to convey meaning
in the place of chatter, as well as the attacks of small-town
grandiosity (a relic of turn-of-the-century boosterism?) and the
constant feuding of people who, despite the immense space out
here, live too much in each other's pockets, this balanced by a
legendary cohesion (a relic of pioneer days, no doubt). A community has matured when it is able to step back and laugh gently at itself, as this show does, as well as doing it with evident
love, not sneering or with anger.


A place, a culture, comes fully alive and rooted when it begins
to produce its own artists who stay to do this work. This is certainly the beginning of the fulfilment of one Western dream—
an indigenous art world.

Of course, by "indigenous" I mean to include those growing
numbers of First Nations artists, many of whom take their
inspiration from their own nations' experiences, especially
since the arrival of Europeans into their world. There is no
reason to discuss First Nations artists separately, as if they
were not part of the "real" art world of Western Canada,
other than to point out that some of them are among the most
significant artists in Canada in their genres: Tomson Highway, the playwright (Manitoba); Jane Ash Poitras, visual artist
(Alberta); the late Bill Reid, sculptor (British Columbia);
Edward Poitras, visual artist (Saskatchewan)—to name a few.
The other reason, perhaps, to mention them independently is

that the best-known of the visual artists here attempt to fuse traditional design elements—sometimes even materials, such as hide and beads—and mythology (although I always remind myself that what Europeans call "mythology" is merely *creation* to Aboriginal people) with contemporary forms and approaches. And the subject matter is often an angry protest about colonialism and its effects, all of this producing some of the most vibrant and powerful art anywhere. (It is also sometimes stunningly beautiful—something that non-Native art, it seems to me, is less and less.) Western First Nations' art sees the West in harsh political terms, while celebrating traditional ways, including spirituality.

The much-loved Saskatchewan Cree painter Allan Sapp stands alone in that his paintings are traditional, representational pictures of life on Saskatchewan reserves when he was a boy, in the thirties and forties of the twentieth century. His work is invaluable as a loving record of—a focus on—a way of life, depicted without anger or hate, because the EuroCanadian world pretty much doesn't exist in his choice of subject matter. Why these pictures should be both so widely instructive (that is, instructive of so much more than merely *this is everyday life on the reserve*) and so moving can only be because they are so genuine, so humble. Sapp's view of the West is purely First Nations, but on the one occasion I spoke to him—it was in a television station in Calgary—I said that his paintings reminded me of my world when I was a child in the forties at the same latitude in Saskatchewan, east of him. Sapp took this to mean I was Native, and I had to say that I was not, though I stand by my comment, excluding, of course, his depictions of the cultural rituals of his people. But I know that countryside, the snow, the teams of workhorses pulling sleighs, wagons, and drays, the pickup hockey games on any available patch of ice.

Tomson Highway's wildly successful plays, as well as being

major critical successes, show the effects of colonialism power-fully, with the difference that he uses humour to make his points, and that he depicts contemporary First Nations people and their battle to survive as Native people in a mostly hostile Canada. His depiction of Western Canada is not flattering to non-Aboriginal people, but he doesn't focus on the non-Aboriginal world. (I once sat alone in the packed audience in a gilded Toronto theatre among a group of Japanese tourists at a production of his *Dry Lips Oughta Move to Kapuskasing* [1989]. The tourists were still and absolutely attentive, not smiling or laughing, though, and I wonder to this day what they thought of it and how they understood it.)

I think it is fair to say that Western First Nations artists, whatever the genre in which they work, view Western Canada with very different eyes than do EuroCanadian artists. They tend to hold the rest of us to account for our crimes against them, and they express the pain, anger, and sorrow of their people. The best of their work tends to be so powerful that most Western non-Aboriginal art pales beside it.

But that wouldn't be true of the work of, for example, the Saskatchewan sculptor and printmaker Joe Fafard. Early on in his career—he taught for years at the University of Regina—he began to sculpt cows, which rapidly caught the attention of the art world. Certainly, they were never exclusively what he did, but they struck a note of such humour and irony (not the cows themselves, which are usually exquisitely exact and radiating *cowness*)—the very idea of a Western artist choosing to depict the animal whose very ubiquity here tends to give the West its reputation as an uncultured backwoods was bold and original. His oeuvre is large and various, much of the sculpture is ceramic, and his subjects are usually, but not exclusively, Western, including ceramic sculptures of Louis Riel and Gabriel Dumont (but there is also one of George Chuvalo and, recently, of Diego Rivera and Frida Kahlo), and bronze works of bison and horses. His art is exhibited around the world, and his cows, placidly chewing their cuds, gaze out at the passing crowds in downtown Toronto. Fafard's view of the West is thoroughly modern and celebratory, but it is a West that is deliberately iconic, unlike that of artists who painted the West in the past.

Like Fafard, Winnipegger Wanda Koop is a talented contemporary artist. Born in Vancouver and trained at the University of Manitoba, she too works with Western subjects. Minimalist as her paintings are, they capture the cities and the vast sweeps of land and sky so characteristic of Western landscape. She, too, is an international star, having had shows in Tokyo and New York City, where her vision of the West— contemporary, stark, but often in the brightest possible colours—show a kind of facelessness (otherwise often depicted as raw and particular) that places the Canadian West in the landscapes of the world.

Although I love the work of the artists I've already mentioned, I am particularly fond of the "environmental art" of Peter von Tiesenhausen, who was raised and continues to live, with his wife and two young sons, on a farm in the Peace River country of northern Alberta. Probably his best-known work is *Forest Figures*. Five larger-than-life men, roughly carved of wood, their faces featureless, stand like soldiers on parade, arms straight at their sides. They have been deliberately scorched by fire, a strange and oddly moving aspect of this work. Von Tiesenhausen has documented stages of this work, including the deliberate fire he set to scorch them and the five men standing in the back of his truck as he moved them across the country, leaving them for long periods to spend the winter standing in snowbanks in the Far North and chained to the rocks above the ocean in Newfoundland.

As well, he has woven boats—canoes, dinghies, it's hard to tell—out of dried limbs of trees, and these too strike a nameless chord in the heart. Spaciousness, again, is a strong element. I think also there is something here about loneliness and the way that each of us stands alone, as well as a comment on the closeness to nature of the Western World. Beyond this last is the enigma of nature and the way that we too come from it and to it will return one day. Von Tiesenhausen's work is as contemporary a view of the world as any in the country today. As a commentary on *Westernness*, it hearkens to the continuing threads of wilderness, nature, and space which are so often used in talking about the essence of *Westness*.[3]

All these artists—and there are certainly others as distinguished and brilliant whom I could have written about—have come to terms with the West, through their own Western eyes rather than through those of the New York City arts community or those of transplanted Europeans. Each sees the West as it is today. Whether they would describe what they do as *dreaming* of the West, I do not know, but while dreaming is certainly an element of what every artist does, I do not see in their work a refusal of what is actually here, but instead a celebration of it, and a delving below surface appearances to find the essence of this place.

The old stereotype of the Prairie provinces lacking in the high arts is simply not true anymore, for if our more remote small-town residents still have to struggle to satisfy that innate human desire, even while they are often at odds with the frankness or the subject matter of contemporary art or do not understand some aspects of it, our cities often lead the country in creation, performance, and production of the highest and best art.

Wallace Stegner, Robert Kroetsch, and other writers have commented on the phenomenon wherein a place becomes real when artists depict it, and do so in a way that all its residents recognize. Through the artists, they see their unspoken dream of the place made real—the one they believe but don't dare to say out loud, or else that, try as they might, they haven't quite managed to formulate. Artists formulate it for them, and say it for them, with the result that then the people of a place cohere around those visions, and, as a result, begin to feel real.

The dream of the West, I think, reveals itself in the work of Western artists as well as it does in history, landscape, or sociology. EuroCanadians came here for adventure, to make fortunes, to make lives; they came, eventually, to make homes here, and they wanted nothing so much as to *feel* at home here, believing, through each period, that the day would come when they would—when the West would truly be home. They painted or wrote about the barriers between themselves and the West as home, about their own sense of alienation and the things they could not quite understand or change, chief of these being the solidity of their claims to the place. Or perhaps I should have put this in the present tense: *We paint, write, sculpt, dance, film, act, compose and sing and play—however wistful, however tentative—our claims on this place.*

# CHAPTER NINE

# The Changing West

*Memory, and the more things change . . .*

A HALLMARK of Western life was once the co-operative societies, which provided Westerners with everything from groceries to a secure, collective place to handle and dispose of grains, as well as their own money-lending institutions called credit unions. I think of these institutions as more prevalent here than elsewhere, and I think of their provenance, grown as they were out of our historical discontent with the free enterprise system as it was evolving during settlement times. Most of these agencies began in hardship and with little capital, and have boards made up of ordinary people. They are owned by their shareholders, also ordinary people, and ownership might even provide, in good years, a cash dividend. In their day they were saviours.

Where once they were omnipresent, today they are just another element of Western life. In the cities, where most Westerners live, co-op grocery stores and service stations compete with chains such as Safeway, Superstore, IGA, and so on. In small country towns where there are co-op stores, there are nearly always independent grocery stores as well. The old notion of co-operative stores as the agencies that truly belong to the community is getting lost in the new fast-paced and competitive West. As a result, in most bigger centres where the people have alternatives, the local co-ops tend to have an older membership and clientele; where they were once also social centres and gathering spots, they remain so, but mainly for the elderly, who are faithful to the old ideal.

Credit unions have grown large and powerful, and—in my opinion, at least—behave more like banks than they ever did in the past, although this may well be the result of changes to the Credit Union Act. Still, there are people who will have nothing to do with them for purely ideological reasons, not even during the period of retrenchment by banks, which shut down dozens of branches in small towns all across Western Canada, whether it left people with a banking institution nearby or not. And yet many others simply transferred their accounts, for the first time in their lives, to the local credit union.

I am an especially strong believer in credit unions because in the late sixties I sat on the board of a newly formed credit union. I remember that we met in a one-room, unlined frame building that wasn't even in a town, in an area in Nova Scotia where there were mostly people with very little money. It was a wonderful experience for anyone to have, because I saw first-hand how people might work together to provide the small loans that many working people need, without usurious rates of interest, unconscionable charges, or implacable repayment schemes.

Our collective memories of our past, too, are undeniably fading and changing, with a new generation that never knew the hardship of the Depression years, and before that, of the homesteading way of life. Such lessons kept the average Westerner frugal and cautious in economic terms. It also kept the average

Westerner dubious of governments in Central Canada and deeply interested in politics as having everything to do with how he or she would live on a daily basis. As these memories fade, along with the expediency of co-operative action, the passion for politics seems to be fading too. Or at least, it does in terms of daily provincial politics.

The old idea that every Westerner had a farm in his or her near past is going too, because it is less and less true. With the memory of the West as a rural, agricultural place vanishing, our collective memories are becoming urban in nature: of rising at 6 a.m. to go to the local rink for coached hockey practice even when one is only five or seven years old (in place of free-for-alls on roads, in backyards, or on unsupervised outdoor rinks); of French immersion school; of trips to see the ocean and the mountains and the United States (when most in earlier generations were grown up before we ever saw even another province); and of a set of beloved television sitcoms different from *The Ed Sullivan Show*.

Most children today will not be remembering the long-lost family farm, as my generation and my parents' generation did: the smell of grass and sage in the earliest spring on the land, the ducks and geese on the slough, the wide fields of wheat ripening in the July heat, the ice for skating on the dugout in minus-zero Fahrenheit temperatures, the steady roar of the combines in the fall. They will not, as their great-grandparents' generation did, be in mourning all their lives for that lost Eden.

Such mourning was absolutely genuine, and it was so despite the endless work, often begun as young as five years old, despite the constant debt and the usual poverty and the terrible uncertainty caused by the danger that happened more often than not (this is a historical fact) of crop failure caused by drought, frost, hail, wind, heat, insects, and crop diseases. What people mourned, I have concluded, was the even-if-often-illusory freedom, and especially the closeness to nature, the life lived in the midst of nature before machinery got so big that people were disengaged from the land, and the days spent outside from the rising of the sun to the rising of the moon, the wide-open spaces free of other humans, the fresh, clean air, the silences except for birdsong and the wailing of coyotes, and the way that families worked together in the single enterprise. That was the West once, but for a very long time it has not been the West. Still, it was a very good way, hardship included, to build a people.

Lost also, or at least drastically changed, is the way we live with our weather. (That our weather is also changing is too uncertain a matter for me to write about.) Weather has always played a surprisingly large part in our self-definition, at least partly because we saw ourselves as extremely hardy: we could survive, especially, the cold and the killing winter storms. When I was a child, it seemed to me that people were always getting lost in blizzards and being found frozen to death. Our houses weren't air-tight, and our central heating systems, if we were lucky enough to have them, were coal-fired furnaces that had to be looked after all night long. Otherwise, we had only wood and coal-burning heaters in the living room and used the cook-stove for heat in the kitchen; bedrooms were unheated.

By the early seventies all that had gone. The thermometer still routinely hit fifty below for stretches and we still had three- and five-day blizzards, but for the most part they didn't stop people the way they had done. We had decent roads, well-heated, reliable vehicles to drive (nobody had to harness the horses or saddle them), and warm garages for those vehicles and for block heaters so that they would start in the coldest weather. Besides that, our houses had begun to be reliably heated, our cars had heaters, the buildings we went to work in were warm. A person could get up on a forty-below morning in his warm house, get into his warm car, drive to work in comfort, park the car, plug in the block heater, and scurry into a warm building. In the cities, councils and businesspeople (too often synonymous for my taste) built covered, heated walkways below or above the sidewalks so that workers and shoppers—especially shoppers—could park in the heated underground garage and go on foot from store to store without ever having to go outside. People—urban and small-town people—stopped fearing winter; often they even stopped taking precautions.

All of this is to say that the weather mythology with which people of my generation and earlier grew up is slowly being vanquished, some would say—or at least, with the advent of modern vehicles, good roads, and warm buildings, eroded. The mythology is going, but for the most part, the weather is not. We still have tornadoes and plow winds, bitterly cold weather, dangerous winter storms, hugely entertaining as well as killing lightning and thunderstorms, and weather sometimes so hot in the summer that Central Canadian visitors can hardly believe it. It is certainly true that modern technology has made life safer in terms of weather for most of us. But faith in technology seems to be such that we older people have learned to just shut up about weather dangers, as it seems to be unfashionable to admit even to their continued existence.

Small-town life is changing as well, and in many cases dying. In the beginning, the West was predominantly rural, as I have noted, and the CPR designated stopping points along its line, usually nine miles apart, where villages and towns would be created. These villages served the surrounding area and acted as feeders for the goods and services that came from the larger towns and cities. Other villages sprang up too, where people found it useful to have a small centre where mail might be picked up, a few provisions purchased of the kind no settler could make or grow herself, and other items of hardware, tack, and building supplies essential to the homestead enterprise. "Feeder" railway lines, or branch lines, were built to these places not on the main railway lines. Nearly always in these towns, however tiny, there would also be a small hotel, with a beer parlour, as they were called in those days, for many years exclusively for the use of the men. And before long, there would be a town hall for weddings and dances, meetings, and imported entertainments. If towns were large, of course, there would also be a church, or two of them (or even more, as towns and villages tended to be well churched), and a school.

Each town had at least one and sometimes four or five grain elevators situated along the railroad track, where grain was stored and then loaded onto the trains, and these large, uniquely designed wooden structures gave the small centres, with their rows of usually modest and undistinguished tiny frame houses, their character and became the symbols of the prairie West. At their historical peak, there were something like six thousand of them across the prairies.

But with the exodus out of the countryside that began as far back as the twenties and has continued more or less steadily, these small towns are fading. Once there were over 300,000 farms across the three provinces; today there are around 125,000. (While the number of farms continues to diminish, the size of those left grows concomitantly larger, more land is in crops than when there were a greater number of farms, and average gross sales also go up.) With the loss of people who provided the business to keep a town alive, towns began to die. Some died very early on, the town of Robsart near where I live being one example. Once big enough to have two garages and even a photography shop and a hospital, it died in the thirties and in the seventies, when I first saw it as a near ghost town, the fact that such a large, thriving town could simply disappear so quickly was something of a local legend.

The real death of the small town began during the Depression, with the exodus of thousands from the countryside. With not enough people to use the services available in towns, and with fewer and fewer taxpayers to support them, towns began to disappear. Fifty years later, when the railroads began to close many branch lines, the grain elevators were emptied and began to be demolished; there were too few farmers in the surrounding countryside to keep the schools and churches alive, and the farmers who were left had no reason to go into those towns, since they could no longer sell their crops there.

My memory of Sunday afternoon drives in the country as a child in the forties and fifties, right after the devastation of the Depression years, is of dilapidated and empty farmstead after farmstead. Not that the land was not in use, but the owners lived elsewhere—on a nearby farm or else in town. Today, most of those empty and collapsing buildings have been burned or bulldozed and buried, so that driving in the countryside now, one sees farmsteads farther and farther apart (depending on, of course, the price and quality of the land and its proximity to cities).

And with the grain elevators crashing down day after day, the landscape has been altered drastically from the time when elevators were a sign of other people to the isolated farm family. Today, along the main highways or on the edge of the large towns on those main highways, there are enormous, depressingly ugly concrete structures called "inland terminals." Farmers must now truck their grain to the nearest terminal, which will be adjacent to a main railway line. The appearance of the countryside—more and more land cleared and broken, small towns gone, small farmsteads gone or going—grows less and less charming with every passing year.

The land around our cities is altering in appearance too, with the trend of well-off urban people packing up their children and pets and household goods and SUVs in favour of a five- or twenty-five-acre piece of land within easy driving distance of cities. Here they keep a couple of horses and try to live a life of peace away from the urban noise and speed, and in the heart of nature (more or less). But that means that outside of our cities there are now something best described as "estates"—very large, attractive, and expensive houses set well back from the road in a bucolic setting, one after the other after the other, usually on prime agricultural land. Sometimes that land is very badly managed, because people with urban backgrounds don't always know how to ration grass for those horses or how to apply land-use principles. Such landowners are regarded by the nearby rural people on genuine working ranches and farms as a nuisance (or an amusement) and an annoying intrusion; only their money gives them the right to be there. On the other hand, those farmers and ranchers who sold them that land now actually have some money in their pockets that farming or ranching could not provide.

As for the towns themselves—those that are left—I suppose they are no different from small towns around the world. On the one hand, they are accused of prejudice and discrimination, of a total lack of privacy for individuals and families, and of being extremely cruel to those perceived as outsiders. On the other, they can be centres of kindness and generosity, safe places to raise children and to be old, places where people take care of one another and where one might feel a powerful sense of belonging not available to city-dwellers. My own experience says that both of these stereotypes are at once true.

Small-town people—those who are left—live a lot like urban people. And we do have rural electrification, the godsend of the farm woman (and which Tommy Douglas said he was the most proud of having achieved), and personal computers, and television, too—thought by many rural and small-town residents to be the chief architect of the demise of a kind of socializing now mostly gone, such as crowded weekly dances. Television and the Internet have changed the West in other, better ways, serving to introduce to even the most benighted villager concepts of the wideness of the world, the undeserved suffering of others around the world, and the sisterhood and brotherhood of all humankind, regardless of skin colour or place of birth.

Governments have concentrated on the prairie problem of providing services to people few and widely scattered. For example, Saskatchewan has one of the best library systems, surely, in the world. Through our marvellous system of free interlibrary loans, no book available elsewhere is unavailable to the resident of La Loche or Eastend. None of the solutions to the access problem is thoroughly satisfactory, but people are pretty much resigned to the fact that if they choose rural and small-town life, they will not have the services so readily available to urban people. In other words, rural life—what is left of it, including village life—is much better than it was when I was growing up.

The West, once seen as the grim hinterland of our country, has joined the world, no doubt about it, and the character of each province, largely determined in settlement days, except for the 1947 discovery of oil at Leduc, Alberta, has, if anything, become more firmly set and is quite different from the other provinces. Even our collective memories are changing from the old "hard times" memories to the new sets of memories our children and grandchildren are acquiring—largely urban, cosmopolitan, full of the sense of opportunity. Our societies will change too, for who we were (or believed ourselves to be) determines who we will be.

The New World, no longer chiefly rural, and the rural now largely agribusiness-oriented, has a great interest in environmentalism and all that that term encompasses, from the handling of garbage to the push to stop pollution, from finding sustainable ways to live to preserving the wilderness, to the desire to return the world outside cities to some modicum of what it was in the distant past. In the Western world, in my opinion there has been, whether right or wrong (and it has been both), no modern movement (except perhaps the second wave of feminism) of comparable significance and power.

If we believed in settlement days (as a result of government propaganda) that the Canadian prairies were millions of acres of "useless" land that it would be our job to change into "useful" land, now, in the twenty-first century, nearly all of us realize that we are living in, at the very least, a once-beautiful place. And growing numbers of us would like to save what natural beauty has been left unchanged by a century of resource-based work. More would like to change back some of that "useful" land into the "useless" land it once was in order to recreate or rediscover not only the beauty, but the ecological balance that was once here.

If there is anything on earth that might make an accord possible between the First Nations people of the prairies and the descendants of the first settlers (the grandchildren, rarely the great-grandchildren) who destroyed their world, it is such an initiative. Here we can at least agree; here we might work together with a single purpose.

This is one way in which accounts of living in the West have changed: from the absolute certainty that we Europeans came to change things for the better—to fix things up and improve them—to the more cautious view held by, so far, a minority of our population that with our burgeoning cities, our agribusiness, and our cars and roads, we are polluting and destroying the best things about this part of the world, and that we had better call a halt, when and where we can, in order to save bio-diversity, ecology, and beauty, to save the Creation that the First Nations people, admittedly not without hardship, once lived in. It is too soon to know for sure which way the wind of change is blowing, but I am inclined to think that at the very least, some sort of compromise between those who would turn the entire Prairie provinces back to the way they were 150 years ago and those who would put to use every bit of resource, from trees and grass to diamonds and uranium, out of every square inch—and those positions in between—will be the struggle of the twenty-first century.

Despite our now-great cities and our emptying countryside where once the opposite was true—small cities and bustling countryside—the West is still, or is once again, about land.

# The Dream of the West

IDENTIFYING MYSELF as a Westerner probably began for me the day I walked across the field at a new elementary school on the outskirts of Saskatoon. The field hadn't yet been plowed and seeded to grass, and as I walked slowly, gazing downward to pick my way, gradually I became aware that the field was full of wildflowers of one kind and another, mostly small flowers, mostly white or yellow, but there were also small pink flowers and even the occasional blue ones. None of them were new to me—I'd seen them all before—but I simply hadn't noticed them since I had been a child living in the St. Louis region.

I was, quite simply, amazed. Until that moment I had identified beauty of landscape with mountains and ocean beaches, with the tropics and hibiscus and orchids and so on. I did not think we had flowers, even though I had been looking at them all my life and in some cases picking them—wild roses, tiger lilies, crocuses, goldenrod, and wild sunflowers stand out especially. And I'd once been familiar with a dozen lovely shrubs and flowers in the bush country: wild hazelnuts, blueberries, strawberries, pincherries, chokecherries, and saskatoons.

After my surprise passed, I began to feel angry—angry that for all my adult life to that point (I was perhaps twenty-nine at that time) it had seemed to me that it was taken for granted that beauty was elsewhere, that we had none that counted any closer than the Rocky Mountains. Most of us took it for granted that when we grew up (if our parents didn't have farms or ranches—that is, land) we would go elsewhere to make our lives; that understanding bred the assumption that the Prairie provinces were not interesting or beautiful or important.

But here was a field full of flowers, real flowers, and as I walked, I thought, *We do so have flowers! This field is full of them, and they are beautiful too!* From that moment I began slowly to change my ideas about the place where I was born, and its own beauty, and its meaning in the world. It would be true to say that on the day many, many years later when I decided that my writerly world would be the world of Saskatchewan and Saskatchewan people, prairie history and the prairie landscape, that decision was really the culmination of the realization I had on the day I walked across that suburban field full of wildflowers on the edge of the city of Saskatoon. I was not alone in this radical new perception of the place I called home; about that time, many, many others were experiencing the same epiphany.

When I began to plan this book, my Irish grandfather's story about being born "under the wagon box" was one of the first to come into my mind. Because it was so central to my sense of myself, I wanted to verify the facts. As I wrote this book, I researched this story.

Of course, in 1880, when he was born, there were no birth certificates, but with the help of one of my elderly aunts, his daughter, I finally received a copy of a document attesting to the fact of his birth in 1880 and, indeed, at Portage la Prairie. It had been completed and signed years after the fact, in May 1947, and was witnessed not by his parents, but by his oldest brother. (A family of eleven children—there was a goodly gap in years between them.) It stated clearly that a certain doctor had been present at our grandfather's birth. I looked again, not wanting it to be true, because I saw at once what this fact meant. It meant that he had been born in a farmhouse, like everybody else. It meant that his story was not true.

The letter from the Dominion Bureau of Statistics says: "In the Census records of 1881 taken as of date April 4th, the following entry appears: 'Frankie Graham, 5 months old, born in November, 1880, in the province of Manitoba and living at the date of enumeration in the Subdistrict of South Western with 'John and Margaret Graham.'"

Why should he have made up such a story? Why did he tell it to his children, so that they passed it on to us? So that it became a family legend, something of which we were all proud? The more I thought about the results of my inquiry into his birth, the more I began to see it as being far more revealing, not just of his sly Irish sense of humour or his life, but of the newness of the West. What a dramatic story of frontier life this was, what an emblematic tale for his descendants to enjoy.


Many Westerners who were never a part of the frontier tradition, and perhaps not even rural, have another dream: it is to see the West as it was perhaps 150 years ago, before large numbers of Europeans came here and changed the face of the Western earth. They dream of great herds of buffalo roaming the grass-covered prairie the way they did until the late 1870s, a prairie very much the way God—or the Creator—made it. They dream of it to such an extent and in such numbers that the first steps toward such a thing happening, albeit on a tiny scale comparatively speaking, have actually happened.

On Friday, December 12, 2003, a year after the "day in the life of the real West" with which I began this book, fifty head of genetically pure plains bison arrived from Elk Island National Park in Alberta to begin their lives on the Old Man On His Back Prairie and Heritage Conservation Area in the extreme southwestern corner of Saskatchewan, the very land from which their ancestors had been driven out and all but extinguished some 125 years earlier.

The groundwork that made that moment in late 2003 possible began in the 1870s with Sam Walking Coyote, who saved a half-dozen bison calves from the Milk River, Alberta, area west of today's Old Man On His Back preserve. The story as reported on the front page of the *Edmonton Journal* on December 14, 2003, goes on: "He sold them to American ranchers Michel Pablo and Charles Allard. They built the herd and sold part of it to the Canadian government." Those twenty-five males and twenty-five females are the actual descendants of the original plains bison, having neither cow genes nor wood bison genes, and having come from the few head saved in Montana by people who understood that if they did not save them, plains bison would be gone from creation forever.

The large number of media representatives who showed up to report on their arrival is evidence of the widespread interest in such an occurrence, and the excited response to the press reports are clear evidence of something—some dream—still lurking in the hearts of countless Canadians, not just Westerners and not just rural. Everybody involved was amazed at the excitement across the country generated by the return of bison. (The difference here from the three hundred or so bison herds already extant in Saskatchewan alone is that these others are commercial herds, with all that goes with that, and that they are not genetically pure, authentic plains bison but a mixture of plains and wood, and often also cattle genes.)

It took place finally after a couple of years of negotiating and planning by the organization that brought the bison home, the Nature Conservancy of Canada, and its scientists and workers and supporters, and by the government of the province of Saskatchewan, through the appropriate departments and agencies. A lot of people were involved, and many more were very excited about the project. It was not merely a few bison calves arriving at Old Man On His Back to begin another commercial herd; it was *the return of the bison to the Great Plains of Canada.*

I think that for thousands of Western Canadians the *dream of the West* is not about oil or farming or even cattle, or block after block of houses that would be palaces in most of the world, but instead, to settle finally into a *real life* that is part of this unique North American world, the one that was here before the first European set foot on it.

The dream is to create a culture that is mindful of the spirits that have always been here, and of their style, understanding, teachings, and voices, so that our failed attempts of the past couple of centuries to recreate the Old World on this soil are forgotten and erased, and our current attempts to be New York or Toronto or Montreal are seen for what they are—foolishness, and a great devaluing of what is already here. For we are not failed Easterners, we are Westerners.

The dream is to recognize at last what has always been here, the very thing First Nations people knew and know, although we've rarely listened to them before, and out of that recognition to make a world grounded—in the literal meaning of the term as well as the metaphoric—in the realities of this place as it is and has always been. A world of the most wondrous physical beauty and accompanying vital and pure spiritual life.

*What is the dream of the West?* I think it is finally, after more than three hundred years of our being in it as traveller, explorer, trader, missionary, and settler, to be able to call it *home*, without irony, fear, belligerence, or pain. For a long time only Europe was home, then only Canada East or Canada West, and then, although we might *say* that the prairie was home, we always had that shadow hanging over us, the shadow of the Aboriginal people of the West whom we had displaced for our own benefit.

No matter what we learned or what we understood—slowly, year by painful year—about our new home, we never could match and never have matched what they knew on the day of our arrival. Even while we prospered and they suffered, we denied them, insisting to ourselves that we had caused no harm by coming, or if we had, it was all a long time ago and it wasn't our fault anyway and could be safely forgotten.

I believe that an unacknowledged shadow can hang over a nation's psyche, where it blights the one thing that its people want most: to belong—fully, wholly, in a seamless match. That is what we Westerners have always wanted. Build giant houses on barren cul de sacs, farm every square inch of prairie, tear down all the trees, mine the earth for every treasure it contains—the West will still not be fully home to us unless we find a way to come to terms with the historical wrong that allowed us to be here.

Still, I offer one more, equally beautiful dream of the West, because we *did* come, and we *did* stay, and through many and great difficulties, we persevered, survived, and eventually even prospered. We are not First Nations people, it is true, but neither are we Europeans anymore. The dreams some of us—many of us—dream at night are not of buffalo covering miles of open, wild prairie, but of a small farm out on the grassland or on the edge of the boreal forest, or a modest house set among streets of houses just like it in a small prairie city or village whose every street ends in a vista of the unique Western landscape—whether mountains, lakes, forests, parkland, or prairie. We dream of the family home where we grew up.

A couple of years ago my older sister, who has lived for more than forty years in British Columbia, most of it in the wet and snowy north, came home to Saskatoon for a visit. I phoned to make sure she had arrived without incident and to enquire about her plans. She told me that she had just returned from a long, slow drive with our brother-in-law through all the places of our youth in the city.

"And the lilacs!" she said. "Oh, the lilacs! They are in bloom everywhere here! They brought back everything," she said, meaning the prairie home she had been missing and dreaming of all those long years she was exiled on the edge of the mountains and the border of the sea. Her voice full of a tender wonder, she said how the lilacs were blooming along the edge of sidewalks, every shade from deep purple to white, and how their unique, exquisite scent rode lightly on the air for blocks in every direction. But mostly, she could hardly articulate the emotion that they stirred in her.

She didn't need to, because I understood completely, and listening to her, I realized how lilacs are, and have been for a hundred years, a symbol of the prairie West. I remembered how there are—among the ordinary people of the prairie West, at least—always lilacs in yards, as hedges along the sidewalk or on farms leaning against the old, original settler's house, abandoned years ago for a more modern one. There they continue to bloom, half-wild, often in rich shades hard to find today, filling the air with their wonderful perfume, and the surest sign (after crocuses) that winter won't be returning for many months.

They are everywhere in the old prairie West, because in a landscape once seen as bare and not pretty, and not *home*, settlers brought lilacs with them from the Old Country, as a plant with showy blooms comparable to the hothouse roses and hydrangea that they had had at home but that would not grow here. Almost certainly those who planted them did not know that they had come from China, by way of Persia, to the Turks, who gave them to Europeans in the mid-1500s, and were first introduced into the United States as far back as 1680, by a French Huguenot physician, John Durand. Nor would most of them have known that there is a native North American lilac called Mountain Balm that was apparently well known to the First Nations people of the Far West.

As settlement spread across the plains, always moving west, women created a trail of lilacs—an image I prefer to that of the fearless, free cowboy on his bronc or its opposite, the kindly yeoman farmer, with the gnarled face and hands, covered in the dust of his fields. Or the dream of my Irish-Canadian grandfather—that he might be seen as a true child of the West, born on the very Western earth.

The West is not now and has never been only a man's country. Women created it too, leaving behind places they knew for one they did not, and bringing with them what they could to remind them of the old home and family that many would never see again. Though they gave their very lives to the male dream, within it they tried to create, as women always have, pleasant places in which to live and raise their families.

So, marking the way across the West, and embedding itself just as firmly as the farmer or the cowboy in the deepest prairie soul, is a scented trail of white, mauve, and purple lilacs, an eloquent emblem of, at first, the home left behind, but today, of *home* itself.

# Acknowledgements

S INCE I BECAME A WRITER, my subjects have been Western life and Western people. Still, despite my years of
reading, it is simply not possible for me to do more than
scratch the surface of all there is to know about Western
Canada. I have relied on the remarkable and generous work
done by an army of true historians who have already identified
the trends, ideas, and ideologies, both conscious and unconscious, that I have pulled partly out of my own Western psyche
and have observed in my own Western society.

I thank the friend who told me about Chief Peguis and lent
me a book about him; historian John Tobias at Red Deer College; archaeologist David Meyer for his work on place names;
Margaret Hanna of the Royal Saskatchewan Museum; my
aunts Germaine (Le Blanc) Montsion and Helen (Graham)
Finney, distant cousins Murray Elder and Keith Elder, cousin
Luc Le Blanc, niece Amanda Ish; Gerald, Yvonne, and Roger
Schmitz; anthropologist Joan Ryan; Grit McCreath; my local
librarians and those of the Chinook Regional Library office in

Swift Current, Saskatchewan, who dealt with my often difficult requests with something that I identified as genuine enjoyment, and those at the Centre for the Study of Co-operatives (a gem of a library) in Saskatoon. (In a better world, librarians would be treated as gods.) Thanks to all of them and to all my friends and relatives who, when I asked them *What makes a Westerner?* gave me a multitude of interesting answers, which, whether I agreed or not, helped me to divine my way into my subject. Errors, misunderstandings, and misinterpretations are therefore mine and no one else's.

Last, but never least, thanks to my husband, Peter, who makes it possible for me to write, to my sisters, especially Kathy Hollands of Hollands Communications, and to my actor son, Sean Hoy, his wife, Carol, and Declan and Maeve, whose love and support keep me more or less sane. Thanks always to Phyllis Bruce for her astute eye and her professionalism, and to Jackie Kaiser, my agent, for her work on my behalf, and to all of them for believing in the dream of this book.

# Appendix A

*Mother Remembers*

**M**Y MOTHER'S COUSIN, Irvine Graham, now deceased, father of the Calgary cousins (now scattered from Denman Island and the Sunshine Coast, British Columbia, to Saskatoon, Saskatchewan, to Lunenburg, Nova Scotia, and to Addis Ababa, Ethiopia), put together a book in the early sixties about the history of the Grahams. He travelled far and wide to gather the material for it and traces the Graham family back to the fifth century, when a John Graham "breached the Roman Wall between Scotland and England . . . and gave the name 'Graham's Dyck' to this breach." While this is all well and good, I am more interested in his inclusion of a family document called "Mother Remembers." Since I am related to both Grahams and Elders, and since the "Mother" of the story was born a Graham and died an Elder, I have in my keeping a copy of the original version given to me by the Elder side of the family, as well as a copy of Irvine Graham's book.

The story seems to have been recorded originally in 1959 and begins: "This true story was told by Annie Graham (Elder) to her daughter, Lexie Elder (Griffith) about pioneer life in Canada." Annie Graham (1875–1975) was a sister to my grandfather Francis, or Frank, and my mother's cousin Lexie, who died in 1989. This is the story of a specific family, told from the point of view of a female child, and as such she focuses more on her mother's world than on her father's. Because it is both specific and generic, and therefore able to stand in very well for thousands of other Canadian settlers' family stories, I include part of it here.

> What Mother seems to remember best, about her early childhood, is the great adventure of moving west. The starting point was the family home in the Ontario bush. They lived in a log house at Howick, about six miles from the town of Wroxeter. The farm belonged to Mr. Gibson, who, to the Graham children, was a real ogre. Their father was to have the crop, in return for clearing the land. He worked at the backbreaking job, through the long days, and well into the evenings, until he had completed his contract; only to be turned out of the house. There was a baby due in a few months, and the only available place to make a temporary home was a building which had been used as a sheep-fold. This was cleaned, and they lived there for several months.
>
> The new baby thrived and was given the name of "Harry." The family now totalled eight; Robert, thirteen years old, and Johnnie, Noble, Willie, Lizzie, Annie, Mary and Harry.
>
> Early in the spring of 1878, when Harry was three months old, the Grahams decided to move to Manitoba. John's friend, Mr. Colin McKay, had a quarter section farm at Portage-la-Prairie, which he agreed to rent to

them for two years. In the meantime, John was to locate a homestead.

So preparations were set afoot, Margaret washed the fleeces from several sheep, and had blankets made at the woollen mill. She made more new feather ticks. All the children were outfitted with new clothes, bought or made with an eye to durability and warmth, more than beauty.

John's two maiden cousins the Misses Strong made many of the children's garments and knitted them all two pair of heavy black stockings, that came up over the knee. That would be at least thirty-six stockings. How the knitting needles must have flown.

When the people in the old country heard of this rash proceeding they sent a large trunk full of blankets and other warm wearables. To them Western Canada seemed nothing but a howling wilderness.

When everything was assembled, it was hauled to Wroxeter, and loaded into a box car of settlers' effects. The CNR gave settlers a special rate, but just one car to each settler, so everything must be crammed in. They had a yoke of oxen, a good milk cow, a dog, and a cat. At the last, it was found to be impossible to load everything, so the sturdy homemade high chair and chamber chair had to be left.

Their many Ontario friends gave them gifts and Godspeed. The children set out in high glee, but their parents must have felt a pang at pulling up their roots from a friendly neighbourhood. The Graham family travelled in a colonist car where they could make shakedown beds and use the stove to cook their food. It took eight days to travel from Wroxeter to St. Boniface, which was the end of the steel. By that time the car was dirty. Everyone was tired of being so crowded and of the close confinement. Margaret and the new baby were feeling poorly.

The ice had not gone out of the Red River, but it was breaking up; so it was not considered safe for the train to cross the river. Planks had been laid over the crevices in the ice, and brawny men hired to help the passengers over. The younger children were to be carried. A huge swarthy half-breed with braids of black hair hanging over his shoulders approached Annie. When he stooped to pick her up, he grinned, showing two rows of glistening teeth, she turned and fled; her mother said, "Come back here Annie," and when mother said "come back," it was the thing to do. The half-breed carried her and many other children across the treacherous cakes of ice that day.

The family stayed in Winnipeg about a week or ten days, resting and being outfitted for the remainder of the journey. John secured a Red-river Cart for the family to travel in. They were huge wooden vehicles, built like a wagon. There were no springs whatever, and the wheels turning on the wooden axle gave out a dismal squall, which could be heard for miles over the prairie. There were three bows over the top which were covered with canvas.

He also bought a team of work horses and a wagon. The lunch for the trip was packed by "Pauline's Biscuit Co.", in huge cans (holding four gallons) and with tight fitting lids; the lids were removed at meal times only.

Margaret and the children rode in the cart, with the oldest boy, Robert, driving the oxen. John and some of the other boys drove the team and wagon hauling the household effects. The girls took turns holding the cat in their laps. The dog trotted happily behind, investigating the occasional gopher. The cow was tied on behind and led along amiably. Sometimes a boy would throw another's fur cap out, and the procession must be stopped to get it.

At night they made camp and for the first time heard the coyotes howling. They saw many bands of Indians, and they were all friendly, only wanting a handful of tea.

They were blessed with pleasant weather, and after about five days travel, they reached the Portage plains and the farm, which was their destination.

The two years at Portage la Prairie seem to have been happy ones. The children played with half-breed and Indian children and the older ones attended school. The baby born here was named Frank. The farm paid well, these two seasons, and it is said Margaret would like to have stayed at Portage; but it was "on to the homestead."

Again there was the job of packing all the household goods and clothing. This along with a large stock of staple provisions, farm implements, and livestock, was again loaded into a settler's car, for the second time.

By 1881 the railroad had been built to Brandon and in due time the train with settler's car and colonist car arrived there. The next move was twenty miles to Rounthwaite. This was accomplished behind the horses and oxen again. They arrived at Rounthwaite in a pouring rain. There was no house on the homestead so they took shelter with a neighbour, bachelor Chris Cook.

He lived on the farm now owned by Evan Roberts. Although his shack had just one room and a sod roof, he made his new neighbours very welcome. Mother remembers being lifted from the wagon by him. He made a fuss over each child, and the welcome was warm even if the accommodation left something to be desired.

The sod roof was leaking badly and the earth floor was

quite muddy. However, he put down more straw and Margaret put her feather ticks on it. The lovely blankets from Ontario and Ireland were used to bed down the whole family.

Everyone woke early with ravenous appetites. The cooking utensils had been left in Brandon for the second load, so it was a problem to feed so many. Mr. Cook's porridge pot was pressed into service. Margaret (like a true pioneer) mixed pancakes in the mouth of the flour bag, and cooked them on the top of the stove. Each one came off imprinted with "BLACK GIANT," the trade name of the stove. Mother remembers they were the best she has ever eaten.

When the rain finally stopped, the ravine near the shack was running full. The children spent many happy hours wading in the more shallow parts.

The homestead was where Charles Duce now lives. John and his neighbours soon had built a house of sorts. The three girls, Lizzie, Annie, and Mary, slept snuggly in one bed. They could look out through the cracks in the roof and count the stars. The rain came in at times and a huge chest containing books and the last mementos of the old land [Ireland] was saturated and destroyed.

John was a healthy strong man, and when it was discovered that a big cupboard had not been shipped from Portage, he walked there and had it forwarded. He was at last satisfied and had no desire to move again. John wrote glowing accounts of the beautiful west, home to his relatives, but they were not interested and none of them came to Canada for many years, and then only for a short visit.

The second year on the homestead John was very ill. He had typhoid fever and was weak nearly the whole summer. The teenage boys carried on the farming and broke more land. There were no bluffs then, only a few poplars near the house, which the children were forbidden to break.

The CNR branch line was not built for many years after this, and the grain was all hauled to Brandon during the winters. It meant starting before daylight and returning after dark. The farmers always went in a group and many from south and east of Grahams stopped in at their place for a second breakfast, and to feed their teams.

Some of the near neighbours were George Findlater, S.B. Flower and Bill Andrews and later the Donaldsons. The happy family was increased for the last time in 1883 when Florence was born. She was everyone's pet.

About this time there was a family on nearly every quarter section. Even without communication, and mostly "shanks pony" for transportation, the people were not lonely. Many of them were refined, educated people from the British Isles, who were wholly unsuited to pioneering and soon gave up the venture.

East Brandon School was opened in 1881 with an attendance of forty or fifty pupils. The young Grahams of course went to school, but there was nothing compulsory about it. In fact, John kept George and Annie out of school for weeks on end to herd the cattle, and the other children too, for various work. Robert had a love for learning, and often read aloud to the younger children. He read Dickens and other classics. Some of the school teachers of this period were Tom Beavington, Hugh Blain, Tom Lockhart, Miss Schillinglaw, Miss Pratt and Boyd from Toronto and Miss Smith, who was to become Mrs. Wm. Morgan.

In 1885 John bought the farm just east of East Brandon

school and had a large brick house built on it. It was considered quite elegant, with a verandah all around, and back and front stairs.

The boys were becoming young men, and were famous (or infamous) for their practical jokes. The farm work was varied by hunting trips. The boys took a special delight in hunting and were known to be excellent marksmen. The girls found plenty of household duties. Lizzie learned to sew, while she was quite young, and made clothes for everyone. Annie acquired her mother's talent for making wonderful bread. On the whole the family got along very well.

In February 1907, Margaret went to a neighbour's funeral, and caught a severe chill, which developed into pneumonia. Before the members of the family still at home realized how sick she was, she was gone. She died February 28th, at the age of sixty-three.

John went to live with his daughter Annie Elder in 1910, where he remained for the rest of his days. He busied himself about the garden, and always raised a bountiful supply of vegetables. He also planted many trees which are flourishing today (1959) on the farm now owned by Wallace Elder.

John was not always easy to get along with, but his lot was made pleasanter by the unfailing patience of his son-in-law, Andrew Elder. John was a healthy old man. He lived to be over 90 years, he did not have any disease, he just wore away. He died in June, 1926, and was buried beside Margaret in the Rounthwaite Cemetery.

# Appendix B

*Key Dates in Western History*

| | |
|---|---|
| 1670 | Hudson's Bay Company is founded |
| 1680s | (possibly earlier) Unnamed French visit the West |
| 1690–91 | Henry Kelsey journeys through the West |
| 1734 | La Vérendrye builds his first of five forts in Manitoba |
| 1754–55 | Anthony Henday travels through the West |
| 1780 | North West Company is formed |
| 1812 | Arrival of first Selkirk settlers |
| 1816 | Battle of Seven Oaks |
| 1821 | Merging of the Hudson's Bay and North West Companies |
| 1857–59 | The Palliser Expedition across the West |
| 1869–70 | The first Riel Rebellion/resistance in Manitoba |
| 1870 | Manitoba Act creates the province of Manitoba |
| 1871 | Treaty 1, Treaty 2: Ojibway, Cree |
| 1871 | Land survey begins using American system, based on square-mile units |

| | |
|---|---|
| 1872 | Dominion Lands Act provides for settlement of Prairie provinces |
| 1873 | Treaty 3: Cree, Ojibway |
| 1873 | Cypress Hills Massacre |
| 1874 | Arrival of North-West Mounted Police |
| 1874 | Treaty 4: Assiniboine, Cree |
| 1875, 1908 | Treaty 5: Ojibway, Cree, Chipewyan |
| 1876 | Treaty 6: Cree |
| 1877 | Treaty 7: Sarcee, Blackfoot, Blood, Stoney, Peigan |
| 1877 | Separate territorial government established at Battleford |
| 1877 | University of Manitoba founded |
| 1883 | Buffalo at near-extinction |
| 1883 | Regina becomes capital of North-West Territories |
| 1885 | The second Riel Rebellion, this one in Saskatchewan |
| 1885 | Completion of Canadian Pacific Railway |
| 1897 | Institution of Crow's Nest Pass Freight Rates |
| 1899 | Treaty 8: Chipeweyan, Beaver, Sekani, Cree |
| 1905 | Alberta and Saskatchewan become provinces, Manitoba expanded |
| 1905, 1929 | Treaty 9: Cree, Ojibway |
| 1906 | Treaty 10: Chipeweyan |
| 1907 | University of Saskatchewan founded |
| 1908 | University of Alberta founded |
| 1916 | Manitoban, Saskatchewan, and Albertan women receive the right to vote |
| 1919 | Winnipeg General Strike |
| 1930 | Natural Resources Transfer Act (from federal to provincial governments) |

1932    Co-operative Commonwealth Federation (CCF) founded at Calgary meeting

1935    On-to-Ottawa Trek takes place, culminating in the Regina Riot on July 1, which resulted in two deaths

1935    Social Credit Party first wins office in Alberta (held until 1971)

1944    CCF, led by Tommy Douglas, first elected in Saskatchewan

1947    Oil discovered at Leduc, Alberta

1957–63    John Diefenbaker, from Saskatchewan, is prime minister

1962    Saskatchewan establishes medicare

1975    Alberta Heritage Savings Trust Fund introduced

1979–80    Joe Clark, from Alberta, is prime minister (for nine months)

1980    National Energy Program instituted

1983    Crow's Nest Pass Freight Rate ends

1984    John Turner, from British Columbia, is prime minister (for three months)

1987    Tornado in Edmonton, Alberta, kills twenty-seven people

1993    Kim Campbell, from British Columbia, is prime minister (for four months)

1995    Gun control legislation enacted

1997    Flooding in southern Manitoba causes $260 million in claims for lost homes

2000    Tornado at Pine Lake, Alberta, kills twelve people

2000    Nisga'a (British Columbia) Finals Agreement/ Treaty is ratified

2003    BSE Crisis (bovine spongiform encephalopathy) strikes, American border is closed to Canadian cattle, causing devastation in the Western beef industry

2003 First Nations University opens on University of Regina campus

2004 Stephen Harper of Alberta (Conservative Party of Canada) becomes federal leader of the Opposition

# Notes

**Chapter Two**   **The Last Great Wilderness**

1. Quoted from *Forging the Prairie West*, p. 5.
2. As do all her thirteen grandchildren, I have a copy of Grandmother Graham's memoir, in typescript only, which ends too soon, around 1950, with the birth of her last grandchild.
3. I do not recall this ever being mentioned when I was a child, but Irvine Graham, son of Noble Graham, who was the son of Margaret Grady and John Graham, my great-grandparents, did the research on the Graham family and self-published a book about them. In it, Irvine quotes from a manuscript titled "Mother Remembers" (see Appendix A, where most of it is quoted). As well, Annie Graham (who became an Elder by marriage) tells Margaret Grady's (her mother's) story and quotes her as saying that her father, John Graham, "often received generous remittances from Mr. William Graham Sr., in Ireland."
4. At its incorporation in 1873, Winnipeg had a population of 3,700. Western historian Gerald Friesen remarks that in 1941, the population of Winnipeg, including its "suburbs and satellites . . . was as large as the

combined totals of Regina, Saskatoon, Calgary and Edmonton." By 1951, it had a population of 357,000; by 1971, 540,000.

5. Calgary is arguably the most vibrant city on the prairies today, and I for one expected it to be one of the oldest of the five main Prairie cities (or city states, as George Melnyk has suggested). In 1884 Calgary's population was between 400 and 500 residents; two years later it was 2,000; by 1912, 63,000; by 1965 it was 325,000; by the end of the seventies it was over a half million; by the 1990s, 727,000; and in the 1996 census it had reached 822,000. The latest estimate says the city is growing at 3 percent per year and estimates that "within four decades it could triple to three million" (*The Western Producer*, March 4, 2004, p. 81).

6. Edmonton, almost as old as Winnipeg and a good bit older than Calgary, had as its earliest population, recorded in 1878, 148 people; by 1904, when it was incorporated as the city of Edmonton, its population was 8,350; only seven years later it was nearly 25,000; by 1970, 430,000. Today it too is just under one million people.

7. Historically, like Edmonton and Calgary, Saskatchewan cities Regina and Saskatoon raced to see which could be the biggest the fastest. As late as 1901, Saskatoon is recorded as having only 113 people.

   The "water to wash a sheep" remark about Regina is quoted in Archer, *Saskatchewan: A History* (p. 76). Regina's population in 1883 isn't recorded, but it had 3,000 people in 1903 (when Edmonton had over 8,000 and Winnipeg well over 100,000).

8. As for the rural versus urban percentages over the years since the beginning of settlement, in 1911 the populations of the five Prairie cities of Edmonton, Calgary, Saskatoon, Regina, and Winnipeg were already a substantial 20 percent of the total prairie population. By 1941, more than half of Manitoba (51 percent), 80 percent of Saskatchewan, and two-thirds of Alberta (66 percent) were rural. By 1981, Manitoba was 71 percent urban, Saskatchewan 58 percent, and Alberta 77 percent. Today, more than 70 percent of the total prairie population live in cities and towns.

Even in Saskatchewan, this most agricultural of provinces, the proportion of rural to urban began almost at once to diminish: in 1901, almost 91 percent of the population of Saskatchewan was rural, but seventy years later only 47 percent was; by 1996 it had diminished to a mere 36.7 percent. In 2001, 528,000, or a good half of Saskatchewan's people, lived in its fourteen cites alone, never mind those in its towns and villages. It's no secret that with every passing day (and with the exception of the well-to-do who move out of the city limits to acreages) the countryside is growing emptier.

From the *Globe and Mail*, Saturday, February 23, 2002:

> The number of people employed in agriculture has dropped 26 per cent since 1998. . . . and is a mere shadow of the post–Second World War farming work force, when 1.2 million Canadians made their daily bread by working the land. . . . Meanwhile, inflation-adjusted net farm income has fallen to a quarter of its 1975 peak. . . . When adjusted for inflation, net farm income was $2.6 billion in 2000, which pales when compared with the $11.1 billion achieved by Canadian farms in 1975. [Canada-wide, the number of farms has dropped from 425,000 in 1998 to 313,000 in 2001.] The number of Canadians eking out a living from farming last year plummeted to about 1 per cent of the population . . . even though the amount of land put to work growing crops has increased.

### *Chapter Three* **Shadows and Stars**

1. On February 20, 2003, then-Justice Minister Eric Cline called an inquiry into Neil Stonechild's death, to be chaired by Justice David Wright of the Court of Queen's Bench of Saskatchewan. After hearing from many witnesses, police, friends and family of the deceased, social workers, and experts, the report of the $2 million inquiry was released by Justice Minister Frank Quennell on October 27, 2004. It concluded that Neil Stonechild had been in police custody the night of November 24,

1990, and that certain members of the Saskatoon Police Service then attempted a cover-up of what they knew or suspected had happened. (On September 1, 2004, Deputy Police Chief Dan Wiks was charged under the Police Act with disreputable conduct for lying about the investigation into Stonechild's death.) But the inquiry could find no evidence that Stonechild died as the result of action by the specific police officers who had him in custody. The Saskatchewan Justice Department concluded that there was not enough evidence to lay any criminal charges against the police officers. Subsequently, Saskatoon Police Chief Russell Sabo fired the two officers, who are now appealing this decision and will have a hearing under the Police Act. The RCMP file on the investigation "remains open."

2. By comparison, Ontario has only 1.8 percent and Quebec 1.3 percent Aboriginal population. As far as cities go, Toronto has a minuscule .5 percent, and Montreal less, at .3 percent, while Winnipeg has 8.5 percent, Regina 10.7 percent, and Saskatoon 8.7 percent. Certainly, in these Western cities we see much more of Aboriginal people than do the inhabitants of the two major Central Canadian cities. According to Statistics Canada (where these other statistics also came from), the total Aboriginal population is about 3.4 percent of the total Canadian population, but in Western Canada it is 8.8 percent. (Ontario and Quebec added together have a proportion of Aboriginal people of less than 2 percent.)

## Chapter Four    *Le pays d'en haut*

1. These figures are 6,500 French speakers out of 11,400 and, by 1891, 11,102 French speakers out of 152,506 (see Silver, "French Canada and the Prairie Frontier, 1770–1890," p. 141).

2. "Language education across Canada has had a stormy history." So writes John Sokolowski of the (then) Alberta Ministry of Education in a 1999 paper posted on the Internet called "Language and Education: Canada and Alberta."

3. According to the 2001 census, 44,340 out of 1,103,695 Manitobans, or about 4 percent, give French as their mother tongue; 17,775 people in

Saskatchewan out of 963,150—2 percent; and 54,500 out of 2,941,150 Albertans—2 percent. This is an average of about 2.67 percent today in the three Prairie provinces, while the average for the entire country is 23 percent. In Ontario it is 4.5 percent; New Brunswick reports 33 percent.

4. Sixteen percent of Albertans, 12 percent of Saskatchewanians, and 20 percent of Manitobans give another (non-official) language as their mother tongue.

5. At the moment in Alberta, out of an approximate total of 590,000 students from kindergarten through grade twelve, 114,000 are studying French as a second language, 28,200 are in French immersion programs, and beyond those totals there are a number of students whose mother tongue is French who are studying in French.

Manitoba has a total of just over 200,000 K–12 students, of whom 49.4 percent are studying in "basic and exposure" French programs and in French immersion programs. That is, in Manitoba, one child in every two is learning French.

Saskatchewan statistics show that close to 9,000 students are in French immersion programs in 2002–3. Out of a total school population of over 180,000 (over 72,000 of them in core French programs), over 81,000 children are studying French.

## Chapter Five   A Loaf of Bread, a Piece of Sausage

1. More precisely, "The rate of attrition—the failure of the homesteader to 'prove up' and thus obtain a patent for his quarter-section—was extraordinary. Chester Martin long ago calculated that four in ten prairie homestead applications were never fulfilled. . . . This led him to note in his ironic fashion that 'in some respects "free" homesteads have been costly beyond computation'" (p. 309).

2. "Careful estimates place the acreage entered for on a homestead basis in Western Canada in the period from 1870 to 1927 at 99 million acres and the corresponding patents, to 1930, at approximately 58.2 million. These data indicate a gap of over 40 per cent between expectation and fulfilment in the first critical phase of homesteading in Canada. In terms of human beings, four out of every ten Canadian homesteaders

failed to 'prove up,' to secure title to their claim. The regional record was even worse. In Alberta, from 1905 to 1930, nearly 46 per cent of homesteaders failed to prove up and in Saskatchewan, in the period from 1911 to 1931, approximately 57 per cent—nearly six out of every ten—homesteaders abandoned their claims before securing title" (Fowke, p. 285).

3. The Crow Rate: Prairie farmers had campaigned hard for equal freight rates across the country; the Crow's Nest Pass Freight Rates of 1922 (first introduced in 1898 but taken away during the First World War) constituted an agreement by which Western producers of cereal grains got cheap freight rates. The original agreement also included the cheap transportation of settlers' goods, but this was not in the 1925 agreement, when the Crow's Nest Pass Freight Rates were reinstated by statute. The agreement was changed in 1983 and removed in 1995.

## *Chapter Six*   **Tough Stock**

1. According to the 2001 census, only about 3 percent of the slightly more than 21,000 farms in Manitoba are operated solely by women; Saskatchewan, with fewer than 51,000 farms, has between 4 and 5 percent operated by women, and Alberta, with just under 54,000 farms, has about 5 percent operated by women.

2. In Saskatchewan more than 60 percent of the men and around 55 percent of the women hold off-farm jobs; in Alberta nearly 50 percent of both men and women and in Manitoba, in 2000, 51 percent of women and 44 percent of men had off-farm jobs.

3. Manitoba, first on January 28, 1916; Saskatchewan, March 14, 1916; Alberta, April 19, 1916. (The other provinces followed: British Columbia, 1917; Ontario, 1919; Nova Scotia, 1918; New Brunswick, 1919; P.E.I., 1922; Newfoundland, 1925; and Quebec, notoriously, on April 25, 1940.)

4. Veronica Strong-Boag writes:

> Prairie women knew, often only too well, the special nature of their situation. Loyal as they were to their region's interests, they

could not ignore the claims of their sex. Their own surveys, the region's papers, and their own experience demonstrated that the crux of women's oppression lay in their heavy responsibilities for work in the private sphere. This essential insight nourished both elite and grassroots feminism. (*The Prairie West*, p. 417)

5. "One of the most visible strike organizers was Helen Armstrong, president of the city's Women's Labour League. Its members provided up to 1500 meals daily to women strikers and others in need. In addition, the League gave cash grants to women on strike to cover . . . their rent" (Prentice et al., p. 219).

6. According to the government's 1999 General Social Survey, which included physical, sexual, financial, and/or emotional abuses, the rate of abuse ranged from 20 to 25 percent across the country, with Alberta women reporting the highest rate and Ontario women the lowest. Saskatchewan and Manitoba were at the lower end, at 21 percent. The rate for self-identified Aboriginal women in the Prairie provinces, however, was reported at around 57 percent. There were no statistics reported for Aboriginal women in the rest of the country ("Rate of Violence Against Women by Partner or Ex-partner in the Previous 5 Years, Canada and the Regions, 1999").

7. Per 100,000: Manitoba, 1.61; Saskatchewan, 1.44; Alberta, 1.40.

8. The authors of the report *Assessing Violence Against Women* suggest that this might be because of,

> among other things, increased community-based supports, mandatory charging policies and improved training of police officers. . . . Also . . . the fact that women may have developed a lower tolerance for spousal violence and an increased tendency to leave relationships before the violence reaches a critical and deadly stage. (p. 17)

The report goes on to say:

Just as spousal assaults were higher for Aboriginal people, spousal homicide rates for Aboriginal women were more than eight times the rate for non-Aboriginal women. (p. 19)

### Chapter Seven  The West Wants In—or Out

1. This is not a history book, and how we came up with co-operatives, credit unions, wheat pools, and other agencies of that sort that are so important in prairie life is very well documented in dozens of other places and by some of the best scholars in this country: Garry Fairbairn's *From Prairie Roots: The Remarkable Story of the Saskatchewan Wheat Pool*; Brett Fairbairn's *Building a Dream: The Co-operative Retailing System in Western Canada, 1928–1988*; Vernon Fowke's unmatched classic, *The National Policy and the Wheat Economy*; Paul Sharp's *The Agrarian Revolt in Western Canada*; books about Western women's history, from Seena Kohl's *Working Together* to Mary Kinnear's *A Female Economy* and Sylvia Van Kirk's priceless *Many Tender Ties*, and much not published in book form—yet—such as Georgina Taylor's work on Western farm women leading the fight for equality and their influence on Prairie politics. As well, there is an increasing body of important books about Aboriginal history and culture written by Aboriginal scholars, such as the several indispensable books by Olive Dickason, *Protecting Indigenous Knowledge and Heritage* by Marie Battiste and James Youngblood Henderson, and *Thunder in My Soul: A Mohawk Woman Speaks* by Patricia Monture-Angus. Check my admittedly limited bibliography for a fraction of the available literature.
2. Quoted by Lynne Bowen in *Muddling Through: The Remarkable Story of the Barr Colonists*.

### Chapter Eight  Visions of the Prairie West

1. The opera was a co-production of Calgary Opera and the Banff Centre for the Arts, with a budget of $1.2 million (also from private donors and corporations), and it took a surprising only two years of hard and unrelenting work to bring it to the stage in February 2003, at the Jubilee Auditorium in Calgary.
2. Currently, though, the Prairie provinces have nothing to be ashamed

of when it comes to institutions whose purpose is to bring high culture to the community. The Royal Winnipeg Ballet Company was founded in 1939 (the National Ballet of Canada came twelve years later) and still claims, with good reason, to be Canada's premier company (as does the National). Winnipeg's Le Cercle Molière says that it is *"la plus ancienne troupe de théâtre du Canada,"* founded seventy-eight years ago, and the Winnipeg Jewish Theatre, founded in 1987, claims to be "the only professional theatre in Canada producing a full season of plays on Jewish themes." Saskatchewan had the first arts board in Canada (1948)—in fact, second only to the British Arts Council. The Saskatchewan Writers' Guild was not only the first in the country, but also has been so successful, it's a template for others started subsequently across the nation.

Besides this, Edmonton has (arguably) the most active and successful theatre community in the country. It was here that the first Canadian Fringe Festival took place in 1982; the most successful in Canada, it still attracts as many as 300,000 theatregoers for its nine-day run. In 1985 Saskatoon launched "Shakespeare on the Saskatchewan," which still does a long summer run of two Shakespearean plays, presented in a more or less permanent large tent, complete with a low stage and chairs on risers, situated on the banks of the South Saskatchewan River.

3. An independent Ontario-based television company, Zephyr Films, has made a half-hour documentary on von Tiesenhausen and his art on the Peace River land where he lives and works and where many of his pieces stand in fields and in the forests, changing with the weather and the seasons. This documentary, one of a series called *Down to Earth*, is probably the best place to get an understanding of what he is doing.

# Selected Bibliography

Allen, Richard, ed. *A Region of the Mind: Interpreting the Western Canadian Plains*. Regina: Canadian Plains Studies Centre, University of Saskatchewan, 1973.

Archer, John Hall. *Saskatchewan: A History*. Saskatoon: Western Producer Prairie Books, 1980.

Battiste, Marie, and James Youngblood Henderson. *Protecting Indigenous Knowledge and Heritage: A Global Challenge*. Saskatoon: Purich, 2000.

Boe, Roger. Research Branch, Correctional Service of Canada, "Future Demographic Trends May Help Canada's Aboriginal Youth," September 2002.

Bowen, Lynne. *Muddling Through: The Remarkable Story of the Barr Colonists*. Vancouver: Douglas & McIntyre, 1992.

Breen, David H. *The Canadian Prairie West and the Ranching Frontier 1874–1924*. Toronto: University of Toronto Press, 1983.

Bumsted, J.M. *Trials & Tribulations: The Red River Settlement and the Emergence of Manitoba, 1811–1870*. Winnipeg: Great Plains Publications, 2003.

Campbell, Marjorie Wilkins. *The Saskatchewan*. Toronto: Clarke, Irwin & Company, 1950.

Cleverdon, Catherine. *The Woman Suffrage Movement in Canada*. Toronto: University of Toronto Press, 1950.

Cohen, M.M., and H. Maclean. *Women's Health Surveillance Report*. Toronto: Centre for Research in Women's Health, 2003.

Creighton, Donald. *Dominion of the North: A History of Canada*. Toronto: Macmillan, 1944.

Dickason, Olive. *Canada's First Nations: A History of Founding Peoples from Earliest Times*. Toronto: Oxford University Press, 1992.

————. *The Myth of the Savage: And the Beginnings of French Colonialism in the Americas*. Edmonton: University of Alberta Press, 1984, 1997.

Dyck, E.F., ed. *Essays on Saskatchewan Writing*. Regina: Saskatchewan Writer's Guild, 1986.

Dyck, Noel. *What Is the Indian "Problem": Tutelage and Resistance in Canadian Indian Administration*. St. John's: Institute of Social and Economic Research, Memorial University of Newfoundland, 1991.

Eccles, W.J. *The Canadian Frontier, 1534–1760*. Revised edition. Albuquerque, NM: University of New Mexico Press, 1983.

Fairbairn, Brett. *Building a Dream: The Co-operative Retailing System in Western Canada, 1928–1988*. Saskatoon: Western Producer Prairie Books, 1989.

Fairbairn, Garry. *From Prairie Roots: The Remarkable Story of the Saskatchewan Wheat Pool*. Saskatoon: Western Producer Prairie Books, 1984.

Ferguson, Niall. *Empire: The Rise and Demise of the British World Order and the Lessons for Global Power*. New York: Basic Books, 2003.

Fowke, V.C. *The National Policy and the Wheat Economy*. Toronto: University of Toronto Press, 1957 (rpt. 1973, 1978).

Francis, R. Douglas. *Images of the West: Changing Perceptions of the Prairies, 1690–1960*. Saskatoon: Western Producer Prairie Books, 1989.

Francis, Douglas. *The Imaginary Indian: The Image of the Indian in Canadian Culture*. Vancouver: Arsenal Pulp Press, 1992 (rpt. 1993).

Francis, Douglas, and Howard Palmer, eds. *The Prairie West: Historical Readings*. Edmonton: University of Alberta Press, 1992.

Friesen, Gerald. *The Canadian Prairies: A History*. Toronto: University of Toronto Press, 1990.

Gibbins, Roger, and Sonia Arrison. *Western Visions: Perspectives on the West in Canada*. Peterborough, ON: Broadview Press, 1995.

Gillmor, Don, Achille Michaud, and Pierre Turgeon. *Canada: A People's History*, Vol. 2. Toronto: McClelland & Stewart, 2001.

Harrison, Dick. *Unnamed Country: The Struggle for a Canadian Prairie Fiction*. Edmonton: University of Alberta Press, 1977.

Hasselstrom, Linda (text), and David Fitzgerald (photography). *Bison: Monarch of the Plains*. Portland, OR: Graphic Arts Center Publishing Company, 1998.

Heath, Terrence. *Uprooted: The Life and Art of Ernest Lindner*. Saskatoon: Fifth House, 1983.

Hildebrandt, Walter. *Views from Fort Battleford: Constructed Visions of an Anglo-Canadian West*. Regina: Canadian Plains Research Centre, 1994.

Hill, Douglas. *The Opening of the Canadian West: Where Strong Men Gathered*. London: Heinemann, 1967.

Keahey, Deborah. *Making It Home: Place in Canadian Prairie Literature*. Winnipeg: University of Manitoba Press, 1998.

Kinnear, Mary. *A Female Economy: Women's Work in a Prairie Province, 1870–1970*. Montreal: McGill-Queen's University Press, 1998.

Kohl, Seena. *Working Together: Women and Family in Southwestern Saskatchewan*. Toronto: Holt, Rinehart and Winston of Canada, 1976.

Kreisel, Henry. "The Prairie: A State of Mind." In the *Transactions of the Royal Society of Canada*, Vol. 6., 4th Series. Ottawa: Royal Society of Canada, 1968.

MacEwan, Grant. *Mighty Women: Stories of Western Canadian Pioneers*. Vancouver: Douglas & McIntyre, 1995. (First pub., 1975, Western Producer Prairie Books, as *And Mighty Women Too*).

———. *The Sodbusters*. Toronto: Thomas Nelson & Sons, 1948; Fifth House Ltd., 2000.

Marsh, James H., editor in chief. *The Canadian Encyclopedia*. Toronto: McClelland & Stewart, 2000.

Melnyk, George. *New Moon at Batoche: Reflections on the Urban Prairie*. Banff, AB: Banff Centre Press, 1999.

———. *The Urban Prairie*. Saskatoon: Mendel Gallery/Fifth House Publishers, 1993.

Meyer, David. *The Red Earth Crees, 1860–1960*. National Museum of Man Mercury Series, Canadian Ethnology Service Paper No. 100. Ottawa: National Museums of Man, 1985.

Millar, Nancy. *The Famous Five: Emily Murphy and the Case of the Missing Persons*. Cochrane, AB: Western Heritage Centre, 1999.

Monture-Angus, Patricia. *Thunder in my Soul: A Mohawk Woman Speaks*. Blackwood, NS: Fernwood, 1995.

Morton, Desmond. *A Short History of Canada*. 5th edition. Toronto: McClelland & Stewart, 2001.

Morton, Dr. F.L. (Ted). "How the Firearms Act (Bill C-68) Violates the Charter of Rights and Freedoms." http://members.shaw.ca/lufa98/CharterChalleges.pdf

Newlove, John. *Black Night Window.* Toronto: McClelland & Stewart, 1968.

Newman, Peter C. *The Acquisitors.* Vol. 2 of *The Canadian Establishment.* Toronto: McClelland & Stewart, 1981.

———. *Merchant Princes.* Toronto: Viking, 1991.

Norrie, Kenneth. "A Regional Economic Overview of the West Since 1945." In *The Prairie West: Historical Readings, 1690–1960,* edited by R. Douglas Francis and Howard Palmer. Saskatoon: Western Producer Prairie Books, 1989.

Owram, Douglas. *The Promise of Eden: The Canadian Expansionist Movement and the Idea of the West, 1856–1900.* 1980; Toronto: University of Toronto Press, 1992.

Poirier, Thelma. *Grasslands: The Private Hearings.* Regina: Coteau Books, 1990.

Pratt, Larry, and Garth Stevenson. *Western Separatism: The Myths, Realities & Dangers.* Edmonton: Hurtig Publishers, 1981.

Prentice, Alison, Paula Bourne, Gail Cuthbert Brandt, Beth Light, Wendy Mitchinson, and Naomi Black. *Canadian Women, a History.* Toronto: Harcourt Brace Jovanovich, 1988.

Rees, Ronald. *New and Naked Land: Making the Prairies Home.* Saskatoon: Western Producer Prairie Books, 1988.

Schmitz, Gerald. "The Paradox of Prairie Radicalism." Master's thesis, Department of Economics and Political Science, University of Saskatchewan, Saskatoon, 1974.

Siggins, Maggie. *Riel: A Life of Revolution.* Toronto: HarperCollins Canada, 1994.

Silver, Arthur. "French Canada and the Prairie Frontier, 1770–1890." In *The Prairie West: Historical Readings, 1690–1960,* edited by R. Douglas Francis and Howard Palmer. Saskatoon: Western Producer Prairie Books, 1989.

Smillie, Ben. *Beyond the Social Gospel: Church Protest on the Prairies.* Saskatoon: Fifth House Publishers and the United Church Publishing House, 1991.

Stegner, Wallace. *Wolf Willow: A History, a Story, and a Memory of the Last Plains Frontier.* New York: Viking Press, 1962 (and many reprints).

Stonechild, Blair, and Bill Waiser. *Loyal Till Death: Indians and the North-West Rebellion.* Calgary: Fifth House, 1997.

Strong-Boag, Veronica. "Canadian Feminism in the 1920s: The Case of Nellie L. McClung." In *The Prairie West: Historical Readings, 1690–1960*, edited by R. Douglas Francis and Howard Palmer. Saskatoon: Western Producer Prairie Books, 1989.

Taylor, Georgina. "Ground for Common Action: Violet McNaughton's Agrarian Feminism and the Origins of the Farm Women's Movement in Canada." Doctoral thesis, Carleton University, Ottawa, 1997.

Thompson, Chief Albert Edward. *Chief Peguis and His Descendants.* Winnipeg: Peguis Publishers, 1973.

Van Herk, Aritha. *Mavericks: An Incorrigible History of Alberta.* Toronto: Penguin Canada, 2001.

Van Kirk, Sylvia. *Many Tender Ties: Women in Fur-Trade Society, 1670–1870.* Winnipeg: Watson & Dwyer, 1980.

Waiser, Bill. *All Hell Can't Stop Us: The On-to-Ottawa Trek and Regina Riot.* Calgary: Fifth House, 2003.

Wiebe, Rudy. *The Temptations of Big Bear.* Toronto: McClelland & Stewart, 1973.

Wiebe, Rudy, and Yvonne Johnson. *Stolen Life: Journey of a Cree Woman.* Toronto: Knopf Canada, 1998.

Wood, L.A. *A History of Farmers' Movements in Canada: The Origins and Development of Agrarian Protest 1872–1924.* Toronto: University of Toronto Press, 1975.

# Index

Aberhart, William, 175
Aboriginal languages, 101
Aboriginal people, 24–25. *See also* Métis
  in the arts, 190, 199–202
  history, 27–29, 34, 36–37, 40, 61–62, 79–80
  and nature, 27, 77
  poverty, 51–52, 72–73, 78, 81
  racism, 53–60, 71–72, 74–82
  spirituality, 77–78, 81–82, 214–15
Aboriginal women, 72–76, 158–60
Acadians, 87, 88
Adams, Samuel, 43
Alberta, xvi, 41, 46, 103, 158, 159, 236
  history, 47, 89, 94, 121, 149, 154, 172
  politics, 171, 172, 174
Allard, Charles, 219
Andraj (guide), 111–14, 115, 117
Archer, John, 92, 126
arts, 183, 185–204

Bad Arrow, 70, 71
Bagman, Paula, 148
Baker, Jacqueline, 187–88
Barr, Isaac, 172–73
Batoche, Sask., 68, 90, 93
Bellevue, Sask., 89, 90
Benedictsson, Margret, 152
Bennett, Richard, 176
bilingualism, 92–93, 94, 100–104
boosterism, 122–25
Brandon, Man., 48
Brandt, Di, 189
Breen, David, 135–36
British Columbia, xv–xvi, 10, 151
Broadfoot, Barry, 132
buffalo, 27, 68, 140, 218–20, 236
Bumsted, J.M., 63
Butala, Peter, 1, 6, 8, 9, 18–19, 21, 45, 110,
  114, 116–18, 141
  family, 100, 106, 109, 110, 117, 119–20,
  146, 161–64
Butala, Sharon, xi–xii
  childhood, 24–25, 35–36, 44–45, 54–55,
  56–57, 83, 96–97, 99, 191

family, xii–xiii, 28–34, 43, 49–50, 52–53,
  56, 69, 83–92, 95–99, 102, 104–5, 165,
  185, 217–18, 228–34

Calgary, 41, 45, 48
Calvert, Lorne, 79–80
Cameron, Angus, Sr., 69
Campbell, Kim, 180, 237
Campbell, Maria, 72, 73–74
Campbell, Marjorie Wilkins, 91
Cardinal, Douglas, 80
Catholics, 66, 93, 94
CCF, 173, 175, 176, 237
Charter of Rights and Freedoms, 94, 180, 181
Chinese, 144–45
Chrétien, Jean, 181
cities and city-dwellers, 4, 9–10, 39–46,
  47–49, 50, 78–79, 209–13
Clark, Joe, 177, 180, 237
Cochrane Ranch, 135–36
co-operatives, 171–72, 205–6
*Corner Gas*, 198–99
cowboy gear, 7, 11, 13
cowboy poetry, 195–96
cowboys, 12–13, 16, 19
CPR (Canadian Pacific Railway), 144–45,
  167–68, 169, 178, 209, 229, 236
credit unions, 171–72, 205, 206
Crow Rate, 137, 168–69, 170, 177–78, 237
Crozier, Lorna, 189

Dauphin, Man., 48
Depression, 42, 130–33, 137, 171, 176, 185, 211
Dewdney, Edgar, 69
Dickason, Olive, 58–59, 60, 68, 77–78
Dill, George, 70
Dominion Lands Act, 55, 89, 120–21, 125,
  148, 149, 171
Domremy, Sask., 88
Doucet, Father, 41
Douglas, Tommy, 212, 237
Doukhobors, 126, 172
Duck Lake, Sask., 68
Dumont, Gabriel, 68–69, 90

Dunsmuir, Robert, 144
Durand, John, 223
Dyck, Noel, 76

Eastend, Sask., 49, 191–94
Eccles, W.J., 38, 91
Edmonton, 41, 47, 48
education, 93, 94–95, 103–4, 141, 191, 233
Edwards, Henrietta Muir, 155
environmentalism, 78, 214–15
Estacio, John, 196–97
"Evangeline," 87

Fafard, Father, 70
Fafard, Joe, 201–2
Famous Five, 155–56, 158
farming, 42, 128–30, 133–35, 138, 149–51,
    153, 184–86, 207–8, 210, 211
Ferguson, Niall, 143
Filumena, 196–97
First Nations University, 79–80
First World War, 95, 154
Fort Carleton, Sask., 68
Fort Garry, 66
Fort la Reine, 55
Fort McMurray, Alta., 48
Fowke, Vernon, 130
Francis, Daniel, 60, 80, 92
Francis, R. Douglas, 183, 186
Franquelin, J.B.L., 38, 91
French Canadians, 38, 60–61, 84, 87, 88,
    91–95, 98
French language, 84–86, 92–93, 94–95,
    99–105, 103–4
Friesen, Gerald, 122, 129, 183

Gimli, Man., 151
Gouin, Charles, 70
Gowan, Lee, 187
Gravelbourg, Sask., 101
guns and gun control, 11, 31, 178–80, 237

Henday, Anthony, 37, 38, 235
Highway, Tomson, 199, 200–201
Hildebrandt, Walter, 142
Hill, Douglas, 121
homesteading, 125–33, 136–37, 141–42.
    See also farming; pioneering; ranching

horseback funeral, 6–9
horses, 6–9, 16
Hoy, Sean, 199
Hudson's Bay Company, 37, 60, 61, 62, 64,
    65, 167, 178, 235
Hutterites, 172

Iceland, 151
Imases, 70
Ireland, 56
Iron Body, 70, 71
Itka, 71

Johnson, Yvonne, 74–75

Kelsey, Henry, 38, 235
Kerr, Don, 39–40, 42
Kinnear, Mary, 156, 158
Kitimat, B.C., 49
Koop, Wanda, 202
Kreisel, Henry, 186, 190, 193
Kroetsch, Robert, 203
Ku Klux Klan, 170–71

labour movement, 157–58, 171
Lac la Biche, Alta., 68, 93
Lacombe, Father, 92
Lagimodière, Marie-Anne, 63–64
land ownership, 121, 135–37, 147–49
landscape, xiii, 1–5, 46, 149, 216–17
Laurence, Margaret, 188
La Vérendrye, Pierre Gaultier, 37, 40, 55, 92
Le Blanc, Daniel, 87
Le Pas, Man., 49
Lethbridge, Alta., 41
Lindner, Ernest, 191
literature, 186–90, 195–96
Little Bear, 70, 71
Losandro, Filumena, 197

MacEwan, Grant, 123–24, 130
Maier, Charles, 168
Mandel, Eli, 186
Manitoba, xvi, 46, 78, 103, 158, 159, 235, 236
    history, 47, 55–56, 62–66, 92–94, 149, 151,
        152, 156, 174, 176
    politics, 171, 174
Manning, Ernest, 175

Man Without Blood, 71
Martin, Paul, 181
Maskepetoon, 65
McClung, Mrs. J.A., 152
McClung, Nellie, 152, 155, 158, 160
McKay, Colin, 228–29
McKinney, Louise, 155, 158
McNamee, Mildred, 39
McNaughton, Violet, 160–64
Medicine Hat, Alta., 41
Medicine Hat Ranch, 137
Melnyk, George, 39, 42
Mendel family, 144
Mennonites, 172
Merenerie, Father, 92
Métis, 47, 55–56, 61–71, 90, 93, 173, 174
Meyer, David, 35–36
Miserable Man, 70, 71
Montreal, 78–79
Moore, Michael, 180
Morrison, Lee, 179–80
Morton, Desmond, 27–28, 94
Morton, F.L. (Ted), 180
Mulroney, Brian, 181
Murphy, Emily, 155
Murrell, John, 196–97

National Energy Program, 178, 237
National Policy, 169
New Iceland, 151
Newlove, John, 185, 189
Newman, Peter C., 144
Nikki (student), 112, 114, 115, 117
Nipawin, Sask., 28, 35, 40
Nisbet, James, 28–29
Norrie, Kenneth, 169–70
North West Company, 64, 235
North-West Mounted Police, 41, 236

Old Man On His Back Prairie and Heritage
    Conservation Area, 130, 219
Ontario, 66–67
On-to-Ottawa Trek, 132, 171, 176, 237
opera, 196–97
Orange Order, 56, 67, 96–97, 174
Osborne, Helen Betty, 74
Owram, Douglas, 142, 169, 183

Pablo, Michel, 219
Palliser, John, 128, 235
Paper Wheat, 197–98
Parlby, Irene, 155
Pasquatinow, 40
Payne, James, 71
Peguis, Chief, 63–64
pioneering, 10, 25, 36, 122, 145–46. See also
    homesteading
place names, 35–36
Poirier, Thelma, 195–96
Poitras, Edward, 199
Poitras, Jane Ash, 199
political culture, 144, 169–78, 180–82, 206–7
Portage la Prairie, Man., 48, 55–56, 66
Prague, 106–7, 108
Prairieaction Foundation, 159
Prentice, Alison, 154, 159
Prince Albert, Sask., 28–29, 48
Prince Edward Island, 159
Prohibition, 158

Quebec, 93, 95, 178
Quinn, Tom, 70

racism, 53–60, 71–72, 74–82
railways, 130, 177, 233. See also CPR; Crow
    Rate
ranching, 133–38
RCMP, 142
Red Deer, Alta., 48
Red River settlers. See Selkirk settlers
Rees, Ronald, 183
Regina, 41, 48, 236
Regina Riot, 132, 237
Reid, Bill, 199
Richards, John, 169
Riel, Louis, 53, 55–56, 64, 65, 68–69, 71, 104
Riel Rebellions, 55–56, 65, 68–69, 90, 235
Robertson, Beverly, 70
Robinson, Mansel, 198
Roblin, Rodmond, 152
Robsart, Sask., 210
rodeo, 11–20
Rodwell, Lloyd, 125–26
Rogers family, 144
Ross, Sinclair, 186, 189
Round the Sky, 70, 71

Roy, Gabrielle, 102–3

Sapp, Allan, 200
Saskatchewan, xvi, 46, 78, 103, 236
    history, 47, 89, 94–95, 121, 149, 151, 159,
        170–71, 176
    political culture, 171, 172–74
Saskatoon, 41, 47, 48
Saulteaux, 63–64
Schmitz, Gerald, 170, 172
Scofield, Gregory, 80
Scott, Thomas, 56, 152
Second World War, 176–77
Selkirk, Lord, 62, 64
Selkirk settlers, 29, 47, 62, 63, 65, 94, 235
settlement and immigration, 120–22, 125, 143,
    151. See also homesteading; pioneering
Seven Oaks Massacre, 64, 235
Shumiatcher, Morris, 144
Slavs, in Canada, 109
Slovakia, 106–11, 114–16, 118
Smillie, Ben, 173, 174
Social Credit, 175
social gospel, 173–74
Sokolowski, John, 94
Sons of Freedom, 126
spirituality, 77–78, 81–82, 214–15
spousal abuse and homicide, 158–59
Sproxton, Birk, 188
St. Albert, Alta., 68, 93
St. Boniface, Man., 102–3, 104
St. Laurent, Sask., 68, 93
St. Louis, Sask., 68, 93, 173
St. Paul des Métis, Alta., 68, 93
Stegner, Wallace, 144, 193–94, 203
Stenson, Fred, 187
Stonechild, Blair, 69–70
Stonechild, Neil, 57–58, 71–72, 79
stories, 29–30, 33, 131, 138–39, 217–18
Strong-Boag, Veronica, 153, 155–56, 158
Sweatman, Margaret, 188
Swift Current, Sask., 48, 49, 101, 145

Taché, Archbishop, 104
Taylor, Georgina, 160
television, 198–99
theatre, 197–99, 200–201

The Forks, 40
Thomas, Mrs. A.V., 152
Thompson, Man., 48, 49
Thompson, David, 26
Thompson, John Herd, 27
Toews, Miriam, 188
Tolstoy, Leo, 126
Tomison, William, 91
Toronto, 45, 78–79
towns, 209–13
Trail of Tears, 75
treaties, 71, 235, 236, 237
Trial of Louis Riel, The, 71
Trudeau, Pierre, 104, 177, 178, 180–81
Turner, John, 180, 237

Upstream: le pays d'en haut, 86–87, 90, 95

Vancouver, 45, 48, 49, 79, 158
Vanderhaeghe, Guy, 187
Van Herk, Aritha, 38, 189
Van Kirk, Sylvia, 61
Verigin, Peter, 125–26
visible minorities, 144–45
von Tiesenhausen, Peter, 202–3

Waiser, Bill, 69–70, 132, 176
Walking Coyote, Sam, 219
Wandering Spirit, 70, 71
weather, 2, 26, 133, 208–9
western alienation, 169–70, 174–75, 177–78,
    180–82
West Vancouver, B.C., 49
White Fox, Sask., 35–36
Wiebe, Rudy, 74, 190
wilderness, 27, 34, 50, 142, 183–84
wildlife, 21–24, 26–27, 36, 49, 140
Winnipeg, 40–41
Winnipeg General Strike, 157–58, 171, 176,
    236
Wiseman, Adele, 157, 188
Wolseley, Col., 65, 67
women, 72–76, 147–56, 158–60, 165–66, 236
Women's Parliament, The, 152
Woodsworth, J.S., 175

Yeomans, Amelia, 152